Recht in Ostasien

Herausgegeben von
Prof. Dr. Kristin Boosfeld
Prof. Dr. Jan von Hein
Prof. Dr. Hanno Merkt
Prof. Dr. Alexander Bruns
Prof. Dr. Bu Yuanshi
Prof. Dr. Silja Vöneky
Prof. Dr. Michael Pawlik und
Prof. Eiji Takahashi

Band 22

Young-Whan Kim | Hyun Jung Lee [Hrsg.]

Die juristische Methodenlehre in Korea

Nomos

Onlineversion
Nomos eLibrary

Die Deutsche Nationalbibliothek verzeichnet diese Publikation in der Deutschen Nationalbibliografie; detaillierte bibliografische Daten sind im Internet über **http://dnb.d-nb.de** abrufbar.

ISBN 978-3-7560-3168-9 (Print)
ISBN 978-3-7489-6053-9 (ePDF)

1. Auflage 2025

Vorwort

Der vorliegende Band enthält nahezu vollständig die Texte der Referate, die im Rahmen des Special Workshops „The Legal Methodology in Korea“ auf dem 31. Weltkongress der Internationalen Vereinigung für Rechts- und Sozailphilosophie(IVR)(7 bis 12. Juli 2024 in Seoul/Rep. of Korea) gehalten wurden.

Das Thema des Workshops war bewusst offen formuliert worden; Im Vordergrund steht nicht nur die Frage, wie der Interpreter bei der Auslegung sowie der Lückenfüllung des Gesetzes theoretisch vorgehen soll. Darüber hinaus werden auch die richterlichen Entscheidungen in der Praxis detailliert analysiert. In der Tagung sind 12 Referate vorgetragen worden, wobei zwei davon leider nicht veröffentlicht wurden,

Wir bedanken uns vor allem bei Prof. Dr. Bu an der Universität Freiburg sowie Prof. Dr. Rux im Nomos Verlag für Ihren Ratschlag, diesen Band in die Reihe „Recht in Ostasien“ veröffentlichen zu lassen. Frau Stoll gebührt auch Dank für ihre wertvolle Hilfe bei der technischen Gestaltung der Manuskripte und der Erstellung der Korrekturen. Es ist auch zu erwähnen, dass dieses Buch mit dem Preis, den Dr. Dae Hwi Kim in der 15. Koreanischen Rechtskultur 2024 gewonnen hat, veröffentlicht wurde.

Seoul in Juli 2025

Young Whan Kim
Hyun Jung Lee

Inhaltsverzeichnis

Function of "Normative Judgment" in Legal Reasoning

Bumjin Kim

Abstract

Legal interpretation and the application of law are core topics of legal methodology. However, while a vast amount of research has been accumulated on legal interpretation, there is a dearth of research on applying the law to individual cases. In this paper, I examine the process of applying laws to specific cases using the frame of "normative judgment." As seen in this paper, legal reasoning in our practice does not simply consist of legal interpretation and fact-finding. There are numerous detailed decisions that connect legal interpretation, fact-finding, and final conclusions. Normative judgment is a conceptual tool used to explain these detailed decisions. If we compare legal reasoning to the human body, normative judgments are like capillaries that supply oxygen and nutrients while penetrating all areas of the human body. As is well known, modern laws are based on general abstraction and, therefore, cannot cover all individual cases. Nevertheless, the existing legal methodology excessively focuses on legal interpretation issues and neglects legal application and normative judgment, which inevitably has clear limitations in understanding the complexity of legal reasoning. In this paper, I sought to find ways to get closer to the reality of legal reasoning in our practice by examining the functions and types of normative judgments.

Keywords

legal reasoning, normative judgment, legal interpretation, legal methodology, application to specific cases.

A. Introduction

I. Questions

Interpretation and application of law and legal formation[1] are central topics in legal methodology. Extensive research has been accumulated on legal interpretation methodology,[2] regardless of whether it is continental law or Anglo-American law. It is expected that continued research will be conducted in the future. In comparison, although legal reasoning is said to be a process of "interpreting the law" and "applying it to a case," the reality is that research on the specific application process is insufficient. Moreover, there is a lack of research on fact-finding as well as on the application of the law.[3] In other words, this means that the legal methodology is excessively focused on issues of legal interpretation.

Today, it is believed that legal reasoning cannot be explained by mechanical syllogisms.[4] In most cases, the cause of this is found in the "obscurity of the law" or the "ambiguity of the law" resulting from the "open texture" of the legal language, which ultimately results in a legal interpretation

1 This term is a translation of the German word "Rechtsfortbildung" but it is sometimes translated as "further development of the law".

2 Books summarizing recent discussions on legal interpretation methodology in Korea include: Do-gyun Kim, Korean Legal Order and Legal Interpretation Theory (2013) (In Korean); Legal Methodology (Kye Il Lee ed. 2017) (In Korean); For an article on the recent trends in American legal interpretation theory, *see* Bong-cheol Choi, *The Methodologies of the Statutory Interpretation in the US*, 176 Just. 204 (2020) (In Korean).

3 In legal methodology, there are many indications that legal interpretation and law formation do not depend on abstract interpretations of laws but are accomplished through interaction with concrete cases. For example, Engisch's point about "the eternal back and forth of the gaze between norms and situations" and A. Kaufmann's famous point about "the hermeneutical cycle of law and issues" are representative examples. However, as far as I know, it is difficult to find articles in domestic literature that empirically analyze the specific meaning of these statements. For the general concept of hermeneutical circularity, *see* Sang-don Lee, New Legal Theory 201–31 (3d ed. 2005) (In Korean).

4 Roberto Alexy, Legal Argument Theory (Jong Pil Byun et al. trans., 2d ed. 2007) (In Korean), the introduction states, "No one anymore believes that the application of legal rules depends on logical subsumption into conceptually formed higher-order propositions." It begins with Karl Larenz's statement, "I cannot seriously claim that it is anything else." There are many domestic literatures critical of syllogism, most notably Cheon-soo Yang, *Criticism of syllogism-based legal interpretation – Referring to "Using Supreme Court Precedents as Examples* – 28 Yeongnam L. Stud. 1 (2009) (In Korean).

problem. But are the uncertainty of legal text and the difficulty of legal application the same thing? If the text of the law is clear, are any difficulties noted at the application stage? It is difficult to give an easy answer to these questions. This is because the essence of the law is general abstraction; therefore, no matter how clearly its contents are defined, there are bound cases in which its application is difficult in specific cases.[5]

With this awareness in mind, this paper seeks to examine the issue of "legal application to specific cases" through the framework of "normative judgment." As we will see in detail in this paper, in legal methodology or legal reasoning, an element as important as legal interpretation is the issue of legal application, and the intellectual process that accounts for the most weight in the legal application process is "normative judgment." If we compare legal reasoning to the human body, it is no exaggeration to say that normative judgments are like numerous capillaries that flow throughout the body and supply oxygen and nutrients. In this paper, we will examine in detail the functions that normative judgments perform in legal reasoning.

II. What "Normative" Means

Before further discussion, I would like to briefly mention the meaning of the word "normative." Broadly speaking, it can be approached from the following two perspectives.

First, the expression "normative" contrasts with the word "factual."[6] It is the distinction between existence (sein) and ought (sollen). A trial is the task of determining whether specific facts meet abstract legal requirements. Therefore, simply thinking about it, a trial can be said to be the task of confirming the facts of a case and determining whether the facts meet the requirements set by the law. However, in many cases, the process is not simply a mechanical application of acknowledged facts. In addition to normative legal requirements, even in the case of factual legal requirements, it is not uncommon to reach a conclusion that differs from the facts recognized from a normative perspective.

---

5 Legal Methodology 551 (Kye Il Lee ed. 2017) (In Korean) ("Even if legal interpretation is the priority task of law oriented towards legal practice, legal science cannot stop at interpretation. Because even the most carefully crafted laws do not contain solutions to every problem that may arise.").

6 For an academic paper that addresses this issue, *see* Jong-gu Kim, *Objective and Normative Interpretation of Criminal Law – Related to recent Supreme Court Cases –*, 13(3) Hongik L. Stud. 461 (2012) (In Korean).

Let us take an example. According to Article 111 of the Korean Civil Code, a declaration of intent becomes effective when it "reaches" the other party. However, the Supreme Court interprets the meaning of "reach" as "reachability" or the "possibility of reaching the point" rather than reaching in the factual sense.[7] What is the reason? It is nothing other than a normative judgment that takes into account the purpose of the system. If we look at it purely as a factual concept, if the other party deliberately refuses to receive it, even though the notice and proof of contents have arrived in the other party's controlled area, there will be no effect of arrival. This is typically an example of modifying a factual concept by the "normative element" of "the purpose of the system," and such examples are not uncommon in the interpretation of substantive law.

Second, the word "normative" is also a concept that contrasts with the word "logical." How logical is the legal argument? It is often said that the basic form of legal argument is a syllogism, but as mentioned earlier, no one today believes that legal reasoning can be easily solved by a syllogism. R. Alexy also points out that the reason is that the problem of "evaluation" cannot be avoided in legal reasoning,[8] and that such an evaluation is nothing but "normative judgment." Logic is the basis of legal reasoning, but the final conclusion is never resolved through logic alone, and normative elements sometimes distort the conclusion reached by a logical process.

In the end, the meaning of the word "normative" in legal reasoning is to reach the optimal conclusion based on "acknowledged facts" or "logical reasoning" but without being limited by them, taking into account the purpose of the legal provisions, legal principles, and constitutional spirit, among others.

B. Specifics of How Normative Judgments Work in Legal Reasoning

Below, I will analyze the specifics of how normative judgments work in legal reasoning by dividing them into four categories, which include more detailed sub-categories.

---

7 Korean Supreme Court, 10. 23. 1983, 82Daka439 ("The arrival of a quasi-legal act such as a notice of transfer of claims, like a declaration of intent, refers to when the debtor is in an objective state where he can know the contents of the notice, according to social concepts, it is not necessary that the debtor actually received the notice or knew the contents of the notice.").

8 Alexy, *supra* note 4, at 27–45.

I. Basic Type: "Evaluation" of Facts

First, the most basic type is the "evaluation" of facts. Simply put, the evaluation of facts is to determine whether the facts admitted at trial are included in the relevant legal requirements. Can this or that act of the defendant be considered "fraud," "embezzlement," or "sexual harassment"? Under a series of facts, is it possible to recognize "justifiable cause" or "gross negligence"? The facts were evaluated at the beginning and end of the trial.[9]

Mostly, this evaluation is not directly derived from the interpretation of abstract legal texts. Of course, there are legal requirements that can be subsumed relatively easily, such as sales and gifts, etc., but in many cases, automatic subsumption is not possible, and in such cases, various types of normative judgments are bound to be involved, as we will see later. In such judgments, the text of the law is, of course, the core standard, but it is not limited to it, and various factors play an overlapping role.

For instance, in a sexual harassment case, the court must first determine what happened in the past through evidence. Afterwards, it is necessary to determine how to evaluate such facts in terms of legal requirements. However, this fact-finding process is mostly not separated from the evaluation process. While reviewing the case records, examining witnesses, listening to the statements of the defendant and the victim, and studying the facial expressions and attitudes of those making statements in court, the judge determines how the defendant placed his hand on the victim's shoulder, the intensity of the contact, what happened before that, and so on. Since the task of determining facts itself is ultimately for evaluation, evaluative judgment is never excluded at the fact recognition stage.

This process of evaluation overlaps with legal interpretation but is not completely the same thing. Forcible sexual harassment refers to an act that infringes upon the sexual freedom of another person through assault or intimidation and causes feelings of sexual shame or disgust. When interpreting the law narrowly, it reveals the general meaning of the law, so it

---

9 This point can be easily confirmed in Supreme Court rulings. For example, *see* Korean Supreme Court, 04. 29. 2021, 2020Da227455 ("the person claiming it must prove that an act that is assessed as constituting an illegal act by invading the protected area of rights is not illegal"); Korean Supreme Court, 02. 16. 2017, 2016Do13362 ("However, in order to say that there is a dispositional act by the victim, the objective aspect that an act that can be evaluated as a dispositional act was performed by the victim is not enough, and the corresponding intention to dispose of it must also be recognized."). In this way, the issue of "evaluation" can be said to be a core issue in legal judgment.

is natural that this general definition of forced harassment must be the basis. However, the final judgment of the case is not automatically derived from the abstract meaning of the legal text. The relationship between the two people at the time the defendant placed his hand on the victim's shoulder, the intent to harm as read from the defendant's and the victim's attitudes, and the degree of shame and psychological shock on the victim are subject to a normative evaluation after confirming the specific facts. It is something that is determined and not automatically derived through legal interpretation alone. Let us look at the Supreme Court decision below (Supreme Court 2018). 2. 8. 2016Do17733).

> "① In the crime of forcible molestation, molestation objectively means causing sexual shame or disgust in the general public and violating the sexual freedom of the victim as an act that goes against good sexual morality.
> ② Whether this applies is determined by the victim's intention, gender, age, previous relationship between the actor and the victim, the circumstances leading to the act, the specific nature of the act, the surrounding objective circumstances, and the sexual moral concepts of the time. "It must be decided comprehensively and carefully."

In the above judgment, sentence ① refers to the general interpretation of forcible molestation and sentence ② explains how the court evaluates the act in question. In this way, there are many examples of Supreme Court rulings that distinguish between issues of legal interpretation and normative evaluation.

In a nutshell, the issue of evaluation is inextricably linked to fact-finding on the one hand and legal interpretation on the other. However, this is a separate thought process that is clearly differentiated from the two. In other words, "legal interpretation → normative evaluation → fact-finding" are closely interlinked but are not the same.[10]

10 Regarding the specific process, *see* Bum-jin Kim, *A Study on the Interaction between Syllogism and Normative Judgment in Legal Reasoning*, 199 Just. 305 (2023) (In Korean).

II. Evaluation Target Expansion

1. Judgment of Sub-Requirements Derived Through Legal Interpretation

The second area where normative judgment plays a central role is the judgment of detailed sub-requirements that specify abstract legal requirements. Normative judgment plays a larger role in these detailed sub-requirements than judgment of the main requirements in type 1.

For example, consider a tort case according to the famous "Hand Formula," which determines whether the duty of care has been violated by comparing the probability of the occurrence of an accident (P), the degree of damage (L), and the cost of preventing an accident (B).[11]

However, determining the probability of an accident occurring (P), the degree of damage (L), and the cost of preventing an accident (B) and comparing them are mental processes that combine fact-finding and normative judgment, for which the court is fully responsible. It is not derived from the interpretation of any legal text.

Moreover, the above formula is only a general theory, and independent judgment is required for each individual case. For example, the duty of care in cases of compensation for damages due to facility defects, the duty of care of financial institutions in financial accidents, and the degree of duty of care of information processors in hacking incidents on the internet are individual and different for every case. Therefore, the B, L, and P elements necessary for the final judgment of these cases must be judged based on the facts of each case.

2. Evaluation of Various Ancillary Requirements Accompanying the Determination of Legal Requirements

Another subtype in which normative judgment plays an important role is judgment regarding various types of indirect facts or collateral requirements. It is not a core legal requirement but an ancillary requirement that must be predicated for a trial, such as the judgment on whether a building under construction should be regarded as independent real estate or is still merely a movable property,[12] and determining whether a specific facility is

11 United States v. Carroll Towing Co., 159 F.2d 169 (2d. Cir. 1947).
12 Korean Supreme Court, 05. 30. 2003, 2002Da21592,21608.

integrated with movable property or real estate and would require excessive costs to separate, as well as whether an advertising leaflet with specific content is "subscribed to" or an "inducement to subscribe."[13] There are cases where the judgment is clear without much disagreement, but there are also many ambiguous limit cases. These judgments start with recognizing facts, but that alone is not enough, and the final judgment is always bound to be influenced by normative factors, such as the purpose of the laws.

3. Judgment of Additional Issues That Arise When Multiple Laws Are Applied

Another type of case in which normative judgments come to the fore is that which requires additional judgments, as multiple requirements overlap. In trials, it is not unusual that multiple legal requirements are applied in an overlapping manner. In such cases, the legal interpretation of the two laws is basic, but that is not enough. In most cases, it does not specify which law takes precedence in such conflicts. Therefore, in such cases, various normative judgments that take into account the purpose of the system determine the conclusion of the trial.

For example, let us look at the Supreme Court's decision that disputed whether a title trust constitutes performance for illegal causes.[14] According to the Act on the Registration of Real Estate under Actual Titleholder's Name, title trusts are prohibited unless they fall under exceptions. Therefore, there is no doubt that title trust is illegal. The issue is whether the title trust is not just a violation of the law but also constitutes performance for illegal causes (Article 746 of the Civil Act). In the above case, that point was disputed, and for this judgment, Article 746 of the Civil Act, Article 103 of the Civil Act, and the legislative purpose of the Act on the Registration of Real Estate Under Actual Titleholder's Name must be taken into consideration, but they alone are not enough.

In order to make such a judgment, the court must make judgments as to (i) whether the harmful effects caused by the misuse of title trusts, such as real estate speculation, tax evasion, etc., have reached a level that our society cannot tolerate; (ii) the degree of property damage suffered by the title trustors if performance for illegal cause is recognized, which results in

13 Korean Supreme Court, 05. 29. 2001, 99Da55601,55618.
14 Korean Supreme Court, 06. 20. 2019, 2013Da218156.

the loss of ownership; and (iii) balancing judgment between the two, and such judgments are not derived automatically from the law.

For these judgments, it is necessary to go beyond the recognition of facts or legal interpretation in the case at hand and make normative and evaluative judgments about the social reality of real estate title trusts in our society at the time of judgment, their side effects, and the need to respond to them. In fact, in the above case, even among the Supreme Court Justices, their evaluations on this point were polarized. A comparison of the judgment in this part of the majority opinion and the dissenting opinion can be drawn as follows.

Judgment of majority opinion	Judgment of opposite opinion
"As a result, the rights to the trust real estate are always definitively vested in the title trustee, and the title trustee loses the rights to the real estate. In this case, the title trustor must bear the consequences of being directly deprived of his or her property, which is highly likely to infringe upon essential aspects of property rights."	"Even if there is a possibility that the property rights of the title trustor may be slightly infringed, it is inevitable in order to contribute to the sound development of the national economy and establish social order by preventing activities such as speculation and tax evasion, normalizing real estate transactions and stabilizing real estate prices."

4. Cases in Which Supreme Court Adopts "Comprehensive Consideration Theory"

There are countless cases where the Supreme Court ruled that in order to determine specific legal requirements, A, B, C, D, etc., must be comprehensively considered. For example, (i) judgment on whether to reduce the amount of expected damages,[15] (ii) judgment on whether disclosure

15 The Supreme Court requires the consideration of "the economic status of the creditor and debtor, the purpose and content of the contract, the circumstances (motive) for predicting the amount of damages, the ratio of the expected amount to the amount of the debt, the size of the expected damages, the transaction practices and economic conditions at the time, and whether the debtor entered into the contract." It is said that "the circumstances of the violation, etc." must be comprehensively considered (Korean Supreme Court, 12. 26. 2013, 2013Da213090).

of personal information infringes on personality rights,[16] (iii) judgment on whether to grant the right to cancel the contract in case of delayed creditor,[17] (iv) automobile. This includes whether liability for compensation for catastrophic losses is acknowledged.[18] Since these issues are intended for the Supreme Court to give up the conclusive declaration of legal doctrines that will be applied to all subsequent cases and to recommend taking into account, as much as possible, the characteristics of each individual case, the function of normative judgment is bound to be further emphasized.

16 The Supreme Court mentions the following – "Whether an individual is a public entity, the public nature and public interest of personal information, the appropriateness of the purpose, procedure, and use form of personal information collection, the necessity of using personal information, and the nature and content of interests infringed by the use of personal information, etc." It is said that the decision must be made by taking into account the "circumstances" etc. (Korean Supreme Court. Full Bench Decision, 09. 2. 2011, 2008Da42430).

17 The Supreme Court requires the consideration of "the purpose and content of the contract, the nature of benefits, transaction practices, the intentions of the parties to the contract expressed objectively and externally, the circumstances of contract conclusion and performance, the proportion of creditors' receipt or cooperation in the process of performance of benefits, etc." It is said that "each judgment must be made individually after comprehensive consideration" (Korean Supreme Court, 10. 28. 2021, 2019Da293036).

18 The Supreme Court said, "In this case, whether it is an accident with serious damage that leaves a potential disability depends on the circumstances and extent of the accident, the area and severity of damage, the repair method, the age and mileage of the car, and the ratio of repair costs to the car value at the time of the accident." It is said that the decision must be made by comprehensively considering the circumstances, such as whether or not there have been repairs to the extent required to be recorded as an accident history in the used car performance and condition inspection record (Korean Supreme Court, 05. 17. 2017, 2016Da248806).

III. Other Areas in Which Normative Judgment Works

Other areas where normative judgment plays an important role in legal reasoning include the following:

1. Contract Disputes and Normative Judgments

Another area where normative judgments play a tremendous role is contract disputes.[19] Contract disputes are one of the largest types of cases in civil disputes, where, compared to any other type of case, normative judgments are more significant than legal interpretations or precedents. In contracts entered into between non-lawyers, it is common for the meaning to be unclear, and even in cases where the meaning seems clear, both parties often have different interpretations. In such cases, the court must supplement the parties' intentions from a normative perspective and make a final conclusion based on this. These normative judgments also have the characteristic of crossing between legal issues, such as the interpretation of a contract and fact-finding, such as the parties' intentions (i.e., the distinction is ambiguous).

2. Role of Normative Judgment in Fact-Finding

One of the vast areas in which normative judgments play a central role is fact-finding. It is easy to think that fact-finding is based only on evidence, but this is not the case at all. Although it cannot be discussed in detail in this paper, the role of normative judgment in fact-finding is overwhelming, such as the evaluation of the credibility of evidence, and the composition and reconstruction of an overall storyline composed of evidence, etc., not to mention the rules of logic and experience.

Depending on which aspect of the evidence the judge focuses on, the evaluation of the various factors seen above may vary, and such differences may also affect the final conclusion of the trial. In that very sense, the role of normative judgment in the fact-finding process may be much more important than expected.

---

19 For research on this, *see* Jun-gyu Choi, Study on Contract Interpretation Methods – Focusing on the Normative Character of Contract Interpretation-] (2020) (In Korean). The title of this book itself shows how important a role normative elements play in contract interpretation.

3. Judgment of Balancing, Sentencing Judgment

Balancing and criminal sentencing judgments are also prominent examples of normative judgments. We have seen some examples before, but there are countless other cases that require such quantitative thinking in trials. Some examples are as follows: (i) lawsuits regarding neighboring relations must compare the interests of the landowner and the surrounding area in each specific case,[20] (ii) in the case of an injunction claim for violation of personal rights, the necessity of the prohibited act and the interests of protecting personality rights,[21] (iii) the collective interests of the company and the interests of workers in labor cases, such as confirmation of invalidity of dismissal,[22] (iv) the interests of freedom of expression and the right to reputation in defamation lawsuits, (v). Furthermore, countless matters need to be compared in a trial, such as whether to issue an order to submit documents according to procedural law, as well as the need to compare the confidentiality of the documents of the document holder and the interests of the claimant.

IV. Final Conclusion of Trial and Multi-Layered Normative Judgment

Lastly, there is the issue of "multi-layered normative judgment" for the final conclusion of the trial. This is an easy case if the final conclusion is automatically determined by legal interpretation. On the other hand, legal interpretation itself is not easy for difficult issues, but in the process of reaching a final conclusion, not only the meaning of legal terms but also legal principles, constitutional grounds, comparative law review, and various types of policy arguments that support a specific conclusion are reviewed in an overlapping manner. In the case of the Supreme Court's en banc rulings, which typically have difficult issues, the length of the judgment alone includes dozens or even more than a hundred pages. In the case of rulings on such difficult matters, no conclusion can be reached based on a single issue of legal interpretation. Most debates begin with the theory of legal interpretation, but in difficult cases, a comprehensive and multi-layered judgment of the various factors considered determines the final conclusion of the trial.

---

20 Korean Supreme Court, 11. 10. 2016, 2013Da71098.
21 Korean Supreme Court, Full Bench Decision, 09. 2. 2011, 2008Da42430.
22 Korean Supreme Court, 11. 7. 1995, 95Nu9792.

For example, the case of the famous ruling on conscientious objection to military service[23] began with a debate on the interpretation of Article 88 of the Military Service Act but also included issues of freedom of conscience under the Constitution, the ramifications of acknowledging this (confrontation between South and North Korea and the issue of national defense obligations), and alternative service. There are always conflicting and majority opinions on a variety of issues, ranging from the possibility of abuse of the ritual system to debates over the differences between Eastern and Western cultural traditions. In difficult cases, a comprehensive and multi-layered judgment of these various considerations determines the final conclusion of the trial.

Meanwhile, the norms applied in multi-layered normative judgments can be broadly classified into past laws and regulations, various judgments related to the current normative situation, and consideration of results or policy judgments, which will be examined in detail in Section C.

V. Conclusion Drawn from This Section

As mentioned above, the detailed areas in which normative judgments intervene in legal reasoning are diverse. Although there are differences between laws, in many cases, laws do not provide detailed and specific guidance on what conclusions should be reached in a specific case. The point is that there is not much difference, even if we decide on methodological positions, such as literal interpretation and teleological interpretation, subjective interpretation and objective interpretation. Normative judgment fills in the empty space in various ways and allows legal reasoning to reach its final conclusion. So what is the content of the norms that make up normative judgments? Let us change the item and take a look.

C. What Is the Content of Norms Considered in Normative Judgments?

The most important aspect of normative judgment is, of course, legal text. But it does not stop there. Various values and policy elements, such as morality, ethical requests, and the maximization of social welfare, also constitute the content of normative judgments. Additionally, changes in the

23 Korean Supreme Court, Full Bench Decision], 11. 11 2018, 2016Do10912.

normative situation that serve as a premise for normative judgment should also be stressed. There may be diverse standards for classifying the contents of normative judgments in detail, but below, I will briefly summarize them based on the temporal standards of the past, present, and future. This is because such a classification most clearly shows the cause of the difficulties facing legal reasoning.

I. Past: Legal Interpretation Methodology, "Normative Judgment" on How to Understand the Law

The most important aspect of legal reasoning is, of course, the legal norms established in the past. There is no doubt that the starting point of legal argument or legal reasoning is the legal text itself. However, even if you look at the contents of the law, there are many cases in which the exact meaning of the law is unclear. As discussed in the introduction, the legal interpretation theory that legal methodology focuses on is the controversy surrounding this point. As is well known, literal interpretation, teleological interpretation, subjective interpretation, and objective interpretation are discussions of methodologies surrounding how to interpret the law. However, there is no correct answer in such a conflict of opinion. In academic terms, there are conflicting views on whether it is possible to theoretically establish the hierarchy of legal interpretation,[24] but there is no consensus, and in practice, it is especially difficult to find a case where one position is superior.

However, if you think about it carefully, the choice of such a legal interpretation methodology is also a "normative judgment." The position that chooses literalism is the position that stresses values such as separation of powers, judicial passivity, and legal stability. On the other hand, the position that emphasizes objective and teleological interpretation is the position that emphasizes flexible adaptation of the law according to changes in times. While the subjective and historical interpretations emphasize the legislator's will, the objective and teleological interpretations emphasize specific validity. As with all value issues, there is no known answer. In this regard, a more important issue than one might think is the temporal conflict between the past and the present, and we will examine it by changing the topic.

---

24 *See* Gye-il Lee,*A Critical Study on the Hierarchy Theory of Legal Interpretation Standards]*, 18(3) J. Legal. Phil. 125 (2015) (In Korean).

In practice, this conflict unfolds in various ways, and it is difficult to say what a uniform answer is. Even looking at the Supreme Court's en banc ruling, even in cases where the majority opinion takes a judicially passive stance based on literalism, there is an opposing opinion that an interpretation that goes beyond the literal is required based on a teleological interpretation theory based on justice and equity. Even in cases where theoretical interpretation is required, there is an opposing opinion that such an interpretation is beyond the authority of the judiciary.[25] Ultimately, behind the judgment on the scope of legal text lies another normative judgment called judicial philosophy.

II. Present: Changes in Normative Situations and Various Normative Judgments

An indispensable element when discussing normative judgments is a change in the normative situation. All legal reasoning presupposes legal texts established in the past, but on the other hand, it presupposes the current normative situation. The normative situation has numerous legal reasoning issues.

First, the examples previously mentioned in Section B, such as the detailed requirements (subtype 2, Hand Formula case), additional requirements (subtype 3, title trust case), and ancillary requirements (subtype 5, building under construction case), are strictly current. In order to determine whether a real estate title trust is an illegal benefit, the degree of social harm and property rights infringement of the real estate title trust "at the time of judgment" must be reviewed. In tort cases where the Hand Formula is applied, the elements of B, P, and L are those of the present and not of the past. This is a critical difference from the legal interpretation governed by the wording of legal norms enacted in the past. Since the legal text is the starting point for legal interpretation, literal interpretation is the basic rule, and the legislator's intention cannot be ignored. On the other hand, the detailed, additional, ancillary requirements, etc., seen above, are all premised on the current situation. Legal reasoning is always bound

25 For example, *see* Korean Supreme Court, Full Bench Decision, 11. 11 2018, 2016-Do10912 (the ruling on conscientious objection to military service) or Korean Supreme Court, Full Bench Decision, 6. 22. 2006, 2004Seu42 (the decision to correct family status for transgender people).

to involve contemporary ethical and social norms and moral and social requests in various ways.

This also applies to the legal principles and moral norms discussed in legal philosophy. The long-standing conflict between legal positivism and natural laws over whether morality should be viewed as a part of positive law can only be a discussion about the tension between the legal norms of the past and the moral norms of the present when viewed from a time frame. Unlike laws, in the case of moral norms, only the moral concepts of the time are at issue, and there is no reason for past ones to be questioned at trial.

Even from the perspective of legal interpretation, which constitutes a major requirement, there are many cases in which the Supreme Court changes precedents, even though there is no change in the legal text.[26] Even if it is not a Supreme Court precedent, there are many cases in which the overall flow of lower courts changes. Why does the conclusion of legal reasoning change, even though the text of the law has not been revised? If you approach legal reasoning with a focus on legal interpretation, there are limitations in explaining this point. This is because it is none other than a "change in the normative situation" and a corresponding change in the "normative judgment." It may be said that it is a change in legal interpretation due to a change in the normative situation, but the fundamental cause of the change in legal interpretation, even though there is no change in the legal text, is a change in normative judgment due to a change in the normative situation. Ultimately, the change in legal interpretation is due to a change in legal interpretation. It is the end result, not the cause.

This gap between past and present provides crucial clues as to the question of why legal reasoning is so difficult. As seen in this paper, legal reasoning, starting from laws enacted in the past, provides a final conclusion through numerous normative judgments, and such detailed normative judgments are thoroughly premised on the normative situation of the present, about which legal texts do not say anything.

Among American legal interpretation theories, "dynamic statutory interpretation" follows this thinking. This theory emphasizes that the interpretation of laws should take place within the political, social, and legal context

26 Korean Supreme Court, Full Bench Decision, 11. 20. 2008, 2007Da27670 ; Korean Supreme Court, 5. 11. 2023, 2018Da248626 (Most notably, the Supreme Court recently issued two en banc rulings in the past 15 years regarding the method of selecting the presiding officer of ancestral rites, thereby discarding previous precedents.).

at the time of interpretation, not at the time of enactment.[27] However, this theoretical position is closer to a descriptive theory than a normative theory. As we saw in detail earlier, all trials and legal reasoning reflect the current normative situation in various ways.

III. Future: Policy Argument or Outcome Consideration Argument

Lastly, the normative judgment that matters in legal reasoning is a consideration of the effect that the judgment will have on our society in the future. Another area where there is intense theoretical debate as to whether it can be a factor in legal reasoning, similar to legal principles and moral norms in existing legal theories, is the so-called policy argument and outcome consideration argument.

In principle, this is to consider whether the result of the ruling is in the direction of maximizing social utility, but this too is conflicting between those who oppose it from the standpoint of the principle of separation of powers or respect for rights and those who actively accept it.[28] It is widely known that extralegal arguments are widely accepted in mainly American pragmatism[29] and that Dworkin's legal theory is a Kantian counterargument to such a position.[30]

Although it cannot be discussed in detail in this paper, our practice also accepts policy arguments or outcome consideration arguments in various ways. In particular, looking at recent Supreme Court rulings, there are cases that mention transaction costs and use social utility maximization as the basis for judgment and rulings that consider the negative ripple effects of decisions, etc., which shows that our practice also accepts the ripple effects of rulings in various ways.

---

27 William N. Eskridge Jr., *Dynamic Statutory Interpretation*, 135 U. Pa. L. Rev. 1479 (1987).

28 For this theoretical conflict, *see* Doo-hyun Kong, *Models of Legal Interpretation in the Korean Supreme Court: Legal Positivism, Legal Realism, and the Theory of Legal Principles*, 22(2) J. Legal. Phil. 185, 201–07 (2019) (In Korean).

29 R. Posner says that the emphasis on consideration of results in American jurisprudence dates back to John Dewey, the founder of pragmatism, and that the core of Justice Holmes' book The Common Law is also the consideration of results. Richard Posner, Beobgwaneun Eotteohge Sagohaneunga [How Judges Think] 338 (Gye-moon Baek & Jong-hyun Park trans., 2008) (In Korean).

30 Kong, *supra* note 28, at 206.

IV. Conclusion

This classification over time clearly demonstrates the difficulty of legal reasoning compared to the classical legal interpretation methodology. As seen earlier, legal interpretation, which is the starting point of legal reasoning, begins with laws enacted in the past. However, the law does not tell us how to solve the various problems currently facing us. It also does not tell us how much to consider future outcomes. However, legal reasoning must always address current problems and take into account future consequences despite the extent to which this may be disputed. Such judgments are normative judgments rather than legal interpretations. As seen in Section B, normative judgments also play a role in determining legal requirements and various auxiliary requirements, but if you look at the specifics of such actions, legal interpretation and consideration of the present and future ultimately constitute substantive content.

D. Summary of Discussion

As seen above, judging legal reasoning or legal syllogisms in simple forms, such as legal interpretation, fact-finding, and conclusion, is not in line with reality. Ultimately, it is the various types of normative judgments that connect legal interpretation and fact-finding and constitute the details of the long journey to the final conclusion. As mentioned earlier, if we compare legal reasoning to the human body, normative judgments are like thousands or tens of thousands of capillaries. Nevertheless, the existing legal methodology had a strong tendency to understand legal reasoning only through the framework of legal interpretation, which inevitably had clear limitations in understanding the realistic complexity of legal reasoning. This is especially true considering that according to modern legislative principles, legal provisions are essentially general abstraction and, therefore, cannot contain all individual cases.

It is true that legal interpretation is the starting point for legal reasoning, but the legal text says much less than you might think. Not to mention indeterminate and abstract concepts, even relatively clear legal terms often only vaguely indicate direction. In such cases, in order for legal reasoning to reach a final conclusion, numerous detailed decisions are needed to fill the empty space to finish a long journey, and normative judgment is a conceptual tool that explains such detailed judgments. Further study on the detailed content, operation, classification, and limitations of normative judgments should become a central theme of legal methodology.

Taking Purpose Seriously: Radbruch and Jhering in the Supreme Court of Korea*

Doo Hyun Kong

Abstract

Teleological interpretation, or purposive interpretation, has grown recently in the Supreme Court of Korea. Along the way, the German legal philosophers Radbruch and Jhering were cited directly or indirectly in the Korean Supreme Court's decision. Accordingly, it is timely to examine the judicial philosophy on which the Court has applied such expression. The development of purposive interpretation can be categorized into two approaches.

The first is an approach that uses the entire legal order as the normative criterion for legal interpretation and aims at it. This approach has something in common with Radbruch's theory based on the objective theory of interpretation. Justice Kim Jae Hyung promoted this approach at the Supreme Court.

Second, it is an approach that extracts and synthesizes specific legal objectives from the Constitution, statutes, and provisions of the law and applies them to legal interpretation. This approach is similar to Jhering's discussion. Also, Justice Ahn Chul Sang solves the problem through this approach in hard cases.

This paper examines the strengths and weaknesses of the two approaches based on the influence the two approaches had in the Supreme Court en banc Decision ruling on Article 92-6 [indecent act] of the Military Criminal Act.

Keywords

legal methodology, teleological interpretation, purposivism, purpose of law, Radbruch, Jhering

---

* This chapter was originally published in Journal of Korean Law, vol.23, no.2 (August 2024), pp. 247-266.

A. Introduction

Studying the Supreme Court's methodology to resolve cases is essential for understanding a judicial system. Of course, the same methodology does not apply to all cases. So-called "easy cases" are mostly resolved according to the text of the law. However, in "hard cases", the conclusions may vary depending on the judicial philosophy of the justices.

This article briefly outlines the legal methodology of the Supreme Court of Korea and then examines how teleological or purposive interpretation has recently developed. Note that Radbruch and Jhering were cited directly or indirectly in the Korean Supreme Court's decision. In that case, it is desirable to examine the judicial philosophy on which the Court based such an expression.

In particular, I focus on two theories. The first is an approach that uses the entire legal order as the normative criterion for legal interpretation. This approach has something in common with Radbruch's theory and can be found in the opinion of Justice Kim Jae Hyung.

The second is an approach that extracts and synthesizes specific legal objectives from the Constitution, statutes, and provisions of the law and applies them to legal interpretation. This approach resembles Jhering's discussion. In addition, Justice Ahn Chul Sang solves the problem in hard cases using this approach.

After briefly describing the approaches, I examine the strengths and weaknesses of each based on their effects on the Supreme Court en banc Decision ruling on [indecent act] of the Military Criminal Act. The two theories of legal interpretation, which are in a dynamic relationship where they compete with or complement each other in the context of the case, show a new form of purposivism distinguished from textualism, intentionalism, and legal pragmatism. Furthermore, this analysis more clearly elucidates the significant role legal methodology or judicial philosophy plays in the judicial process.

B. Legal Methodology in the Supreme Court of Korea

Until the 1990s, the debate on legal interpretation theory in the Supreme Court was characterized by a conflict between judicial activism and judicial restraint. The primary issue was whether to interpret a statute strictly according to its literal meaning or to interpret it flexibly, considering the law's purpose.[1] During this period, Supreme Court justices were appointed through a vertical hierarchy, with few differences in judicial philosophy among them.

In 2005, the need for justices with diverse opinions was recognized, and the composition of the Supreme Court began to diversify. The first female justice was appointed, Supreme Court justices with various careers and philosophies were appointed, and the theory of legal interpretation changed.[2] At the beginning of the change, the pro-constitutional interpretation, which considers the "entire legal order with the Constitution as the supreme norm," began to be emphasized.[3]

The Supreme Court's interpretation of the law was synthesized in the Supreme Court Decision 2006Da81035, which was decided on April 23, 2009. In interpreting the concept of 'tenant' entitled to benefits under the Rental Housing Act, the Supreme Court explained the goals, methods, and limitations of statutory interpretation:[4]

> Since the law is, in principle, a universally valid norm of society that is equally binding on an unspecified number of people, the interpretation of the law must be made objectively valid by identifying the standard meaning of the law and, as far as possible, maintaining consistency that is acceptable to all, so that legal stability is not compromised. In addition, since positive law is often formulated with universal and typical cases in mind, it is necessary to interpret the law in such a way that it has concrete feasibility, i.e., the most plausible solution for the specific case, in order to apply it to the various cases that arise in real life. In short, the goal of legal interpretation should be to find concrete feasibility without compromising legal stability.
>
> In the process, the interpretation should be based on the principle of faithfulness to the ordinary meaning of the words used in the law as far as possible, and should additionally employ a systematic and logical method of interpretation that takes into account the legislative intent and purpose of the law, its history of enactment and amendment, its harmony with the entire legal order, and its relationship with other laws, in order

1 Kong 22(2) Korean. J. Leg. Phil. 2019, 185 (190–191).
2 D. Kim 13(1) Korean. J. Leg. Phil. 2010, 95 (111–112).
3 Kong, supra note 1 (210–212).
4 Korean Supreme Court, 04.23. 2009, 2006Da81035.

> to arrive at a reasonable interpretation that meets the aforementioned requirements.
>
> On the other hand, if the text of the law itself is composed of relatively clear concepts, in principle, other methods of interpretation are no longer necessary or can only be limited even if the terms used in the provisions of law are to be interpreted differently from the ordinary meaning of the text by considering the legislative intent and purpose of the law and regulations, the systematic relevance of other provisions in the law and other laws and the harmony with the entire legal system cannot be ignored so there are certain limitations.

The decision declared that the goal of legal interpretation was to determine concrete feasibility without compromising legal stability (Rechtssicherheit). As a method of legal interpretation, it proposed a two-tiered interpretation theory based on the principle of faithful interpretation of the text's ordinary meaning that may additionally employ logical-systematic interpretation, historical interpretation, and purposive interpretation. Lastly, as a limit on legal interpretation, the decision urged that harmony with the entire legal system be considered. This represented a comprehensive acceptance of the various concepts of legal interpretation developed by the Supreme Court up to that time. An example is the legislative intent and purpose of the law and harmony with the entire legal order,[5] rather than the traditional textualism, which considers the possible meanings of the text (möglicher Wortsinn) as the limit of legal interpretation. The thrust of the judgment has been frequently cited as the Supreme Court's theory of legal interpretation ever since.

In the early 2010s, a trend of legal pragmatism emerged that centered on policy considerations and social pragmatism.[6] However, in the late 2010s, a legal interpretation theory that emphasized the entire legal order and pro-constitutional interpretation again formed the majority opinion in significant cases.[7] Meanwhile, Supreme Court justices who support textualism have continued to be influential.[8] These changes in the Supreme Court's legal interpretation theory reflect the diverse judicial philosophies of the

5 Kong, *supra* note 1 (217).
6 Kong, *supra* note 1 (224).
7 Kong, *supra* note 1 (227); *See also* K. Lee 18(2) J. Korean L. 2019, 335 (342).
8 *See* Park 1 J. Juris 2022, 381 (381–418).

Justices at the time. They will continue to be discussed and developed in the future.

Recently, the significance of purposive interpretation has surged. There was a sharp rise in the number of cases that addressed purposive interpretation from 2018 to 2023. Ten decisions were handed down in just three years: four in 2018, three in 2019, and three in 2020. Eight were handed down in the last three years: three in 2021, three in 2022, and two in 2023. This represented a significant increase given that only six decisions applying purposive interpretation were issued between the creation of the Supreme Court in 1948 and the 1990s. There were eight decisions in the 2000s and only five from 2010 to 2017.[9]

However, the rise of teleological interpretation did not completely contradict constitutional interpretation. Rather, the combination of teleological interpretation and pro-constitutional interpretation spawned new approaches.

This article examines two approaches to purposive interpretation. The key issues involved are how to construct the purpose of the law and how to link the purpose of the law to the interpretation of the law.

From now on, I will research on the influence of Radbruch's theory of legal interpretation, which presents purposiveness (Zweckmässigkeit) as the ideal of law (Rechtsidee) and constructs the purpose of law in terms of normative value within the framework of objective interpretation theory. Next, I will review the influence of Jhering's concept of law. That concept understood the general purpose of law as maintaining the community's social living conditions. It emphasized the appropriate balance between autonomy and coercion while respecting the purposes of various agents.

C. Radbruch's Purposiveness and Justice Kim Jae-Hyung

The influence of Radbruch can be traced to a judicial philosophy that focuses on the entire legal order. Radbruch based his theory of legal interpretation on the objective theory of interpretation. The distinction between subjective and objective theory is essentially whether the goal of legal interpretation is to reproduce the subjective intention of the legislator or to realize the inherent purpose of the law itself in the entire legal order.

9 Kong, Ph.D. dissertation, Seoul National University 2024, (1–2).

Thus, from the perspective of objective theory, what the framers of a law may not have been aware of at the time of its enactment can be ascertained by the interpreter of the law. "The interpreter can understand the law better than its legislator, and the law can be wiser than its legislator," Radbruch emphasisedemphasized.[10]

Justice Kim Jae Hyung[11] has led the approach centering on the pro-constitutional interpretation (Verfassungskonforme Auslegung) and the entire legal order.[12] In particular, Justice Kim Jae Hyung refined Radbruch's famous aphorism to coin the expression, "The law can be said to be wiser than the legislator."[13] This short sentence contains the core of objective theory.

The objective theory of interpretation has implications for other issues. First, the meaning of the law can change according to the context of the times even after it is enacted. Second, the law can be interpreted beyond the meaning of the text. Creating or interpreting laws is widely justified for judges. Furthermore, rather than accepting legislative supremacy, objective theory favors horizontal relations between the legislature and the judiciary.

Justice Kim Jae Hyung observed that the specific meaning, content, and scope of application of the law may vary depending on changes in social and economic conditions and changes in legal consciousness.[14] He emphasized that there is no need to be bound by the subjective intentions of the legislator when interpreting indeterminate concepts that inevitably involve normative judgments.[15] He identified the relationship between the legislature and the judiciary as a horizontal partnership[16] and consistently emphasized the need to consider the integrity of the entire legal order.[17]

Although the opinions of Justice Kim were not always in the majority, he pushed for change and provided direction based on the combination

10 Radbruch, Rechtphilosophie [legal philosophy] 211 (5th ed. 1956).

11 Justice Kim Jae-Hyung has been a judge since 1992, a professor of civil law at Seoul National University for 21 years since 1995, a Supreme Court Justice from September 2016 to September 2022, and a professor at Seoul National University since 2023.

12 Kong, 21(2) J. Korean L. 2022, 311 (312).

13 Korean Supreme Court, 11.01. 2018, 2016Do10912 (Justice Soon-Il Kwon, Jae Hyung Kim, Jae-Youn Cho, and You-Sook Min, concurring).

14 Korean Supreme Court, 04.21. 2022, 2019Do3047 (Justice Jae Hyung Kim, Jeong-Hee Noh, Dae-Yup Chun, and Kyeong-Mi Oh, concurring).

15 D. Kim/J. Kim, 2 J. Juris. 2023, 25 (39).

16 *Id.* at 39.

17 Legal Times, Retirement Speech of Justice Kim Jae-Hyung (Sept. 4, 2022), https://www.legaltimes.co.kr/news/articleView.html?idxno=68497 (In Korean).

of objective theory and the Constitutionally conforming interpretation. Specifically, Justice Kim's theory can be seen in the following excerpts from his decisions.

> Purposive interpretation is a method of interpretation that seeks to find the meaning of a statute in accordance with the rational purpose objectively required by the legal order. Interpretation does not simply reiterate what the legislator has already considered, but rather attempts to find the meaning and spirit of the law that the legislator is aiming for in a new context.[18]

> Legal norms cannot perfectly regulate all matters that occur in reality. Due to its general and abstract nature, the law is inherently bound to contain flaws in it. Interpretation of law is therefore not simply a matter of recognising and finding the law as it exists. In certain cases, it is necessary to actively shape the law by clarifying its scope of application through analogy or purposive reduction. This is the call of the substantive rule of law. Courts should declare 'law,' not 'statute.'[19]

> The interpretation of a law should not be limited to the subjective intention of the legislator at the time of enactment, but should explore the possible meanings of the text, reflecting the content and value of the Constitution, the highest norm, and clarify the legitimate meaning of the law suitable for the present era, considering the current legal situation and changes in legal consciousness over time.[20]

On the other hand, Radbruch identifies purposiveness (*Zweckmässigkeit*) as the ideal of law (*Rechtsidee*), along with justice and legal stability. In proposing purposiveness, Radbruch said that the content of the purpose of the law would be determined in the competition between democracy, socialism, liberalism, etc. from a relativistic perspective.[21]

However, Justice Kim Jae Hyung considers 'the unity of the legal order with the Constitution as the supreme norm' as the content of the purpose

---

18 Korean Supreme Court, 06.18. 2020, 2019Do14340 (Justice Jae Hyung Kim, concurring with the Dissenting Opinion).

19 Korean Supreme Court, 09.03. 2020, 2016Du32992 (Justice Jae Hyung Kim, concurring).

20 Korean Supreme Court, 04.21. 2022, 2019Do3047 (Justice Jae Hyung Kim, Jeong-Hee Noh, Dae-Yup Chun, and Kyeong-Mi Oh, concurring).

21 Radbruch, *supra* note 10 (156).

of law. Dworkin's concept of 'law as integrity'[22] is influential here.[23] This is because pro-constitutional interpretation can be linked to Dworkin's legal theory by expressing the unity of the legal order.

In this regard, Justice Kim Jae Hyung has proposed a constitutionalist interpretation, which goes beyond pro-constitutional interpretation that removes unconstitutionality and adopts constitutionally-oriented interpretation. The notion of the most appropriate interpretation for realizing the Constitution illustrates how purposive interpretation can be combined with constitutionally conforming interpretation.

> The interpretation of the law should reflect the constitutional provisions and their purpose. If several branches of interpretation are possible for certain legal provisions, a pro-constitutional interpretation that removes unconstitutionality by adopting a meaning consistent with the Constitution must be made, and furthermore, a constitutionally-oriented interpretation that adopts the meaning that best realizes the principles and values of the Constitution among interpretations consistent with the Constitution must be made.[24]

Because constitutionally-oriented interpretation has a structure that sets out a particular purpose and considers whether it is the most appropriate way of achieving that purpose,[25] Justice Kim Jae Hyung combined purposive and pro-constitutional interpretation to develop constitutionally-oriented interpretation. In a broad sense, this theory of legal interpretation is a kind of objective purposive interpretation. However, it is also differentiated from another form of purposive interpretation focusing on the law's specific purpose.

D. Jhering's Purpose and Justice Ahn Chul Sang

Jhering, who drew attention to the purpose of law before Radbruch, is the founder of purpose jurisprudence (*Zweckjurisprudenz*) and is famous

---

22 Dworkin, p. 226.

23 D. Kim, *supra* note 2 (110–11); D. Kim/J. Kim, *supra* note 15 (40–41).

24 Korean Supreme Court, 09.03. 2020, 2016Du32992 (Justice Jae Hyung Kim, concurring).

25 Eveline T. Feteris, 22 Argumentation 2008, 489 (490).

for the expression, "The end of the law is peace, the means to that end is struggle" in his book, *The Struggle for Law* (*Der Kampf ums Recht*).[26]

Whereas Radbruch's purpose of law is 'Ought' as the ideal of law (*Rechtsidee*), Jhering's purpose of law has a more concrete and individual substance, in which Jhering sees law as pursuing relative ends that are shaped by the needs of diverse people, groups, communities, and states.[27] In Jhering's view, the purpose of various subjects coexist in the law.

Furthermore, Jhering believes that law is a creation of purpose and contains purposiveness (*Zweckmässigkeit*) and that exploring the purpose of law is the greatest task of jurisprudence.[28] Therefore, for rational legal interpretation, it is essential to explore the purpose of the law and put it into judgment.

While Justice Kim Jae Hyung presents a theory of legal interpretation that focuses on the entire legal order, Justice Ahn Chul Sang argues that the more specific purpose of the law should be the focus of legal interpretation. This position was more evident when Justice Ahn cited Jhering.[29]

Accepting the conventional definition of law, which states that "law is the total of coercive norms enforced by a state," Jhering derives the elements of coercion and normativity as components of the law. At this point, Jhering asserts that "law without coercion is a contradiction in terms, a fire that does not burn and a light that does not shine."[30] Justice Ahn cites this in his argument on whether procedural regulations are compulsory: "A law without coercion is not a complete law as a 'bladeless knife' that Rudolph von Jhering said."[31] This led to the conclusion that the judiciary must give deference to what the legislature has made relatively clear as mandatory rules.

---

26 Jhering, 1877, p. 1.

27 Jhering, 1893, p. 440.

28 *Id.* (442).

29 Justice Ahn had served as a judge since 1986 and served as Justice from January 2018 to January 2024. He has been a chair professor at Konkuk University since March 2024.

30 Jhering, *supra* note 27 (320).

31 Korean Supreme Court, 03.18. 2021, 2018Du47264 (Justice Chul Sang Ahn , concurring). The main issue and Holding of this decision are as follows: Legal nature of the period within which the right to seek payment of childcare leave benefits prescribed in Article 70(2) of the former Employment Insurance Act can be exercised (held: prescriptive period), and the significance of the above provision as a norm (held: imperative provision).

In addition, Jhering said, "The sword without the scales is brute force, the scales without the sword is the impotence of law."[32] This means that coercion must be justified, and a balance to judge correctness is necessary for justification. Citing the analogy of the scale, Justice Ahn defined, "Trial is a process of weighing conflicting values with a scale of law and finding a balance" and explained that "The balance struck by the scale ought to ensure that the social system is functioning at the most appropriate condition and operating at the highest efficiency level, while keeping in mind the impact on members of the society, based on our experienced historicity and actuality."[33] Justice Ahn Chul Sang used the metaphor of the sword and the scales to describe the fate of the law in regulating society, saying that it is the essence of the law to pursue social goals through coercion.

Moreover, Jhering believes that the guarantee of social living conditions is the general purpose of the law.[34] He explains that individuals, groups, communities, and the state, which exist as independent subjects with their own purposes, can interact through various activities to achieve their purposes. As a result, the maintenance and development of society takes place.[35] Jhering posits that law serves as a mechanism to enforce societal objectives that cannot be achieved through autonomous actions in a society of self-interested individuals. Therefore, he presupposes that the law does not need to intervene in areas in society that can be resolved autonomously by individuals. For this reason, Jhering even emphasized the need for autonomous problem-solving in society.

Justice Ahn Chul Sang also emphasized the autonomous problem-solving of individuals and communities through the principle of proportionality for balancing public interest and self-interest. In particular, he distinguished between the legitimacy and justifiability of laws and expressed the attitude that laws must be validated as time progresses.

> Law is always legitimate, but it is not necessarily *ipso facto* justifiable. Law cannot be autotelic, and its reasonableness must be verified. Also, law cannot be permanent. There are times when a statute is wrong from the outset, but there are also times when a statute has become corrupted as time progresses, as we have frequently witnessed thus far.

---

32 Jhering, *supra* note 26 (1).

33 Korean Supreme Court, 03.18. 2021, 2018Du47264 (Justice Chul Sang Ahn , concurring); Korean Supreme Court, 03.11. 2021, 2018Oh2.

34 Jhering, *supra* note 27 (443).

35 *Id.* (565).

> The people have freedom to express disagreement with unreasonable laws or institution. They can seek recourse through filing a petition or lawsuit for repeal in an effort to make demands for improvement. Nonetheless, it is not so unusual for an unjustifiable law to be rectified in the process of assessing blame.[36]

Justice Ahn Chul Sang stated that the legal sanctions for wrongdoing should be appropriate, and that even if there is a problem with the ideological bias of an organization, it can be corrected by a free market of ideas based on the common sense promoted by the people. "Judicial judgments should aim to resolve disputes and conflicts and achieve social integration through legal peace," he emphasized.[37]

Justice Ahn Chul Sang's judicial philosophy, citing Jhering, has a more realistic view of pursuing legal peace and social integration by exploring the purpose of specific laws in terms of resolving social disputes and conflicts.[38] Also, it can be understood based on a sociological perspective and a purpose-oriented attitude toward the law. First, it is necessary to distinguish and respect the compulsory realm of the state and the autonomous realm of society in detail. Second, the law is a means of pursuing a certain social purpose. Third, interpreting the law derives specific norms based on the purpose of the law and pursues harmony of various values.

E. Hard Cases and Deeper Justification by Judicial Philosophy

While Justice Kim Jae Hyung's view is represented by a constitutionally-oriented interpretation that aims at the entire legal order, Justice Ahn Chul Sang's view places the specific purpose of the law in the history of society at the center of legal interpretation. The question raised by these two opinions is whether to develop a purposive interpretation with more emphasis on the entire legal order, including the Constitution as a supreme norm or

---

36 Korean Supreme Court, 09.03. 2020, 2016Du32992 (Justice Chul Sang Ahn, concurring).

37 Korean Supreme Court, 09.03. 2020, 2016Du32992 (Justice Chul Sang Ahn, concurring). In his retirement speech, he also emphasized, "The role of the judiciary, as mandated by the Constitution, is to achieve social integration by resolving conflicts and disputes in society peacefully in accordance with legal proceedings." See Retirement Speech of Justice Chul Sang Ahn Lawtimes, (Dec. 29, 2023), https://www.lawtimes.co.kr/news/194544 (In Korean).

38 Lawtimes, *supra* note (37).

to develop a purposive interpretation with more attention to the specific purpose of the law.

In most cases, these two approaches to statutory interpretation appear as a concurring opinion that reaches the same conclusion but on different grounds. This relationship differs from the confrontation between purposivism and textualism, which leads to different conclusions, sometimes in controversial cases. This is because pro-constitutional interpretation has the character of a systematic interpretation and accepts most of the principles and values of the law. On the other hand, purposive interpretation can eventually be abstracted to the purpose of the relevant constitution or the law's general purpose, even if it begins with the purpose of individual laws and legal provisions. This abstraction of the law's objective purpose will lead to combining the two perspectives, but these two positions often diverge in individual and specific cases.

This confrontation can be seen more clearly in the Supreme Court en banc Decision 2019Do3047 Decided April 21, 2022. The en banc decision concerns the scope of the offense provided for in Article 92-6 [indecent act] of the Military Criminal Act. The decision held that:[39]

> [1] Whether Article 92-6 of the Military Criminal Act applies in a case where anal intercourse or any similar act between same-sex servicemen have taken place in a private space with the voluntary consent of both parties and it is difficult to consider such sexual engagement a direct and specific infringement of healthy cultures and discipline of the military community (negative)
>
> [2] In a case where Defendant A and Defendant B, both military servicemen, were accused of violating the Military Criminal Act consisting of: (a) Defendant A's commission of acts of indecency by mutually kissing and performing oral and anal sex with Party C, who is also a military serviceman, in his bachelor enlisted quarter; and (b) Defendant B's commission of indecent acts with Defendant A in the same manner as above in Defendant B's bachelor enlisted quarter, the case holding that the Defendant's conduct does not constitute "anal intercourse or any other indecent act" subject to criminal punishment under Article 92-6 of the Military Criminal Act, in light of the circumstances that the Defendants and Party C are all male military servicemen and that they engaged in consensual oral and anal intercourse based on their freely formed intent

39 Korean Supreme Court, 04.21. 2022, 2019Do3047.

at the Defendant's bachelor enlisted quarters after duty hours and on weekends

The majority opinion of the Supreme Court, joined by Justice Kim Jae Hyung, concluded that "In light of the aforesaid legal normative assessment of same-sex sexual acts, imposing criminal punishment for consensual sex between same-sex military servicemen, especially in a case where such sexual engagement does not constitute a direct and concrete infringement of the healthy cultures and discipline of the military community, is prohibited in light of the entire legal order, including the Constitution of the Republic of Korea."[40]

The majority opinion concluded that the purpose of the provision was to protect both the 'healthy cultures and discipline of the military community' and the 'right to sexual self-determination of soldiers' and that a case of consensual sexual act in a private space could not be considered an infringement of both interests. Therefore, it was determined that punishment could not be applied based on the provision. Furthermore, through the concept of 'the entire legal order, including the Constitution,' the majority opinion clearly explained what kind of approach their legal interpretation theory is taking.[41] This approach is oriented toward abstractness and universality.

On the other hand, the concurring opinions of Justices Ahn Chul Sang and Lee Heung koo contend that "the current provision needs to be interpreted in a reasonable manner by sufficiently taking into account the distinctive purpose of the Military Criminal Act, which is to sustain combat strength for complete victory, within the framework of the constitutional order based on the guarantee of fundamental rights and separation of powers, and the legal value the current provision intends to protect, which is the healthy cultures and discipline of the military," and that, based on the situation of the act, "it is reasonable to understand that the current provision basically applies to a situation in the face of the enemy and during wartime or disturbance; conversely, in time of peace, the current

40 *Id.*

41 The majority opinion considered that "consensual sexual act in a private space" cannot be punished in that none of the two protective legal interests of this provision were violated, but it is not yet clear what judgment should be made if only one of the protective legal interests is violated.

provision applies only when there are concerns about a direct and concrete infringement on military discipline during military exercise or on guard."[42]

The concurring opinions of Justices Ahn Chul Sang and Lee Heung koo frame the purpose of the law differently from the majority opinion. At the constitutional level, they emphasize maintaining national security as one of the nation's most important responsibilities. At the level of the Act, it defines the distinctive purpose of the Military Criminal Act as 'securing combat power for victory in battle.' Lastly, it explains that the legal value intended to be protected by the provision is 'healthy cultures and discipline of the military community.' As a result, the purpose of the three levels is combined to serve as a criterion for solving the case. This approach is directed toward particularity and concreteness.

In this case, even though it may seem that the constitutional right to sexual self-determination is opposed to the purpose of the law, the concurring opinion of Justices Ahn and Lee strongly declared that "courts have a duty to provide a reasonable statutory interpretation that removes the unconstitutionality of the current provision and preserves the legal value protected thereby." So, 'the ultimate purpose of maintaining the military discipline' presented the standard that the right to sexual self-determination can be guaranteed in private areas that are less related to the core work of the military. Thus, the current rules do not apply during free time or on holiday. This distinction has the clearest logical structure in terms of a purposive interpretation. It is an alternative that realizes the objectives in a way that is harmonized with constitutional rights.

Two recent developments in legal interpretation in the Supreme Court have gone beyond textualism[43] and legal pragmatism to seek the legitimate and justifiable meaning of the law by interpreting the purpose and spirit

---

42 Korean Supreme Court, 04.21. 2022, 2019Do3047. *See* Ahn, 3 J. Juris. 2024, 45 (63). In addition, there was a concurring opinion by Justice Seon-soo Kim that sexual acts mutually agreed upon by the two cannot be criminally punished in any case based on the interpretation of the text "against" used in the article, and there was also a Dissenting Opinion by Justice Jae-Youn Cho and Justice Dong-Won Lee that anal intercourse or any other indecent act should be punished regardless of whether they agreed upon or were committed in private space.

43 The relationship between pro-constitutional interpretation and literal interpretation is not straightforward. In cases where a literal interpretation of the text is consistent with the Constitution and protects the rights of individuals, there have been rulings that deny what the text says in consideration of political judgments regarding national finances and so on. Particularly when textualism is used to secure constitutional rights, and Supreme Court judges who favor a pro-constitutional interpretation

of constitutions, statutes, and provisions. Moreover, Judicial philosophy, including these theories of interpretation, is an important basis for deciding hard cases and providing deeper justification for the conclusion.

F. Reflection on the Two Approaches

It is also necessary to recognize the weaknesses of each approach to legal interpretation. In the case of pro-constitutional interpretation centered on the entire legal order, 'entire legal order' is described as encompassing the general public's perception of law, which has been formed with the Constitution, the supreme norm, at the center.[44] Therefore, identifying and confirming the perception of law by the general public becomes an important task of legal interpretation. The strength of this approach is that it can reflect the changes of time and social circumstances in the interpretation of the law. Even if legislation is delayed, the changes in value and legal perception can be reflected in the process of interpreting a statute that contains the concept of ethics and morals of the community.[45] It could provide a solid basis to justify changing existing precedents. Therefore, judges should play a role in communication in society to identify and confirm the perception of law.[46]

However, there is a concern that unclear and invisible moral judgments may penetrate the abstract concept of 'the entire legal order.' The Constitution must be interpreted in detail, and the values and principles contained in the Constitution may conflict with each other. It is difficult to demonstrate how legal judgments made in various cases can be specifically evaluated considering the entire legal order. These are the limitations of uncertainty, vagueness, and invisibility.

On the other hand, an approach that develops purposive interpretation with more attention to the specific purpose of the law has the advantage of making the interpretation of the Constitution and the law relatively clear. The Constitution is interpreted and applied focusing on the part related to the case. The statute's purpose can also be constructed from the

---

also emphasize the importance of the legal text. This context can lead to different approaches depending on the issue of the case.

44 Korean Supreme Court, 04.21. 2022, 2019Do3047 (Justice Jae Hyung Kim, Jeong-Hee Noh, Dae-Yup Chun, and Kyeong-Mi Oh, concurring).

45 *Id.*

46 Un Jong Pak, 16(1) J. Korean L. 2016, 147 (156–57).

perspective of realizing this constitutional purpose. Finally, if the purpose of the Constitution and statute can be achieved, the provision's text can be interpreted in a limited way. This is how to harmonize the achievement of the objective with constitutional considerations. Furthermore, since the purpose of the law is often specified in the purpose-provision of the statute, it also has the advantage of realizing the value of democracy by respecting the purpose stated by the legislator.

However, there are also weaknesses in this approach. It would be difficult to find a normative standard that can critically evaluate the purpose of the statute. Moreover, another weakness is difficulty of making the standard determining the compatibility of the two conflicting values. Even in this case, the standard established by the purpose do not completely resolve the conflict in situations where military values and the right to sexual self-determination contradict each other.

In other words, although the concurring opinion of Supreme Court Justices Ahn and Lee stated that the current provision could apply in cases of combat or wartime, it is questionable how to judge other cases. For example, even in wartime, a soldier may take leave and engage in consensual sexual acts in a rear area where there are no battles. Therefore, another criterion is needed to determine the extent to which the purpose will be realized through what means and to what extent.

At this stage, it is impossible to define a sequence on the superiority of the two approaches to legal interpretation because they have their own strengths and weaknesses. It is necessary to continue to explore and develop to overcome their limitations in the context of specific cases. However, it is essential for the current Supreme Court to explore more specific and distinctive purposes of law. The limitations of presenting the entire legal order as arguments must be supplemented through clearer arguments; for this, it is necessary to provide more specific criteria.

G. Conclusions

Teleological interpretation is not about arbitrarily manipulating the meaning of the law to suit the interpreter's personal preferences. Instead, it is a method and argumentative tool that sincerely explores the purpose of the law, forecasts the potential outcomes resulting from its application and assesses these outcomes in light of the purpose. Moreover, it serves as a crucial mechanism for overcoming the linguistic constraints of legal texts.

Thus, it is neither feasible nor desirable to entirely divorce the purpose of law from the process of legal interpretation.

The legal interpretation theory developed by the Supreme Court in recent years has branched off from textualism, intentionalism, and legal pragmatism. Furthermore, two approaches have emerged on how to set the purpose of the law. One is based on German objectivist interpretation theory, which establishes the entire legal order as the normative standard for legal interpretation and the Constitution as the core of the entire legal order, exerting profound influence on issues related to fundamental rights. The objective purpose is abstracted and combined with constitutional values. Justice Kim Jae Hyung, who led this trend, combined the theories of Radbruch and Dworkin to present the unity of the entire legal order with the Constitution as the highest norm.

On the other hand, another trend attaches more importance to the purpose of specific laws. It calls for understanding the nature of the law as a means to realize its purpose. This perspective has been underscored by Justice Ahn Chul Sang, who draws upon Jhering's legal thought. Justice Ahn also considered it desirable to curb excessive intervention by the penal or administrative powers if an autonomous solution by the social community is possible. Furthermore, this attitude is also linked to the issue of legal interpretation. Justice Ahn made the purpose of the law an important basis for legal interpretation. This approach seeks to address practical feasibility from a more specific perspective.

The difference between the two approaches can also be seen in whether the direction of development is toward abstractness and universality or particularity and concreteness. This difference eventually returns to the question of how to construct the purpose of the law.

Therefore, the question of what constitutes the purpose of law is at the heart of legal interpretation. Radbruch and Jhering had different ideas about the purpose of the law, but Radbruch held Jhering in high esteem. Likewise, the two theories of legal interpretation discussed here will continue to evolve with respect for each other and the pursuit of the 'rule of law.'

These jurisprudential philosophies play a significant role in justifying conclusions in challenging cases. Jurisprudence is not only 'the general part of adjudication, silent prologue to any decision at law,' as Dworkin said,[47] but the final justification for the decisions in hard cases.

---

47 Dworkin, *supra* note 22 (90).

Bibliography

Ahn, Chul-Sang, Beob, Beobwon, Panlye [Laws, Courts, Precedents], 3 J. Juris 2024. 45 (In Korean)

Dworkin, Ronald, Law's empire, Belknap Press, 1986

Feteris, Eveline T., The Pragma-Dialectical Analysis and Evaluation of Teleological Argumentation in a Legal Context, 22 Argumentation 2008, 489

Jhering, Rudolf von, Der kampf ums recht [the struggle for law], 5th ed. 1877

Jhering, Rudolf von, Der zweck im recht [law as a means to an end], 1893

Kim, Do-Kyun, Taking Integrity Seriously: Recent Trend in Jurisprudence of Korean Supreme Court, 13(1) Korean. J. Leg. Phil. 2010, 95 (In Korean)

Kim, Do-Kyun/Kim, Jae-Hyung, Special Conversation: Professor Jae-Hyung Kim, 2 J. Juris 2023, 25 (In Korean)

Kong, Doo-Hyun, Models of Legal Interpretation in the Korean Supreme Court: Legal Positivism, Legal Realism, and the Theory of Legal Principles, 22(2) Korean. J. Leg. Phil. 2019, 185 (In Korean)

Kong, Doo-Hyun, Notable Supreme Court Decisions on Legal Philosophy: 2019, 21(2) J. Korean L. 2022, 311

Kong, Doo-Hyun, Rational Reconstruction of Teleological Interpretation, Ph.D. dissertation, Seoul National University, 2024 (In Korean)

Lee, Kye-Joung, The Supreme Court Decision on the Liability of Japanese Company for Forced Labor During the Japanese Colonial Era and Its Implications, 18(2) J. Korean L. 2019, 335

Pak, Un Jong, Judicial Justice: From Procedural Justice to Communicative Justice, 16(1) J. Korean L. 2016, 147

Park, Min-Je, An Analysis of Justice Cho Heedae's Judicial Philosophy, 1 J. Juris. 2022, 381

Radbruch, Gustav, Rechtphilosophie [legal philosophy], 5th ed. Koehler, 1956

Retirement Speech of Justice Ahn Chul-Sang, Lawtimes, Dec. 29, 2023 [https://www.lawtimes.co.kr/news/194544 (In Korean)]

Retirement Speech of Justice Kim Jae-Hyung, Legal Times, Sept. 4, 2022 [https://www.legaltimes.co.kr/news/articleView.html?idxno=68497 (In Korean)]

Korean Supreme Court, 04.23. 2009, 2006Da81035

Korean Supreme Court, 11.01. 2018, 2016Do10912

Korean Supreme Court, 06.18. 2020, 2019Do14340

Korean Supreme Court, 09.03. 2020, 2016Du32992

Korean Supreme Court, 03.18. 2021, 2018Du47264

Korean Supreme Court, 04.21. 2022, 2019Do3047

The Law of Balancing applied in Cases from the German Constitutional Court and the Constitutional Court of Korea*

Hyun Jung Lee

Abstract

The principle of proportionality, grounded in German constitutional jurisprudence, has emerged as an important methodology for reconciling conflicting rights and interests. The Federal Constitutional Court ("FCC")'s judgments in cases such *as "Lüth", "Esra",* and *"Künast"* illustrate how a structured four-step analysis - legitimacy, suitability, necessity, and balancing - ensures a careful weighing of fundamental values. In *"Lüth"*, the FCC emphasized the significance of evaluating the motives and contexts of speech, allowing for legitimate restrictions in instances where a call to boycott violated prevailing public interests. *"Esra",* conversely, highlights the tension between artistic freedom and personality rights, compelling a heightened degree of fictionalization when intimate personal spheres are implicated. Meanwhile, the *"Künast"* decision exemplifies how the law of balancing serves as a methodological framework for adjudicating conflicts between freedom of expression and the right to honour, reflecting a growing concern over defamatory online speech. The Constitutional Court of Korea ("CCK") has likewise engaged with the principle of proportionality, though its approach exhibits both convergence and divergence in relation to German jurisprudence. While the CCK acknowledged the legitimacy of preventing deceptive misinformation, critics have noted that it has been less inclined to adopt a carefully contextualized balancing approach, thereby risking unduly restrictive outcomes for democratic discourse. Notwithstanding these variations, the overarching framework of the proportionality

* This work has been translated, revised, and summarised from my articles: *"The Law of Balancing applied in the German Constitutional Court Cases of Lüth and Esra",* published in Korean in the *Journal of HUFS (Hankuk University of Foreign Studies) Law Research* in February 2022; and *"Discussion on the Limits of Freedom of Expression and Insulting Expressions Against Politicians through an Analysis of a Recent German Federal Constitutional Court Case Künast",* published in Korean in the *Journal of Media and Defamation Law* in December 2023.

serves as an essential means of harmonizing competing constitutional values in both jurisdictions. This comparative study highlights that balancing is most effective when applied contextually, considering the political, technological, and cultural factors shaping public discourse, and that refining proportionality in a case-specific manner - particularly in digital communications - can strengthen democratic deliberation while safeguarding freedom of expression and human dignity.

A. Introduction

The principle of proportionality is a fundamental concept in constitutional jurisprudence, serving as a crucial tool for evaluating the rationality and necessity of state actions relative to their aims. This principle ensures that state measures do not disproportionately infringe upon individual rights and freedoms. The German Federal Constitutional Court ("FCC") has played a significant role in establishing and refining this principle through its jurisprudence, notably by developing a structured proportionality test. This test includes four steps: legitimacy, suitability, necessity, and proportionality in the narrow sense (often referred to as 'balancing'). Originating in German administrative law, the principle of proportionality has gained global acceptance in constitutional law, ensuring that any limitation on fundamental rights imposed by the state is justified, appropriate, and not excessive. It stipulates that state actions must pursue a legitimate aim, be suitable to achieve that aim, be necessary (meaning that there are no less restrictive means available), and maintain a balance between the benefits of the action and the rights infringed upon. This approach not only safeguards individual rights but also enhances the transparency and accountability of state actions, thereby reinforcing the rule of law in constitutional governance.

The principle is widely recognized as a standard of fairness and justice, used to argue the reasonableness of the relationship between means and ends, and to ensure that state actions minimize harm to other objectives while achieving their aims. It serves to prohibit excess, to control the excessiveness of state action when it is subject to review, and embodies the principle against insufficiency when passive state action is scrutinized. Despite its central role, the principle of proportionality faces criticism, as it can conceivably be applied irrationally, grant wide judicial discretion, and enhance the power of the judiciary, especially constitutional courts.

Critics argue that it lacks unique content and may not provide sufficient protection for constitutional rights. However, its structured application, particularly as developed by the FCC and effectively employed in European courts, including the European Court of Human Rights, demonstrates its importance in balancing state interests with the protection of fundamental rights.

B. The Proportionality and Law of Balancing

This section explores the European debate on the content and development of the principle of proportionality and highlights how it can be used to detect and remedy violations of fundamental rights in specific cases. Although the European Court of Human Rights and the European Court of Justice are distinct judicial bodies, they apply the principle of proportionality in partially overlapping ways. The principle as applied by European courts is generally less structured or predictable than the version applied by the FCC, which offers a more systematic approach.[1] This article argues for the adoption of the more structured German approach to enhance judicial predictability and fairness.

The principle of proportionality originated in German administrative and constitutional law and has since been adopted by many constitutional courts worldwide, including those in Europe, Israel, Canada, and South Africa, as a key test for assessing fundamental rights.[2] The FCC has developed the principle into a core constitutional principle, recognizing its constitutional status and employing it as a critical tool in rights-related adjudication.[3] The Constitutional Court of Korea ("CCK") has held that the proportionality test for discrimination in the examination of equal rights is not merely an assessment of whether there is a rational reason for the discrimination, but also an evaluation of whether there is an appropriate balance between the weight of the discrimination's purpose and the degree of its impact.[4] The CCK further clarified that this test involves examining whether a strict proportional relationship is established between the ends

1 Lee, pp. 121–128.
2 Mendes/ Gargarella/Guidi/Clérico p. 554 (555).
3 Shelton/Arai-Takahashi p. 446 (447).
4 Constitutional Court of Korea, 12. 23. 1999, 98Heonma363.

and means of discrimination.[5] The FCC, having developed the principle of proportionality as a fundamental constitutional principle, has long recognized its constitutional status.[6] A rights-related adjudication process based on the principle of proportionality thus serves as an effective method for resolving conflicts between competing constitutional values or interests.

Global constitutionalism is understood as a normative theory that centres on the rights of the individual rather than the state and relates to generally accepted constitutional principles such as human dignity, the right to freedom and equality, democracy and participation, the separation of powers, and the rule of law. *Alec Stone Sweet* and *Jud Mathews* argue that the principle of proportionality is one of the fundamental elements of global constitutionalism.[7] They further consider it to be one of the most important characteristics of modern constitutional adjudication.[8] In this context, the structured test of the proportionality applied by the FCC is seen as a crucial means of decision-making in important legal interpretations. The structured approach ensures a meticulous examination of whether the means used to achieve a particular end are appropriate, necessary, and balanced in relation to the intended goal, thereby upholding the core values of constitutional governance.

Restricting fundamental rights before the FCC is only possible if such restrictions pass a structured proportionality test.[9] The structured proportionality test in Germany consists of four steps: legitimacy, suitability, necessity, and proportionality in the narrow sense.[10] The first step, legitimacy, examines whether the purpose of the restriction is justified. To justify a limitation of a fundamental right, the aim must be related to the protection of a constitutional or human right or to the realization of a public interest.[11] The second step, suitability, requires that the means or measures adopted by the law or the state be capable of realizing a legitimate aim. The third step, necessity, is often referred to as the "less restrictive means test." Some constitutional scholars argue that the necessity test is distinct from the less restrictive means test or the least-intrusive-means test. For example, *Gerards* argues that the two tests differ because the necessity test can be

5 Constitutional Court of Korea, 02. 22, 2001, 2000Heonma25.
6 Shelton/Arai-Takahashi p. 446 (447).
7 Stone Sweet/Mathews CJTL 2008, 68 (161).
8 Stone Sweet/Mathews CJTL 2008, 68 (75).
9 Stylianos-Ioannis G. VURÜ 2011, 32 (32–34).
10 Barak/Kalir, pp. 243–370.
11 Barak/Kalir, pp. 245–246, 253–257.

determined on its own, whereas the less restrictive means test necessarily involves a comparison with other means.[12] Nevertheless, in this article, it is assumed that the two tests are equivalent, as the necessity test is ultimately an examination of which of all possible means (including hypothetical ones) is the least restrictive of the fundamental right whose protection is sought.[13] Equally importantly, these less intrusive means must be shown to be equally effective in comparison to the means under consideration.[14]

The final stage of the balancing test is proportionality in the narrow sense, which compares the benefits of protecting a public interest or another right with the harm caused to a fundamental right by the means chosen to achieve the legitimate end.[15] This process of weighing benefits and harms aims to find an optimal solution in constitutional law.[16] Of course, there are those who criticize the application of the principle of proportionality in constitutional courts. For example, some argue that the principle itself lacks rationality and thus grants the judiciary excessive discretion, which may be insufficient to protect fundamental rights.[17] Additionally, it is criticized for being a principle that can be applied in various ways without any unique and distinctive content. At the same time, however, there are counter-arguments to these criticisms. *Sieckmann* refutes objections to the principle of proportionality by arguing that it qualifies as a universal principle in three respects: its categorical structure as a principle, its a priori validity as a norm, and its validity of the norm across divergent legal orders.[18] These arguments are particularly relevant for the constitutional resolution of shared legal challenges not only within Europe but also within the domestic legal systems of individual states. For example, the principle of proportionality can function as a norm of universal validity across jurisdictions by providing a common analytical structure for resolving conflicts between competing constitutional rights and interests.[19] In the context of freedom of expression, this approach offers a coherent framework for adjudicating cases where expressive freedoms come into tension with personal honour, privacy, or public order.

---

12 Gerards IJCL 2013, 466 (482).
13 Barak/Kalir, p. 317.
14 Brems/Lavrysen HRLR 2015, 139 (142).
15 Barak/Kalir, p. 340.
16 Sieckmann/Sieckmann, p. 113 (131–132).
17 Barak/Kalir, p. 340.
18 Duarte/Silva Sampaio/Sieckmann, p. 3 (4–10).
19 Duarte/Silva Sampaio/Sieckmann, p. 3 (4–10).

C. The Law of Balancing in the German Constitutional Court Cases

The following analysis addresses the changes and developments in the law of balancing as reflected in the jurisprudence of the FCC, with particular focus on three landmark cases: the 1958 *"Lüth"* decision[20], the 2007 *"Esra"* decision[21], and the 2021· *"Künast"* decision[22].

I. The Case of Lüth (1958)

The "Lüth" decision by the FCC concerned Erich Lüth, a Hamburg civil servant who called for a boycott of the film *"Immortal Beloved"*, directed by Veit Harlan, a controversial filmmaker from the Nazi era. In 1951, the Hamburg District Court prohibited Lüth's boycott call, citing Section 826 of the German Civil Code[23] which forbids intentionally causing damage in a manner contrary to good morals. Lüth's appeal argued that this injunction violated his freedom of expression under Article 5(1)[24] of the Basic Law. Lüth's call for a boycott arose from his belief that Harlan's continued involvement in the film industry would harm Germany's moral reputation. The FCC's 1958 ruling upheld Lüth's constitutional complaint, overturning the District Court's decision. The FCC held that fundamental rights, including freedom of expression, form an objective value system that

20 BVerfGE 15. 01.1958 – 1 BvR 400/51, Rn. 1–75. (The decision to analyse the *"Lüth"* case is based on its illustrative application of the principle of proportionality and the balancing of interest in situations where the exercise of freedom of expression potentially infringes on higher-priority interests worthy of protection. The case also addresses significant issues such as the third-party effect of fundamental rights and the reflexive effect of the constitution on general law. (Alexy 2010, pp. 352–355; Park PLR 2005, 273 (287)).

21 BVerfGE 13. 06.2007 – 1 BvR 1783/05.

22 BverfGE, 19.12.2021 – 1 BvR 1073/20.

23 Section 826 of the German Civil Code (BGB) addresses liability for intentional harm. It provides that anyone who, in a manner contrary to good morals, intentionally causes damage to another person is liable to compensate that person for the harm caused. This provision is a key aspect of tort law in Germany, focusing on wrongful intent and prevailing moral standards.

24 Article 5(1) of the German Basic Law (*Grundgesetz*) guarantees the freedom of expression, freedom of the press, and freedom of information. It grants every person the right to express and disseminate their opinions freely and ensures the protection of freedom of reporting through the media. This provision is foundational for safeguarding free speech and a free press in Germany.

influences private law and binds civil courts in their application of general laws.

This landmark decision highlighted the critical role of freedom of expression in a democratic society and reinforced its solid protection under German law. The ruling established that civil court decisions in private disputes must consider fundamental rights, setting a precedent for the interplay between constitutional rights and private law. In this decision, the FCC examined whether Lüth's constitutional complaint was well-founded, specifically whether the District Court's ruling infringed his fundamental right. The scope of protection of the right to freedom of expression under Article 5(1) of the Basic Law was the central issue. The FCC also addressed the third-party effect of fundamental rights, which traditionally been viewed as defensive rights against the state and not applicable in private disputes. However, the FCC interpreted fundamental rights as objective principles that influence general law, thereby extending them to civil law disputes. The FCC established a balancing rule in this decision as follows: if a boycott call includes an expression of opinion driven by improper purposes or causing disproportionately severe harm to conflicting interests, it violates public morals under Section 826 of the Civil Code[25]. This rule, guided by legal mandates, necessitates balancing the right to freely express opinions against the rights and legal interests that justify restrictions on this freedom. The FCC concluded that Lüth's motives were not improper ("*nicht unlauter*" in German) and that the conflicting interests were not unreasonably harmed, thereby holding that the District Court's injunction violated Lüth's freedom of expression.[26]

The "Lüth" decision demonstrates the third-party effect of fundamental rights and their impact on general law, emphasising the necessity of balancing different fundamental rights. According to *Alexy*, these values ("*Werte*" in German) are interpreted as principles ("*Prinzipien*") that require optimisation within the realm of possibility, not absolute achievement.[27] This approach allows for conflicts between values or principles to be resolved through balancing, rather than adhering to unconditional priority.[28] In conclusion, the *"Lüth"* case illustrates how fundamental rights, such as freedom of expression, can come into conflict with other rights or public

---

25 BVerfGE 15. 01.1958 – 1 BvR 400/51, Rn. 1 (47).
26 Alexy 2010, pp. 352–354.
27 Alexy 1986, p. 71 ff.
28 Park PLR 2005, 273 (287).

interests, and how such conflicts are resolved through the principle of proportionality and the law of balancing. This approach fosters clarity and intellectual rigour in constitutional adjudication.

II. The Case of Novel "Esra" (2007)

The 2007 *"Esra"* decision by the German FCC constitutes a key precedent that illustrates the application of the law of balancing between artistic freedom and personal rights in contemporary literature. The case originated from a Munich court's prohibition of the novel *Esra* by *Maxim Biller*, published by Kiepenheuer & Witsch, on the grounds of an alleged violation of the freedom of art protected under Article 5(3)[29] of the German Basic Law. The novel, written as a first-person narrative, recounts the relationship between the writer *Adam* and the actress *Esra*, whose life events closely resemble those of *Biller*'s former partner, *Ayse Romey*, and her mother, *Birsel Lemke. Romey* and *Lemke* asserted that the novel infringed their general personal rights under Articles 1(1) and 2(1)[30] of the Basic Law due to its autobiographical character. *Biller* contended that the characters were fictional and any resemblance to real persons was coincidental. Despite this, he sent a copy of the novel to *Romey* with a personal letter, suggesting its connection to their past relationship. Initial legal efforts to prohibit the novel's publication were unsuccessful; however, subsequent proceedings resulted in an injunction issued by the Munich District Court, which was subsequently upheld by higher courts. The FCC dismissed the publisher's claim that this prohibition violated his artistic freedom, emphasising the significant intrusion into *Romey*'s personal sphere. The FCC did not find *Lemke*'s rights to personality to be similarly infringed. In the final litigation related to the novel, *Romey* and *Lemke* filed a claim for damages against the author, *Biller* and the publisher, citing a violation of Section 823 in

29 Article 5(3) of the German Basic Law(*Grundgesetz*) guarantees freedom of the arts and sciences, as well as freedom of research and teaching. It ensures that artistic expression and academic activity are free from state interference. This provision underscores the importance of intellectual and creative freedom in a democratic society.

30 Article 1(1) of the German Basic Law(*Grundgesetz*) states that human dignity is inviolable and must be respected and protected by all state authority. Article 2(1) guarantees the right to the free development of one's personality, provided that it does not infringe the rights of others or violate the constitutional order.

connection with Section 249 of the Civil Code[31]. The Munich District Court ruled that € 50,000 should be paid.[32]

The *"Esra"* case involved the balancing of *Biller* and his publisher's artistic freedom against *Romey* and *Lemke*'s personal rights. *Biller* and the publisher argued that their artistic freedom was violated by the ban on the novel's publication. The key issue was whether the novel *Esra* constituted art protected under the Basic Law. The German FCC had previously defined art using three concepts in the *"Mephisto"* decision[33]: the substantive concept, defining art as 'a free creative design in which the artist's impressions, experiences, and emotions are expressed through a specific form of language'[34]; the formal concept, defining art by the intrinsic characteristics of the work that classify it as a certain type of art[35]; and the open concept, allowing for a broad interpretation of the work's expressive content.[36] Under these definitions, the novel *Esra* was recognized as a piece of art and thus fell under the protection of artistic freedom.[37]

To balance the artistic freedom of the author and publisher against the personal rights of *Romey* and *Lemke*, the FCC conducted a two-step analysis. Firstly, it examined whether the publication of the novel could infringe personal rights by assessing if the fictional characters could be identified as real persons. The FCC established this criterion in the *"Mephisto"* decision, where it held that if the public could easily recognise the characters as real individuals, the identification was likely.[38] In *"Esra"*, the FCC required a clear correlation between the fictional characters and real persons.[39] This standard aimed to protect well-known public figures.[40] The FCC concluded that the alternate Nobel Prize reference in the novel made it likely that *Lemke*'s character could be identified. Additionally, the detailed depiction

---

31 Section 823 of the German Civil Code (*BGB*) establishes liability for damages resulting from unlawful acts, requiring compensation for harm to life, body, health, freedom, property, or other protected rights. Section 249 specifies that the liable party must restore the condition that would have existed if the event causing the damage had not occurred, typically through reparations or monetary compensation.

32 Landgericht München I 13.02.2008 – 9 O 7835/06.

33 BverfGE 24. 02.1971 – 1 BvR 435/68. Rn. 1–117.

34 BverfGE 24. 02.1971 – 1 BvR 435/68. Rn. 1 (58).

35 Mangoldt/ Klein/Starck/ Starck/ Paulus, GG Art. 5, Rn. 1 (423).

36 Jarass/Pieroth/Jarass, Art. 5, Rn. 1 (118).

37 BverfG 13. 06. 2007 – 1 BvR 1783/05 -, Rn. 59–60.

38 BverfGE 24. 02.1971 – 1 BvR 435/68.

39 BverfG 13. 06. 2007 – 1 BvR 1783/05 -, Rn. 1 (76).

40 Obergfell in Conter/Obergefell, p. 65 (69); Obergfell JZ 2006, 196 (198).

of *Adam* and *Esra*'s sexual relationship, and of *Esra*'s daughter's illness, was considered a substantial intrusion into *Romey*'s private sphere. Secondly, the FCC assessed whether the infringement of personal rights could be justified by the importance of artistic freedom. The FCC held that while *Lemke*'s personal rights were not significantly violated, the intimate and highly recognisable portrayal of *Romey*, with detailed reference to her personal circumstances, constituted a serious infringement of her general personality rights that could not be justified by artistic freedom. In its contextual balancing of fundamental rights, the FCC emphasised that even artistic expression must give way where deeply private spheres are intruded upon through such detailed and identifiable depictions.

III. The Case of Künast (2021)

The *Künast* case involved German politician *Renate Künast* of the Green Party, who was misquoted in various publications regarding her stance on paedophilia. In 1986, during a session of the Berlin House of Representatives, *Künast* was recorded as interjecting "As long as no violence is involved!", in a debate about decriminalising sexual acts between adults and children. This statement was later distorted in media and blog posts, implying she condoned sex with children if non-violent. *Künast* filed a lawsuit against a blog owner for defamation and sought to identify Facebook users who had posted abusive comments about her, seeking to prosecute them under Section 185[41] of the Criminal Code. The Berlin Regional Court initially ruled that all 22 comments were permissible under freedom of expression. This decision was heavily criticised for seemingly stripping politicians of their right to honour. In response to public criticism and a criminal complaint against the judges, the Berlin Regional Court revised its decision, identifying six of the comments as criminal insults. *Künast* appealed, and the Berlin Higher Regional Court ruled that an additional six comments could also be prosecuted as insults. The German FCC ultimately found that both lower courts failed to properly balance freedom of expression with personal honour, applying incorrect standards and failing to adhere to constitutional requirements for evaluating the statements.

41 Section 185 of the German Criminal Code addresses insult (*Beleidigung*), which criminalises the act of intentionally offending the honor of another person through insulting words or actions. It provides for penalties including fines or imprisonment.

This case highlights the complex interplay between protecting personal honour and upholding freedom of expression, particularly in the context of political figures and public discourse.[42] According to Article 5(2)[43] of German Basic Law, freedom of expression is limited by the right to personal honour. The right to be respected in one's honour is an expression of the general right of personality (linked to Articles 1(1) and 2(1) of the Basic Law) and derives from the right to human dignity specified in Article 1(1). However, the general right of personality can be restricted in order to protect the rights of others, including the basic rights of third parties, such as freedom of expression in the *Künast* case. Respect for others' personal rights and freedom of expression are not mutually exclusive.[44] In this case, Künast's right to privacy and the Facebook users' freedom of expression came into conflict under Section 185 of the German Criminal Code. Pursuant to the established jurisprudence of the German FCC, conflicts between freedom of expression and the protection of personal honour require a case-specific balancing of interests. This balancing approach has formed a consistent element of the FCC's doctrinal framework since the Lüth decision of 1958.

The criteria for balancing the freedom of expression and the right to personal honour were articulated in the 1994 "*Auschwitz Lie*" decision[45] and the 1995 "*Soldiers Are Murderers*" decision[46]. In narrowly circumscribed categories such as attacks on human dignity, formal insults, and defamation, the protection of personal rights take precedence without requiring individualized balancing.[47] Given their restrictive scope, these exceptions serve as narrowly drawn limitations on freedom of expression.[48] Outside of these categories, conflicts between freedom of expression and personal honour are subject to a case-specific balancing of interests, guided by strict constitutional standards. An erroneous classification of a statement

---

42 BVerfG, 19. 12.2021 – 1 BvR 1073/20.

43 Article 5(2) of the German Basic Law(*Grundgesetz*) states that the rights to freedom of expression, freedom of the press, and freedom of information are subject to limitations provided by general laws, laws for the protection of youth, and the right to personal honour. This clause ensures a balance between freedom and other legal interests worth of protections.

44 Ipsen, J., p. 120 ff.

45 BVerfG, 13. 04.1994 – 1 BvR 23/94.

46 BVerfG, 10. 10.1995 – 1 BvR 1476/91, 1 BvR 221/92, 1 BvR 102/92, 1 BvR 1980/91.

47 BVerfG, 19. 12.2021 – 1 BvR 1073/20.

48 Gerdemann, ZUM. 2022.

as falling within one of these exceptions, without engaging in the requisite balancing, amounts to a serious constitutional violation.[49] In this respect, the contextual approach to balancing requires a careful assessment of the specific circumstances of each case, in order to determine whether the restriction imposed on freedom of expression satisfies the criteria of proportionality and remains consistent with constitutional guarantees.

IV. Concluding Remarks

The jurisprudence of the FCC exemplifies a sophisticated model of adjudication in which freedom of expression is balanced against competing constitutional values through a structured and context-sensitive proportionality analysis. Rather than adopting rigid hierarchies or categorical rules, the FCC applies a principled balancing approach that allows for the accommodation of plural and often conflicting rights claims within the constitutional order. This method not only reflects the open-textured nature of modern constitutional rights but also provides a valuable point of reference for comparative constitutional discourse, where courts are increasingly called upon to navigate the tensions inherent in rights-based democracies committed to both individual liberty and the protection of personal dignity.

D. The Korean cases of Freedom of expression balanced with other competing interests

This section examines how the law of balancing is applied in the case law of the Constitutional Court of Korea ("the CCK"). Drawing upon the contextual balancing approach developed in the German cases of *Lüth* (1958), *Esra* (2007), and *Künast* (2021), this section analyses corresponding decision of the CCK to assess how conflicts between fundamental rights are resolved within the Korean constitutional framework. In doing so, it examines how the contextualized balancing of competing constitutional interests, particularly in the realm of freedom of expression, informs judicial reasoning in both systems, and traces the convergences in their shared commitment to proportionality-based adjudication as well as the divergences arising from distinct constitutional traditions, normative frameworks, and institutional contexts in Germany and Korea.

49 BVerfG, 19. 02.2019 – 1 BvR 1954/17.

I. The decision on criminalizing "false communications" (2010, 2008 Hun-Ba 157)[50]

This case concerns the constitutionality of Article 47(1) of Korean Basic Telecommunications Act ("KBTA"), which stated: "Anyone who makes false communications using telecommunications facilities with the intent to harm public interest shall be punished by imprisonment for up to five years or a fine of up to 50 million Korean Won". The complainant, Dae-sung Park("Park") argued that Art. 47(1) violates the principle of legality (specially the vagueness doctrine)[51] and the principle of proportionality[52], particularly infringing upon his freedom of expression as guaranteed by Article 21[53] of the Korean Constitution.

This decision arose from the case of Park, an online commentator who wrote under the pseudonym *"Minerva"*. During the 2008 global financial

---

50 Constitutional Court of Korea, 12. 28. 2010, 2008 Heonba 157.

51 The Constitutional Court of Korea has adopted the vagueness doctrine, seemingly influenced by the case law of the United States Supreme Court, in its ruling on the unconstitutionality of Article 92 of the Korean Military Criminal Act. (Constitutional Court of Korea, 06. 27. 2002, 2001 Heonba 70). For example, in the cases of *Franklin v. State*, the Florida Supreme Court held that the state's felony ban on sodomy was unconstitutionally vague because an "average person of common intelligence" could not reasonably know, without speculating, whether the phrase "abominable and detestable crime against nature" included oral sex or only anal sex (taken from Supreme Court of Florida, Franklin v. State, 12. 17. 1971, Nos. 40758, 40757; Lee, pp. 188–191.).

52 The Principle of Proportionality can be derived from Article 37(2) of the Korean Constitution, which states: "The freedoms and rights of citizens may be restricted by Act only when necessary for national security, the maintenance of law and order or for public welfare. Even when such restriction is imposed, no essential aspect of the freedom or right shall be violated". This provision provides the constitutional basis for applying the proportionality in assessing the legitimacy, necessity, and minimal impairment of restrictions on fundamental rights.

53 Article 21 of the Constitution of the Republic of Korea states
All citizens shall enjoy freedom of speech and the press, and freedom of assembly and association.
Licensing or censorship of speech and the press, and licensing of assembly and association shall not be recognized.
The standards of news service and broadcast facilities and matters necessary to ensure the functions of newspapers shall be determined by Act.
Neither speech nor the press shall violate the honor or rights of other persons or undermine public morals or social ethics. Should speech or the press violate the honor or rights of other persons, claims may be made for the damage resulting therefrom.

crisis, Park gained considerable public attention for his economic analyses, which he published on an internet forum. His online posts included some accurate forecasts, such as the bankruptcy of U.S. Financial Company Lehman Brothers, but also controversial allegations - for example, that the South Korean government had imposed restrictions on financial institutions' ability to purchase U.S. dollars. While his posts were considered by many to be insightful, they eventually provoked governmental concern over their potential negative impact on public trust in economic policy[54]. The controversy escalated in 2009 when Park was arrested and charged under Article 47(1) KBTA, which criminalised the dissemination of false information with the intent to harm the public interest. His online post alleging the government's intervention in U.S. dollar transactions was found to be false, and prosecutors argued that it had caused panic in the financial markets. At trial, the Seoul Central District Court acquitted Park, finding no evidence of intent to disrupt public order[55].

Following his acquittal in the criminal proceedings, Park filed a constitutional complaint, challenging the constitutionality of Article 47(1) of the KBTA. The applicant argued[56], firstly, that the provision violates the principle of legality, particularly the vagueness doctrine, due to its ambiguous terms. The phrase "public interests" in the expression "with the intent to harm public interests" was criticized, as the concept shifts according to societal perceptions and the related values evolve over time. Park contended that "public interests" lacks definitional clarity, making it difficult for an ordinary person to foresee which actions could be punished. Similarly, the term "false communications" was criticized, as it could encompass not only deliberately false statements but also satire, exaggeration, or even assertions that are later proven false due to new evidence. Secondly, the applicant argued that the provision violates the principle of proportionality by imposing excessive and unnecessary restrictions on freedom of expression.

According to the majority opinion in the decision by the CCK, Article 47(1) of the KBTA is unconstitutional because it violated the principle of legality, specifically the vagueness doctrine. The reasoning of the majority opinion[57] can be summarised in the following three key points. Firstly, the CCK emphasised that the vagueness doctrine is particularly important

54 For the detailed facts of the case, I have referred to "Kim, Press Arbitration 2013, 44(pp. 45–48)".

55 Seoul Central District Court, 04. 20. 2009, 2009 Godan 304.

56 Constitutional Court of Korea, 12. 28. 2010, 2008 Heonba 157.

57 Constitutional Court of Korea, 12. 28. 2010, 2008 Heonba 157.

when restricting freedom of expression. Laws that criminally punish expression must use clear and precise language to avoid a chilling effect on protected speech. Secondly, the terms "public interests" and the phrase "false communications" were considered excessively vague and unclear. The CCK found that "public interests" lacked concrete criteria and was open to varying interpretations, making it difficult for individuals to foresee which actions would be subject to criminal punishment. Likewise, the lack of clarity regarding what constitutes "false" in the phrase "false communications" made it impossible for individuals to reliably determine the legality of their statements. Lastly, the CCK held that Article 47(1) was subject to strict scrutiny under the vagueness doctrine, given that it restricted freedom of expression and imposed criminal sanctions. Under this standard, the provision clearly failed to provide clear and specific guidance on prohibited conduct, rendering it inconsistent with the constitutional requirements of legal clarity and foreseeability.

Although the majority opinion did not examine the potential violation of the principle of proportionality in depth, Article 47(1) clearly violated this principle, as highlighted by the concurring opinion[58]. The concurring opinion criticized the provision for failing to meet the requirement of necessity[59], as less restrictive measures[60] already existed to address the harm caused by false statements. According to the law of balancing, which assesses whether "the importance of the legitimate aim justifies the intensity of the restriction"[61], Article 47(1) disproportionately criminalised internet communications, such that even a legitimate aim could not justify excessive restrictions on a fundamental right such as freedom of expression.

---

58 Constitutional Court of Korea, 12. 28. 2010, 2008 Heonma 157.

59 Barak emphasises the necessity step as a critical threshold, stating that "the legislature must employ the least restrictive measure that can achieve the law's legitimate purpose" (Barak/Kalir, p.317). The applicant's claim that existing legal frameworks were adequate reflects this principle: that redundant restrictions are inherently unnecessary and fail the test of necessity within the principle of proportionality.

60 As alternative mechanisms already existed to address the harm caused by false statements, the concurring opinion invoked the idea of 'self-correcting mechanisms in a free market of ideas', whereby the internet provides avenues for real-time rebuttal and debate, which can mitigate the impact of false statements. Additionally, other laws - such as the Information and Communications Network Act - already regulate harmful online expressions. Thus, further criminal punishment was unnecessary, and the provision failed to demonstrate that criminalizing false communications constituted the least restrictive means of protecting the public interests. (Barak/Kalir, p. 700).

61 Alexy 2010, p. 102.

This case exemplifies the particular importance of a contextualized balancing approach in constitutional adjudication concerning freedom of expression. Rather than abstractly privileging state interests or individual rights, the proportionality analysis demands a careful consideration of the specific normative and factual circumstances in which the regulation operates. In the present case, the absence of clear legal definitions combined with the severe sanctioning of speech created a legal uncertainty incompatible with the chilling effect doctrine, which occupies a central position in the constitutional protection of expression. While the legitimate aim of safeguarding public interests in the stability of financial markets may be acknowledged, the measure imposed was neither sufficiently determinate nor necessary in light of less intrusive alternatives available under ordinary defamation or market manipulation laws. The CCK's reasoning thereby reflects an emerging jurisprudential convergence with broader constitutional traditions that recognize proportionality, when properly applied in a contextualized manner, as a universal tool for reconciling conflicting constitutional interests without abandoning the primacy of individual freedoms in democratic discourse.

II. The decision on criminalizing "public defamation" (2021, 2016 Hun-Ba 84)[62]

This case concerns the constitutionality of Article 307(2) of the Criminal Code, which stipulates: "A person who defames another by publicly alleging false facts shall be punished by imprisonment of up to five years, suspension of qualifications of up to ten years, or a fine of up to 10 million KRW". The complainant appeared on a news programme on 18 March 2013, alleging that Kim, the head of a management company, had made sexual propositions. This was determined to constitute public defamation through false statements, leading to the complainant's conviction at first instance and a fine of 5 million KRW[63]. During the appeal process, the complainant requested a constitutional review of Article 307(2)[64], but the court rejected the request on 15 February 2016. Subsequently, the complainant filed a

62 Constitutional Court of Korea, 11. 30. 2017, 2016 Heonba 157.
63 Seoul Eastern District Court, 05. 13. 2015, 2013 Gojung 2236.
64 Seoul Eastern District Court, 02. 15. 2016, 2016 Chogi 102.

constitutional complaint under Article 68(2) of the Constitutional Court Act[65], arguing that this provision violates freedom of expression.

The CCK unanimously upheld the constitutionality of Article 307(2), concluding that it does not violate the Constitution. The Court's reasoning can be restructured according to the principle of proportionality. Firstly, the provision serves the *legitimate aim* of protecting personal dignity and maintaining trust in public discourse, both of which are essential to a democratic society.[66] Secondly, criminal punishment is an effective means of preventing and deterring defamatory acts involving falsehoods, thereby fulfilling the requirement of *suitability*[67]. Thirdly, the law applies narrowly to cases in which the alleged facts are proven false and the defendant acted with knowledge of the falsehood, thereby minimising undue limitations on freedom of expression. Safeguards - such as the prosecutor's burden to prove both falsity and intent, and judicial interpretation requiring strict scrutiny of the term "false facts" - further satisfy the requirement of *necessity*[68]. Lastly, in terms of the law of *balancing*, the public interest in protecting personal dignity and safeguarding the integrity of public discourse outweighs the restriction on freedom of expression imposed by the provision, since allowing false information to circulate unchecked undermines democratic opinion formation and erodes social trust[69].

However, this decision can be criticized particularly with respect to the requirements of *necessity* and the law of *balancing* under the principle of proportionality. The CCK justified criminal sanctions by citing the inadequacy of civil remedies. Yet civil remedies can be effective, especially when combined with digital-era mechanisms such as content removal or fact-checking platforms. In addition, the provision in question lacked tailored alternatives, thereby failing to satisfy the *necessity* criterion. As Justice Kim emphasized in his concurring opinion[70], the German Criminal Code[71]

65 Article 68 (Causes for Request), Constitutional Court Act: (2) If a request under Article 41(1) for adjudication on unconstitutionality of Act is rejected, the claimant may file a constitutional complaint with the Constitutional Court pursuant to its Regulations. In this case, the claimant may not request another adjudication on the unconstitutionality of the same Act for the same reason as in the original proceedings.

66 Constitutional Court of Korea, 02. 25. 2021, 2016 Heonba 84.

67 Constitutional Court of Korea, 02. 25. 2021, 2016 Heonba 84.

68 Constitutional Court of Korea, 02. 25. 2021, 2016 Heonba 84.

69 Constitutional Court of Korea, 02. 25. 2021, 2016 Heonba 84.

70 Constitutional Court of Korea, 02. 25. 2021, 2016 Heonba 84.

71 Section 186 of the German Criminal Code (*malicious gossip*) stipulates that anyone who asserts or disseminates a fact about another person with the intent to degrade

distinguishes between defamation involving unprovable value judgements and intentional falsehoods, prescribing lighter penalties for the former. This approach could serve as a less restrictive measure for improving Korean law to better balance competing constitutional rights. In the process of balancing of interests, the CCK concluded that the public interest in protecting reputation outweighs the restriction on freedom of expression, without adequately examining the specific context in which rights must be balanced. By contrast, the German Court emphasised the importance of contextual analysis, particularly in the *Esra* (2007) decision. For example, even some offensive or false statements in political discourse may be protected if they contribute to public opinion formation. It is therefore essential to adopt a nuanced, context-sensitive approach that distinguishes between cases involving public figures or matters of public interest and purely private disputes, so as to avoid unduly restricting democratic discourses.

III. Concluding Remarks

The CCK's evolving jurisprudence on freedom of expression reveals both the promise and the persistent challenges of constitutional balancing within a comparative framework. In both the "*False Communications*" and "*Public Defamation*" decisions, the CCK explicitly recognized the necessity of proportionality analysis as the central doctrinal mechanism for reconciling freedom of expression with competing constitutional interests. Yet, the depth and sophistication of the contextual inquiry remain uneven. In "*False Communications*", the CCK adopted a more rigorous contextual approach, carefully considering the indeterminacy of statutory terms and the resultant chilling effects on democratic discourse. By contrast, in "*Public Defamation*", the CCK's balancing remained largely abstract, insufficiently engaging with the specific communicative contexts that are crucial for determining the democratic value of contested speech. Comparative experience, particularly from German constitutional jurisprudence, underscores

---

them or negatively affect public opinion - unless the fact can be proven true - may be punished by imprisonment of up to one year or a fine. If committed publicly, in a meeting, or through disseminated content, the penalty increases to imprisonment of up to two years or a fine. Section 187 (*defamation*) provides that anyone who, despite knowing better, asserts or spreads a false fact about another person with intent to degrade them, harm their reputation, or endanger their honour, is subject to imprisonment of up to two years or a fine; if committed publicly, the penalty increases to up to five years or a fine.

that effective balancing must not only weigh competing interests but must also be embedded in a contextualized assessment of the nature of the speech, its subject matter, and its contribution to public discourse. Without such attentiveness to context, proportionality risks degenerating into a formalistic exercise that inadequately safeguards the democratic function of free expression. The Korean experience thus highlights both the normative convergence on proportionality as a shared doctrinal framework and the continuing divergences in its concrete application across constitutional systems.

E. Conclusion

The comparative analysis of the jurisprudence of the German Federal Constitutional Court (FCC) and the Constitutional Court of Korea (CCK) on the application of the law of balancing reveals both normative convergence and structural divergence in contemporary constitutional adjudication. At the normative core, both courts have recognized the principle of proportionality as the fundamental method to evaluate interferences with fundamental rights, integrating its fourfold structure - legitimacy, suitability, necessity, and proportionality in the narrow sense - into their constitutional review.

The FCC's jurisprudence, exemplified by *as "Lüth", "Esra",* and *"Künast"*, demonstrates a highly contextualized approach to balancing that engages deeply with the communicative function and democratic significance of contested expressions. This approach enables the FCC to weigh and reconcile competing constitutional goods in light of the specific societal, political, and technological contexts in which conflicts arise, thereby ensuring the dynamic protection of freedom of expression while safeguarding personal rights and maintaining democratic order. The precision of this contextual engagement reflects the FCC's broader doctrinal commitment to principled, yet flexible, constitutional reasoning that respects both the normative weight of individual rights and the evolving challenges of pluralistic democracies.

In contrast, the CCK's engagement with proportionality, while structurally aligned with the proportionality doctrine, reveals a more formalistic application, particularly in cases involving freedom of expression. In the *"False Communications"* and *"Public Defamation"* decisions, the CCK affirmed the importance of protecting dignity and public order but often refrained from fully contextualizing the societal and democratic functions of the contested speech. The CCK's reasoning tends to remain focused on the abstract legitimacy of state aims, without sufficiently engaging with the qualitative communicative value of the expression in question or rigorously examining the availability of less restrictive means. This limited contextual engagement risks insufficiently safeguarding freedom of expression, particularly in the digital age where the boundaries between private reputation and public discourse are increasingly contested and overlapping.

Nonetheless, the broader picture demonstrates an ongoing convergence in constitutional doctrine. The shared adoption of the proportionality principle signifies an important harmonization in global constitutional practice. The divergence lies less in formal doctrine than in the depth and sophistication of its application. The German experience illustrates how the law of balancing, when applied in a contextualized and dialogical manner, can provide both normative coherence and constitutional legitimacy. The Korean jurisprudence, while normatively compatible, still faces the institutional challenge of operationalizing this principle with the same level of contextual nuance. In this respect, the comparative dialogue between German and Korean constitutional jurisprudence offers valuable insights for the global constitutional discourse. It highlights the universal utility of the proportionality principle while underscoring the indispensable role of contextual balancing in ensuring that constitutional adjudication remains sensitive to the substantive democratic values it seeks to protect.

Bibliography

Alexy, Robert, Theorie der Grundrechte, Suhrkamp Taschenbuch Wissenschaft, 1986

Alexy, Robert. A Theory of Constitutional Rights, Oxford University Press, 2010.

Arai-Takahashi, Yutaka, Proportionality, in D. Shelton (eds.), The Oxford Handbook of International Human Rights Law. OUP Oxford, 2013, p. 446.

Barak, Aharon, and Kalir, Doron. Proportionality: Constitutional Rights and Their Limitations, Cambridge University Press, 2012.

Brems, Eva/Lavrysen, Laurens, 'Don't Use a Sledgehammer to Crack a Nut': Less Restrictive Means in the Case Law of the European Court of Human Rights. HRLR 2015, 139.

Clérico, Laura, Proportionality and Balancing, in C. H. Mendes/ R. Gargarella/S. Guidi (eds.), The Oxford Handbook of Constitutional Law in Latin America. Oxford University Press, 2022, p. 554.

Gerards, Janneke, How to improve the necessity test of the European Court of Human Rights, IJCL 2013, 466.

Gerdemann, Simon, Ein Stück Rechtsgeschichte zu den Grenzen der Meinungsfreiheit in sozialen Medien?, ZUM 2022, 266.

Ipsen, Jörn, Staatsrecht II: Grundrechte, 24. Auflage, München 2021.

Jarass, in: Jarass/Pieroth (eds.) Grundgesetz für die Bundesrepublik Deutschland 17. Auflage 2022, Art. 5, Rn. 1–158.

Kim, Sun Tae. The Ongoing Minerva Case. Press Arbitration 2013 (ISSN: 2005-2952), 44.

Koutnatzis, Stylianos-Ioannis G. Verfassungsvergleichende Überlegungen Zur Rezeption Des Grundsatzes Der Verhältnismäßigkeit in Übersee. VURÜ 2011, 32.

Lee, Hyun Jung. Discrimination Based on Sexual Orientation: Jurisprudence of the European Court of Human Rights and the Constitutional Court of Korea, Springer International Publishing, 2022.

Obergefell, Eva Inés, Anmerkung zum Urteil des Bundesgerichtshofs vom 21.6.2005 – VI ZR 122/04 – Esra (Persönlichkeitsrecht), JZ 2006, 196.

Obergefell, Eva Inés, Der Fall Esra – Eine Neujustierung des des Verhältnisses von Persönlichkeitsrecht und literarischer Kunstfreiheit?, in: Claude D. Conter (eds.) Justitiabilität und Rechtmäßigkeit – Verrechtlichungsprozesse von Literatur und Film in der Modern, 2010, p. 65.

Park, Zinwan, Fundamental Rights as Rules and Principles, PLR 2005, 273.

Sieckmann, Jan, Proportionality as a Universal Human Rights Principle, in Duarte/Silva Sampaio (eds.), Proportionality in Law: An Analytical Perspective, Springer, Cham 2018, p. 3.

Sieckmann, Jan. To Balance or Not to Balance: The Quest for the Essence of Rights, in Sieckmann (eds.), Proportionality, Balancing, and Rights, Springer, Cham 2021, p. 113.

Starck/Paulus, in: Mangoldt/Klein/Starck (eds.) GG Art. 5, 7. Auflage 2018, Rn. 1–552.

Stone Sweet, Alec/Mathews, Jud, Proportionality Balancing and Global Constitutionalism, CJTL 2008, 68.

Taking conventions seriously*

– The normative status of conventions in multidimensional legal reasoning and the problem of 'bad conventions' –

Hyun Kyung Lee

A. Convention closer than law?

One of the clichés of law is that 'the Fist is closer than the law' [The law is far and the fist is close], which may have been appropriate for pre-modern societies before mature legal systems, and it resonated with many people. However, I wonder if the saying that convention is closer than law is sometimes more relevant to us '*hic et nunc*'. "Convention is closer than the positive law".

As the sentence above shows, there is a very close relationship between law and convention. Today, the question of convention is at the center of the legal order, and convention plays a very important role in the legal world at many levels. This is important not only in relation to the nature of law, but also in the context of legal reasoning. This article aims to explore this issue from a number of different perspectives. In the course of my discussion, I will rely on the idea of 'source of law' as a key concept and transitional mechanism in support of my argument.[1]

On this basis, I will discuss the role and validity of 'convention as a source of law' in legal decision-making or multidimensional legal reasoning, i.e., legislative reasoning, judicial reasoning and the practical reasoning of citizens. In this article, I will combine 'source theory'[2] and 'convention

---

* The full version of this article was published in the Sungkyunkwan Law Review. See Hyun Kyung Lee, "The Normative Status and Validity of Conventions in Multidimensional Legal Reasoning," Sungkyunkwan Law Review 2025, 1–77.

1 Despite its importance, the concept and theme of 'the sources of law' has tended to be overlooked in modern legal philosophy. For a discussion of this phenomenon, see Roger Shiner, *Legal Institutions and the Sources of Law*, Springer 2005, 1. Giorgio Pino, "Sources of Law", in *Oxford Studies in Philosophy of Law* Volume 4, John Gardner · Leslie Green · Brian Leiter (eds.), Oxford University Press 2021, 58.

2 For a monumental work on the sources of law, see Alf Ross, *On Law and Justice*, Holtermann, Jakob v. H. (ed.), Oxford University Press 2019. In this article, however,

theory'[3] to develop a richer understanding of the reality of legal reasoning and propose an improved model of legal reasoning. Chapter 2 discusses the concept of legal convention and the multidimensionality of legal reasoning. Chapter 3 clarifies the meaning and validity of the 'convention as a source of law' [Thesis 1]. In the context of legal reasoning, I distinguish between different types of sources according to their degree of normative power over legal actors and link them to the question of the normativity of conventions. The "principle of deference to conventions" and the "presumptive validity thesis" are proposed as concrete theses, and the question of so-called "bad conventions" is also discussed. Chapter 4 then focuses on specific areas of judicial and legislative reasoning under the heading 'Between law and convention'. In particular, one of the most controversial issues from the perspective of legal methodology is analyzed on the basis of Korean cases. Based on this discussion, Chapter 5 concludes by proposing a 'reflective conventionalism' [Thesis 3] that incorporates the legal theory thesis of 'law as reflective convention' and 'reflective reasoning' [Thesis 2] as an alternative model of legal reasoning.[4]

B. Legal conventions and the multidimensionality of legal reasoning

Let's return our attention to the phrase "conventions are closer than the law." If we revise and refine this rather clumsy sentence to make it more precise, we can introduce the following possibilities:

---

the author will present a more nuanced discussion of the sources of law in the context of legal reasoning. For a detailed explanation, see HyunKyung Lee, The Distinction between 'Sources of Law' and 'Legal Norms' and Meta-Jurisprudence, Korean Journal of Legal Philosophy 2024.

3 HyunKyung Lee, Legal Convention Theory –Focusing on Three Dimensions of Discourse on Normativity of Convention: conceptual analysis, justification, and evaluation, Korean Journal of Legal Philosophy 2017, 7. HyunKyung Lee, A Dynamic Theory of Convention, KWLR 2017, 139. HyunKyung Lee, Conceptual Structure and Constitutive Elements of Coordination Convention –Reconstruction of the Concept of Convention and the Analytic Foundation for an Alternative Theory, Korean Journal of Legal Philosophy 2017, 137.

4 For further discussion of the relationship between law and legal reasoning, see Frederick Schauer, "On the Relationship between Law and Legal Reasoning", in *New Essays on the Nature of Legal Reasoning*, McBride, Mark/Penner, James/Pavlakos, George (eds.), Hart Publishing 2022, 5.

(a) The social origin and source of law is convention.[5]
(b) Law and convention can sometimes be in tension and conflict.
(c) In the context of legal reasoning, convention sometimes has stronger normative force than positive law.

From the perspective of legal reasoning, the three theses above are valid and mutually reinforcing on all three horizons: (i) judicial reasoning, (ii) legislative reasoning, and (iii) the practical reasoning of ordinary citizens. I will take 'convention as a source of law' as a starting point, as a proposition that can integrally capture the normative status of convention in the multidimensional legal reasoning of these different types of legal actors. In order to clarify the meaning of this proposition and to argue for its validity, certain basic preliminary reflections on the two key concepts that make up this proposition, specifically 'convention' and 'source', are necessary.

I. 'Legal convention formula'

1. What is a convention? A convention is an equilibrium agreed upon by rational subjects facing a common coordination or cooperation problem through a process of practical reasoning; it is an implicit normative order that emerges through social interactions among actors without explicit consent or agreement and that persists autonomously. A convention is a special kind of social rule that has as its ontological basis a norm that is practiced and that, by its own mechanism, can provide participants with reasons for action and generate obligations to comply. In other words, a convention is a combination of elements of social norms and social practices that provide actors with reasons for action during the course of practical reasoning. Among the various social conventions, those that are particularly relevant to law and that we must consider important in legal discourse can be referred to as 'legal conventions'. A 'legal convention' is a special kind of social convention. We can call a normative order a 'legal convention' if it satisfies the following conditions of the 'legal convention formula' as proposed here.[6]

5 For a discussion of the role and importance of convention in the foundations of law, see Gerald J. Postema, Coordination and Convention at the Foundations of Law, The Journal of Legal Studies 1982, 165.
6 HyunKyung Lee, The Concept and Requisites of Legal Convention, CHONNAM LAW REVIEW 2017.

A rule R, if all the following conditions apply, is legally conventional.

(1) R is a cooperative practice premised on a specific aim or value.
(2) Members of a group P have a reason (or combination of reasons A) to conform to R under a given circumstance C, but the reason/resolution of such conformity to R need not be clearly perceived/noticed by the members.
(3) Members of a group P in a given circumstance C expect that most people will prefer to conform to rule R on the condition that other people generally conform to it, and most people will conform to R on the reasonable expectation of general conformity to it.
(4) Given one or more potential rule R*, if members of group P actually conform to R* in a given circumstance C, this fact would be a sufficient reason to conform to R* instead of R. If other conditions are identical, it is impossible or pointless to comply with both of them concomitantly in circumstance C.
(5) If some of the actors involved in the formulation and practice of the convention have official status in the legal system or are involved in such a role [① 'legal office-holder convention'], or the content of the convention regulates a constitutional matter [② 'constitutional convention'], or the convention is institutionally supported by established legal norms (that is, the convention is created and admitted thereby) [③ 'positive-legal convention'], or the convention is highly likely to shift to a directly legal rights-duties relationship in case of a dispute thereon [④ 'shifted legal convention'], then the convention is 'legal'.
(6) R needs no initial process of express consent or agreement with regard to its formulation and extinction, and its regularity needs no single-timeline continuation.

A convention qualifies as a genuine legal convention if it satisfies the 'legal convention formula' above. Qualified genuine legal conventions provide reasons for action in the process of legal reasoning and thus function as a source of law.

2. There is a normative hierarchy of legal conventions[7]. If a genuine convention that has passed the convention formula fulfils one or more of the following four conditions, it becomes more powerful, both factually and normatively, and becomes a "strong convention." The "strengthening condi-

7 HyunKyung Lee, Convention as Norm, Hanyang Law Review 2017, 263.

tions" of a convention, which are distinct from the conditions for the establishment and existence of a convention, are ① common knowledge and ② formal articulation; ③ temporal persistence, continuance and repetition[8]; ④ institutional support; and ⑤ moral grounds. A 'strong convention' that satisfies one or more of the strengthening conditions not only provides legal actors with reasons to act in the context of legal reasoning but also generates obligations to comply. In other words, it is strongly binding. This point will be restated in the next section on the language of 'sources of law'.

II. Multidimensional legal reasoning and sources of law

1. The discourse on legal methodology or legal reasoning as a subfield of the philosophy of law has tended to focus too much on judicial reasoning or the theory of adjudication. This phenomenon is evident from the two Latin words that make up the etymology of 'jurisprudence'; '*juris*' and '*prudentia*', the former meaning 'of justice'. Dworkin is probably the best example of this judicial philosophy. In recent years, however, what is known as 'legisprudence' has also been increasingly emphasized in contemporary legal philosophy, with the idea that '*prudentia*', or judiciousness and deliberation, is also required in the realm of legislation. Therefore, in the field of legal methodology, we need to consider not only judicial reasoning but also legislative reasoning, and to strengthen the interaction between the two forms of official legal reasoning through a mutual examination between the two fields.

2. On the other hand, there is a type of legal reasoning which is not the official reasoning of legal institutions but which has a closer impact on our legal reality and everyday life. Depending on the issue at stake, it is also necessary to take into account the reasoning of experts in a specialized field or the domain-specific reasoning of interested parties in certain issues. Thus, from judicial and legislative reasoning to expert and domain-specific reasoning and to citizens' practical reasoning, there is a need fully to recognize the multidimensionality of legal reasoning and pay attention to the interrelationships among these dimensions. On the basis of

8 A prime example of this type is custom. For custom as a source of law, see Roger Shiner, *supra* note 1, Chapter 4. For a multifaceted discussion of the significance of custom in legal philosophy, see HyunKyung Lee, Why does Custom matter in Jurisprudence? –A Fresh Understanding on the Nature and Legality of Custom?, Korean Journal of Legal Philosophy 2021, 441.

such a comprehensive consideration, discussions of the source of law could make more meaningful theoretical and practical contributions.

3. What is the role and function of sources of law within multidimensional legal reasoning? First, I make a conceptual distinction between 'sources of law' and 'legal norms'.[9] Legal norms can be seen as the result of legal interpretations by legal subjects. In other words, the object of interpretation is the source of law, and the question of whether to apply the legal norms derived from the interpretation of the source to a particular case can be regarded as adjudication. The entire process can be broadly described as legal reasoning or legal decision-making.

What is the role of legal sources in the process of legal reasoning and to what extent are they binding?[10] First, the nature and status of sources of law is debated in Korea between those who understand them as the 'mode of existence' of law and those who understand them as the 'ground of recognition' of law.[11] The two positions are not entirely clear-cut, with the distinction depending to a large extent on the perceptual interests of the respective commentators. The discussion of sources of law in the context of legal reasoning in this article is more closely aligned with the latter position. Traditionally, the types of sources of law have been divided into two main categories: formal sources and material sources. Material sources are all of the factors that influence the decision-making of legal actors in the process of legal reasoning. On the other hand, formal sources are those that legal actors are legally required to use during their legal decision-making. According to Pino, the term 'legally required' refers not only to the fact that the relevant legal officials regularly use the source in the course of their legal recognition and legal decision-making, but also to the fact that they themselves are under internal pressure to consult the source and that failure to do so may have legal consequences. This internal and external normative response or normative force is one of the important features of formal sources. The following quotation summarizes this point well.

9 HyunKyung Lee, *supra* note 2, 495.

10 For a study that presents the "source of law" argument and illustrates the rich discussion of sources of law in legal reasoning, see John Bell, SOURCES OF LAW, The Cambridge Law Journal, 2018, 40.

11 For a comprehensive summary of the debate in Korea on the nature and types of sources of law, see ByoungJo Choe, general provision, in *Civil Law Commentary*, 2nd ed., ChangSoo Yang(ed.), PARKYOUNGSA 2022.

> "Something is a source of law in a given legal system if the officials (predominantly, but not exclusively, law-applying officials) in that legal system are legally required to use it in discharging their law-ascertaining activities. As I have already made clear, 'legally required' here means that the relevant officials not only do regularly consult some facts in the course of their law-ascertaining activities, but also take themselves to be required to do so, and that failure to do so engenders legal consequences—as opposed to reactions levelled on sheer moral, political, or even prudential grounds. This means that the status of something as a source of law is ultimately grounded on a practice of recognition shared by the relevant officials."[12]

To use a source is to interpret a source.[13] Accordingly, what is the role of sources in the process of legal reasoning and interpretation, and can their validity be differentiated according to differences in their normative force?

C. The role and validity of 'convention as a source of law' in legal reasoning

I. Normative power and types of sources in legal reasoning

Let's go back to the short definition of convention we gave earlier: "A convention is an equilibrium agreed upon by rational subjects facing a common coordination or cooperation problem through a process of practical reasoning; it is an implicit normative order that emerges through social interactions among actors without explicit consent or agreement and that persists autonomously. A convention is a special kind of social rule that has as its ontological basis a norm that is practiced and that, by its own mechanism, can provide participants with reasons for action and generate obligations to comply". What types of reasons do conventions provide for us as a source of law, and how do they affect the legal reasoning process of legal subjects?

---

12 Giorgio Pino, *supra* note 1, 70.

13 Giorgio Pino, *supra* note 1. For a study presenting a general theory of legal sources from a legal positivist perspective and scrutinizes the concept of 'interpretation', see Riccardo Guastini, Fragments of a Theory of Legal Sources, Ratio Juris, 1996. Riccardo Guastini, On the Theory of Legal Sources: A Continental Point of View, Ratio Juris, 2007. Riccardo Guastini, Legal Realism as a Positivistic Theory of Law, El realism jurídico como teoría positivista del derecho 2021.

In the process of legal interpretation and reasoning, sources of law can be categorized according to the degree or strength of their normative power. Traditionally, a distinction has been made between 'mandatory sources of law' and 'permissive sources of law'. In particular, explanations given by certain authors with regard to permissive sources should be noted here.

·"permissive sources are often characterized as sources which may be used in legal reasoning and decision-making, but which need not be used." ; "Usually the importance of a permissive source varies according to the availability and conclusiveness of applicable mandatory sources." (Shecaira)[14]

·"The legal system does not require [a judge] to use these sources, but it is accepted as perfectly proper that he should do so [...]. [They] are recognized as 'good reasons' for decisions"[15] (Hart)

·"when mandatory sources fail to yield determinate norms, permissive sources may have a more important (gap-filling) role to play."[16] (Gardner)

·"[...] in addition to the sources that courts are clearly if defeasibly bound to apply, there are sources that they are by their own customary practices expressly permitted to apply: practice-based "good reasons" for decision [. . .]. We need to be cautious here, for if they are permissive sources, then they are not, as one might think, mere permissions, for sources are prima facie reasons for courts (and others) to act. But being permitted to φ is not normally any sort of reason to φ (though it may be a reason for others not to interfere with one's φ-ing). Moreover, absent a source, a court is already permitted to act on any reasons that are relevant to the matter; in this way, too, judges are human."[17] (Green)

According to Green, permissive sources are associated with *prima facie* reasons for action. Following Peczenik and Shecaira, I will distinguish three types of sources of law according to their degree of normative power: ① "may-sources[=permissive source]," ② "should-sources[=defeasible source],"

14 Fábio Perin Shecaira, Sources of Law Are not Legal Norms, Ratio Juris *2015, 24.*

15 H.L.A. Hart, *The Concept of Law* 1961, 247.

16 John Gardner, Concerning Permissive Sources and Gaps, Oxford Journal of Legal Studies *1988, 457.*

17 Leslie Green, Law and the Causes of Judicial Decisions, University of Oxford Legal Research Paper Series 14, 19.

and ③ "must-sources[=mandatory source]." I have already argued that there is a normative hierarchy in convention; how therefore does 'convention as a source of law' fit into these three categories, and what types of reasons for action are provided by each type of convention? I would like to summarize as follows. These distinctions apply to both legislative and judicial reasoning.

[Table 1] Normativity and its Types of Convention as a Source of Law in Practical Reasoning[18]

Source	**Invalid sources**	**Valid source**		
		"may-source"	**"should-source"**	**"must-source"**
		permissive source (optional)	**defeasible source**	**mandatory source (strongly binding)**
Convention	bad convention, pointless convention in a strong sense	pointless convention in a weak sense, (mere) convention	(mature) convention, strong convention	strong convention [esp. Codified convention]
Reason-giving normativity	*pseudo*-reason for action	*prima facie* reason for action	authoritative reason	absolute reason
Generating-obligation	X	X	△	O

To cover the grey area not covered by the traditional binary model ("mandatory-permissive sources"), we have added the types "should source" or "defeasible source." "the use of this is not fully mandatory but is not merely permitted either. A defeasible source is a source that should be considered by a law-applying institution, and failure to do so would result in an invalid or otherwise legally wrong decision unless strong reasons are provided to this effect."[19] Here's how Pino explains these three distinctions.

> "The difference between mandatory, permissive, and defeasible sources emerges nicely in the perspective of legal argumentation. From this point of view, the use of a mandatory source does not require to be appositely justified by the law-applying institution (its use is just business as usual). The use of a permissive source, by contrast, usually requires to be appo-

18 For the revised version of this table and further explanation, see HyunKyung Lee, The Normative Status and Validity of Conventions in Multidimensional Legal Reasoning, SungKyunKwan Law Review 2025, 31.

19 Giorgio Pino, *supra* note 1, 84.

sitely justified by the law-applying institution, by making reference to the need to strengthen the acceptability of the overall decision, or to the fact that mandatory sources are indeterminate or incomplete, etc. Lastly, the use of a defeasible source does not require justification, but an opposite argumentative burden falls upon the law-applying institution in order to set that source aside."[20]

In the table above, what is the primary criterion of the distinction between "conventions as a valid source" and "conventions as an invalid source"? According to Pino, the concept of validity of legal norms is material validity, whereas the validity of sources is formal validity.[21] Carpentier, another leading thinker on sources of law and a proponent of legal positivism, defines 'sources' as 'legality-endowing facts', i.e., facts that give legal qualities to a norm, and argues that a legal norm is only possible if it can be traced back to its sources. He proposes the 'simple model' as a model for the role of social sources in modern legal systems. He explains that the simple model not only resolves the ambiguity of the concept of legal validity but also helps to solve a classic jurisprudential puzzle.[22] Waluchow proposed four concepts of legal validity: (i) legal validity as existence (or acceptance), (ii) systemic validity, (iii) systemic moral validity, (iv) moral validity.[23] In the simple model, Carpentier distinguishes between two conceptions of legal validity: 'validity as membership' and 'validity as conformity'. Validity as conformity' is the view that an act must satisfy substantive normative requirements in order to be recognized as valid, whereas 'validity as membership' is literally the recognition of membership of a system.[24] These views essentially reflect the legal positivist position. In my view, however, this distinction is inaccurate and inadequate, at least where 'conventions' are concerned. The final determination of the validity of a convention as a community law or cultural norm cannot be made solely on formal and procedural grounds, irrespective of its materiality. The distinction between

20 Giorgio Pino, *supra* note 1, 84.

21 Giorgio Pino, *supra* note 1, 69.

22 Mathieu Carpentier, "Sources and Validity", in *Legal Validity and Soft Law*, Westerman, Pauline/Hage, Jaap/Kirste, Stephan/Mackor, Anne Ruth (eds.), Springer 2018.

23 W.J. Waluchow, "Four Concept of Validity: Reflections on Inclusive and Exclusive Positivism", in *The Rule of Recognition and the U.S.*, Adler, Matthew/ Himma, Kenneth Einar (eds.), Oxford University Press 2009, 123.

24 Mathieu Carpentier and Torben Spaak, "Sources of Law", in *Jurisprudence in the Mirror*, Kenneth Einar Himma, Giorgio Pino, Luka Burazin (eds.), Oxford University Press 2024.

'formal validity' and 'material validity' in the traditional classification is similarly blurred, inadequate and hybrid in the case of 'convention as a source of law'.

II. "The principle of deference to conventions" and "the presumptive validity thesis"

Conventions are autonomous normative orders formed through the interaction of participants and must be respected first and foremost owing to their democratic origins and functional effectiveness. Let's call this "the principle of deference to conventions". A genuine legal convention that satisfies the legal convention formula is presumptively valid on its own merits. This we can refer to as "the presumptive validity thesis", which translates "the principle of deference to conventions" into a legal proposition. The validity given to a genuine convention is 'presumptive' in that it is not definitive or final, and therefore 'bad conventions' that cross a threshold can be invalidated.

"The presumptive validity thesis" has thresholds. Particularly in the legal domain, the recognition of thresholds and normative judgments is very important. Therefore, I argue that in the legal domain the presumptive validity of conventions may require a process of reconsideration and reassessment. Even a strongly normative convention with a generating obligation can be seen to have crossed the 'threshold of presumptive validity' if it is judged to be a 'bad convention' according to certain criteria; i.e., if it is a 'bad convention', the 'presumption of validity' will be invalidated, with the result that the general obligation to comply with it can be denied. This is the practical implication of "the presumptive validity thesis".

III. The problem of 'bad conventions' in legal reasoning: meaning, validity and duty to comply

The problem of 'bad conventions' in legal reasoning may be seen as a kind of 'appendix', but in reality it is perhaps most critical. It is not only a problem that is frequently encountered in the realm of legal practice by ordinary citizens, but it also poses difficult theoretical and practical problems in the process of legislative and judicial decision-making. On the one hand, in the context of legislative reasoning, it is a question of the 'codification of bad convention'. On the other hand, in the course of judicial reasoning, the question of 'bad conventions' often appears as a question surrounding the conflict between statutory and conventional norms. It is necessary to explain these practical problems theoretically and to consider methodological solutions to them.

In this case, we'll start the discussion by presenting a conceptual distinction between a 'bad convention' and a 'pointless convention'. 'Pointless conventions' can be divided into a weak sense and a strong sense. A weak sense of pointless conventions refers to situations in which people rarely comply with the convention, thus removing the reason for compliance. One of the essential requirements for the establishment of a convention is general compliance; if there is no effective amount of compliance, the convention may be pointless. On the other hand, 'strong sense' is also possible. According to condition (1) of "the convention formula", a convention presupposes certain points as a normative response to certain values, purposes or needs (e.g., the practice of 'first come, first served' or single queuing serves 'egalitarianism'; 'driving on the right' serves the goals of 'safety' and 'arriving at one's destination on time'). However, if a convention is formed or operates in a way that is clearly contrary to the values or purposes that underlie its emergence, then it is not rational and can be considered a 'pointless convention in the strong sense'. How is the relationship between a 'pointless convention' and a 'bad convention' defined? First, not all levels of 'pointless conventions' are necessarily 'bad conventions'; pointless conventions may be a trigger for escalation to bad conventions, but bad conventions are often judged by stronger external criteria. In summary, 'pointless conventions' are mostly conventions that do not rise to the level of 'bad conventions': ① conventions whose effectiveness has been significantly weakened because (for whatever reason) people have gradually stopped following them (the 'effectiveness test'); ② conventions that are contrary to, or have been transformed into, the goals or objectives on which the conventions were originally premised (a violation of condition (1); the 'reasonableness test'); and ③ 'bad conventions' (in the weakest sense). These can be summarized as shown in the table below.

[Table 2] 'Pointless conventions' and 'bad conventions'

	Pointless convention in a 'weak sense'	**Pointless convention in a 'strong sense'**
Content	People gradually stopped complying, significantly weakening its effectiveness.	It violates the purpose and point of the convention in the first place.
Conditions for CF	Condition (3) of "convention formula": 'General compliance dependence'	Condition (1) of "convention formula": 'purpose · value premises'
Judgement criteria	Effectiveness test	Fitting for purpose test
Status	In its own sense of 'pointless convention'	'Pointless conventions' & 'bad conventions' in the weakest sense

[Table 3] What constitutes a 'bad convention'?

Judging criteria	**Conditions that would not be 'bad convention'**	
Fitting for purpose test (Internal criteria)	It does not contradict or distort the purpose, point, or values that the convention is intended to embody.	
Integrity test (extrinsic criteria)	It does not significantly threaten the principle and systemic consistency with the higher normative order and neighboring/allied orders of community P.	
Fairness test (extrinsic criteria)	It does not violate the principles of equity and fairness.	
	A	The realization of common interest through convention does not significantly threaten the public interest.[25]
	B	It is not significantly contrary to democratic publicity.

The fundamental and preferred solution to the problem of 'bad conventions' is a gradual and autonomous approach to the demise of conventions, ideally through the realization of autonomous mechanisms whereby 'bad conventions' are transformed into 'pointless conventions' and finally into 'no convention'. In particular, the collaborative work of judicial decisions and legislative interventions can serve as important catalysts or complements to the resolution process. Ultimately, what is needed is critical reflection and public consensus on bad conventions.

The following chapter examines how the issue of 'bad conventions' has been addressed in legal practice in Korea from the perspective of legal methodology, focusing on specific cases.

25 For the jurisprudential conception and theory of 'public interest', see Dokyun Kim, Das öffentliche Interesse als Rechtsprinzip: Eine liberal-republikanische Konzeption des öffentlcihen Interesses, Seoul Law Journal, 2006.

D. Case analysis: between law and convention

From the perspective of legal methodology, 'convention as a source of law'[Thesis 1] plays an important role in the process of legislative and judicial reasoning. Below, I divide the two areas and briefly present a selection of representative Korean cases in this regard.

I. Conventions and judicial reasoning: 'The validity of a note without a place of issue' Case

One of the most prominent decisions of the Supreme Court in which the legitimacy of the judiciary's legislative power was questioned is the "Validity of a note without a place of issue" (Supreme Court, 23 April 1995, Judgement 95da364666). This case can be seen one in which the validity of a statute was annulled through the recognition of the normativity of a convention that had been drawn up contrary to positive law on the grounds of respect for "trade conventions." Here's the Supreme Court's 'majority opinion'.

> ·"Although the mention of the place of issue in a bill is an important criterion for the interpretation of the Bill Act in the case of international bills and other bills whose places of issue and payment are in different countries or under different jurisdictions, it has no significance in the case of so-called domestic bills issued and paid in Korea, and in general bill transactions, domestic bills without mention of the place of issue are widely issued and transferred between parties as if they were complete bills meeting the requirements of a bill. In view of the fact that it is conventional that such bills are not rejected on the ground that they do not bear the name of the issuer, even in the process of payment through bill exchanges and banks, but are treated as if they did bear the name of the issuer, the parties involved in the circulation of banknotes without the name of the issuer must have intended to perform the same valid acts as those performed by complete banknotes, and therefore, in cases where the face of the note itself is recognized as a domestic note, the absence of

the name of the issuer on the face of the note cannot be regarded as an invalid note."[26]

On the other hand, 'the Dissenting opinions' make the following arguments;

·"If there is a statute to be applied to the matter to be decided and its meaning is so clear that there is no room for any other interpretation, either by the requirement of justice that something else should be treated differently (the so-called "teleological reduction interpretation") or by the requirement of constitutional interpretation (the so-called "constitution-conforming interpretations"), unless there are special circumstances, such as the need for an exceptionally restrictive interpretation of the scope of the statute, even if there is an aspect of the statutory provision that is not in harmony with the convention. The Bills of Exchange Act expressly provides that a bill without a place of issue is of no effect, and there is no special circumstance in this explicit provision which would require the court to give an interpretation which unreasonably departs from or limits the scope of the statutory provision. The majority's view that the explicit provision of the Bills of Exchange Act does not apply to so-called "domestic bills" would mean that the court would be reading into the Bills of Exchange Act a provision which is not there, namely "domestic bills as to place of issue." It is difficult to avoid the criticism that the Court has clearly exceeded the scope of the court's powers of statutory interpretation by attempting to interpret or amend the law contrary to the express provisions of the Bills of Exchange Act. [...] Even if there is inconsistency between the provisions of the statute and the trade convention, it is for the courts to await amendment by the legislature and not to interpret the statute in such a way as to depart unreasonably from or limit the scope of its application."[27]

The following comments are particularly noteworthy from the perspective of 'convention theory'.

·"In particular, it appears that when the Bills of Exchange Act was amended as described above, it was not considered that there had been

26 Korean Supreme Court en banc Decision, 04.23. 1998, 95Da36466, Summary of the judgement [Majority Opinion].

27 Korean Supreme Court en banc Decision, 04.23. 1998, 95Da36466, Summary of the judgement [Dissenting opinions].

> changes in social and economic conditions or in domestic and international commercial conventions. [...] There is no data or evidence to suggest that it has become a convention in the drafting trade for the drawer to pay or assume liability for a draft presented without endorsement, and even assuming that such a convention exists, it should not be permitted if it is contrary to the mandatory law of bills of exchange. If the majority were to allow it, the effect would be to open and close a mandatory rule of law by convention, which is unacceptable in a statutory system of written law."[28]

In the literature and in legal practice, there is disagreement between the view that this case should be understood as a 'teleological reduction', as 'judiciary law-making contrary to the letter of the law', and a 'restrictive interpretation' within the possible meaning of the letter of the law.[29] However, I believe that the uniqueness of this case is that it provides us with a very important point of discussion and debate regarding the role and validity of 'convention as a source of law' in the process of judicial reasoning. Finally, applying the preceding theories of legal convention, this case can be argued in at least two ways: (i) using the 'conflict of legal sources argument' and (ii) using the 'bad convention argument'. First, a 'conflict of legal sources argument' analysis between a 'statute' and a 'strong convention' that satisfies the strengthening condition can identify the destructive power of conventions in judicial reasoning. Second, the validity of a note without a place of issuance can be described as an example of a so-called 'bad convention', as it was formed in contravention of the provisions of Article 1 of the Bills of Exchange Act, which requires the indication of the place of issue as a matter of course; i.e., it can be analyzed under the 'bad convention argument'.

---

28 Korean Supreme Court en banc Decision, 04.23. 1998, 95Da36466, Dissenting opinions of Supreme Court Justice Yoon Kwan, Supreme Court Justice Choi Jong Young, Supreme Court Justice Cheon Kyung Song, Supreme Court Justice Jeong Gui Ho, Supreme Court Justice Kim Hyung Sun, and Supreme Court Justice Lee Im.

29 For a study that provides an in-depth discussion of the system of legal methodology in Korea and its theoretical and practical problems, see Young-Whan Kim, The theory on practice of legal reasoning in Korea—especially the relation between the extensive interpretation and the analogy as well as between the restrictive interpretation and the teleological reduction, Korean Journal of Legal Philosophy 2015, 133. Young-Whan Kim, The theoretical structure of legal interpretation and its practical meaning in the case of GS Caltex, Korean Journal of Legal Philosophy 2015, 5.

II. Convention and legislative reasoning: the 'codification of conventions'

The "Convention as a source of law" thesis also plays a role in the field of legislative reasoning. It can be approached via two aspects. First, in relation to the question of 'what to legislate', normative convention serves as an important democratic source in legislative reasoning. This can be referred to as the problem of the 'codification of convention'. The codification of convention can be assessed in terms of a time axis divided into 'up to codification' and 'after codification'. Moreover, a discussion of the modes and mechanisms of codification is relevant to legislative reasoning. Secondly, in the case of 'bad conventions', the question arises, on the one hand, of the direction of their codification and, on the other, of the evaluation of their effective functioning after codification.

First, as an implicit normative order and legislative source of law, conventions can be codified in the form of statutory rules through legislation. Marmor describes two ways in which conventions can be codified institutionally.[30]

[Table 4] Methods of the Codification of Conventions in Legislative Reasoning

	Legislative codification	**Encyclopedic codification**
Primary role	Actually determining their content for the future	Only purports to report what the rules are
Persistence of conventionality on success	No longer conventional	Still conventional
Relationship to institutional rules	Replaces a convention	Conventional rules are preserved
		Dictionaries, grammar books

However, while the two approaches to the codification of conventions as described above provide a good description of the process and corresponding characteristics of legislative reasoning, they do not provide an explanation of the substantive content or value orientation. In practice, however, when we consider the interrelationship between convention and statute law, it may be the codification of 'bad conventions' becomes a hard case in legal reasoning.

30 Andrei Marmor, *Social Conventions: From Language to Law*, Princeton University Press 2009, 50 – 52.

Through codification by legislative reasoning, we can distinguish between two types of legislative reasoning: ① 'forward (+) codification' and ② 'reverse (-) codification'. Firstly, 'forward codification' reflects the content of existing conventions as they are, elevated to a mandatory source by official recognition by a law-making institution. A recent example of this in Korea is the codification of 'premiums in the commercial building leasing market'. The long-standing and strong convention of a "premium" was legislated as a "premium contract" through the amendment of the Commercial Lease Protection Act in 2015. Second, 'reverse codification' contains content opposite to that of the rule of an existing convention in order to solve a problem of a 'bad convention'. In its strongest form, it is intended to officially 'abolish' an existing bad convention by placing a statutory 'prohibition' on it. The most recent example in Korea is the abolition of the long-standing convention of the taxi payment system through an amendment to the Passenger Carriage Business Act, which introduced an explicit clause ("transport operators shall set a certain threshold of transport revenue and not accept it, and drivers shall not pay it"). To rephrase the issue of 'bad conventions' as discussed earlier, the case of the taxi payment system could be characterized as a 'reverse codification of bad convention'. What is interesting is that even after the 'reverse codification', the existing conventional order in its 'deformed form' still has a strong normative function in the practical reasoning of the field: the legislative solution to eradicate 'bad conventions' has had an unexpected side effect. Here are some of the Supreme Court's rulings.

- "The so-called the fixed taxi commission system, in which a certain amount of money is paid to the transport operator and the excess of the transport revenue over this amount is the driver's own income, creates the problem in which the transport workers' wages fluctuate greatly because the transport revenue is not constant, and because the fixed salary is not large, it can be difficult for the driver to secure even a basic living wage when the transport revenue is low. The law was amended by Law No. 5448 of 13 December 1997, which established the so-called the management system of the total amount of the fare system, but it was often circumvented and a de facto fixed taxi commission was introduced. Subsequently, the Law on Passenger Transport Services was amended by Law No. 16563 of 27 August 1999. As amended by Act No. 16563 of 27 August 2019, new articles 21(1)(2) and 26(2)(2) were added, which explicitly provide that 'the transport service provider shall set a certain amount of transport revenue as a threshold, which shall not be paid by the driver', and these entered into force on 1 January 2020. In light of the history and purpose of the new regulations, which is to correct the abuses of the fixed taxi commission by clarifying that it is prohibited to set and collect a certain amount of transportation revenue, each of the above regulations should be considered as mandatory law, and even if there is an agreement between the employer and the taxi driver's trade union to the contrary, the agreement should be considered invalid."[31]

There are several important implications and lessons to be drawn from these two cases(the codification of 'premiums in the commercial building leasing market' and the ongoing case of 'the taxi payment system').

First, genuine legal conventions, as well as "bad conventions," can be an important source of legislative reasoning in the first instance. Second, 'reverse codification', which relies on the legislature's strong power of control to address the problem of 'bad conventions', is not an effective solution. Third, the valid and desirable approach to the problem of bad conventions requires cooperative interaction between legislative and judicial reasoning, with the institutions engaged in a 'joint cooperative project'. This can be justified by the 'shared authority'[32] argument. Fourth, the problem of bad conventions in particular cannot be solved by the role of the legal institutions alone. More fundamentally, they need to be supported by public dialogue with ordinary citizens who actually shape these sources and bring about change. In other words, if the multidimensional legal reasoning of legislative and judicial reasoning and the practical reasoning of citizens work all together in a cooperative manner, the problem of a 'bad convention' could be solved. This must be justified by the argument of the 'solidarity of responsibility'.

E. Towards 'reflective conventionalism': 'Law as a Reflective Convention' + 'Reflective Reasoning'

Tuori emphasizes the multi-layered nature of law, arguing for 'law as a multi-layered normative phenomenon'. He emphasizes two aspects of law: (i) the legal order as a symbolic normative phenomenon and (ii) legal

31 Korean Supreme Court, 12.07. 2023, 2023Do2318.
32 Dimitrios Kyritsis, *Shared Authority*, Hart Publishing 2015.

practice as a set of concrete social practices.[33] The following statement by Tuori is instructive for our thesis 1 on the 'conventions as a source of law', which has the peculiarity of being both community law and a cultural norm.

> "Law is not exhausted by such concrete legal materials as individual regulations and court decisions but includes 'subsurface' layers. I now call these layers the legal culture and the deep structure of the law." [34]

Southwood once described the nature of law as a conventional norm.[35] Rescorla defines conventionalism as follows. "Conventionalism about some phenomenon is the doctrine that, perhaps despite appearances to the contrary, the phenomenon arises from or is determined by convention."[36] More recently, Owen has proposed what he calls 'modest conventionalism', arguing that there is intrinsic value in being bound by conventions: not 'brute conventionalism', where blindness to conventions implies submission, but 'modest conventionalism', where being bound by and submitting to conventions produces normatively and practically very good values. Owen's argument can be seen as a form of 'normative conventionalism'.[37] There are certainly important insights in Owen's argument, but I think we need to go a step further.

As we have seen, 'convention as a source of law' has strong normative force in legal reasoning, often greater than statutory law. At the same time, due to its democratic origins and the nature of community law and cultural norms, convention is a very powerful source of binding force. This calls for a more cautious approach and a critical and reflective attitude, especially in the case of 'bad conventions': as a democratically created source, convention deserves to be respected for its own sake ("the principle of deference to convention" and 'normative conventionalism'), but at the same time we must always be critical and reflective in order to avoid the extreme arbi-

33 Kaarlo Tuori, *Critical legal positivism*, Routledge 2016.

34 Kaarlo Tuori, *supra* note 33.

35 Nicholas Southwood, "Laws as Conventional Norms", in *Dimensions of Normativity: New Essays on Metaethics and Jurisprudence*, Plunkett, David/Shapiro, Scott J./Toh, Kevin (eds.), Oxford University Press 2019, 23.

36 Michael Rescorla, Convention, Stanford Encyclopedia of Philosophy 2024. (https://plato.stanford.edu/entries/convention/).

37 For the different versions of Conventionalism, see Federico José Arena, "Conventionalism", in *Encyclopedia of the Philosophy of Law and Social Philosophy*, sellers, Mortimer/Kirste, Stephan (eds.), Springer 2023, 599.

trariness and injustice of convention. In conclusion, an alternative model suitable for the question of the 'convention as a source of law' [Thesis 1] in multidimensional legal reasoning is 'reflective conventionalism' [Thesis 3][38] based on 'reflective reasoning' [Thesis 2].

Bibliography

Arena, Federico José, "Conventionalism" in *Encyclopedia of the Philosophy of Law and Social Philosophy*, sellers, Mortimer/Kirste, Stephan (eds.), Springer 2023, 599.

Bell, John, SOURCES OF LAW, The Cambridge Law Journal, 2018, 40.

Choe, ByoungJo, "general provision", in *Civil Law Commentary*, 2nd ed., Yang, Chang-Soo (ed.), PARKYOUNGSA 2022, 40.

Carpentier, Mathieu, "Sources and Validity", in *Legal Validity and Soft Law*, Westerman, Pauline/Hage, Jaap/Kirste, Stephan/Mackor, Anne Ruth (eds.), Springer 2018, 75.

Carpentier, Mathieu/Spaak, Torben, "Sources of Law", in *Jurisprudence in the Mirror*, Himma, Kenneth Einar/Pino, Giorgio/Burazin, Luka(eds.), Oxford University Press 2024, 241.

Dworkin, Ronald, "The Model of Rules II", in *Taking Rights Seriously*, Harvard University Press 1978.

Dworkin, Ronald, "Conventionalism", in *Law's Empire*, Hart Publishing 1998 (2003 printing).

Gardner, John, Concerning Permissive Sources and Gaps, Oxford Journal of Legal Studies 8, 1988, 457.

38 In some respects, the model of 'reflective legal conventionalism' that I propose can be seen as a further development of 'critical legal positivism' in Korea, drawing on the concerns of that theory and applying them to legal conventionalism. For a study of critical legal positivism in Korea, see Hun-sup Shim, "Critical Legal Positivism", *Collected Papers on Contemporary Legal Philosophy*, Bobmun Sa 2001. Daehwi Kim, Theory of Critical Legal Positivism, The Journal of Jurisprudence 2024. HyeonCheol Kim, Reconsidering Critical Legal Positivism, Korean Journal of Legal Philosophy 2024. However, it is important to note that this does not necessarily mean that the alternative model in this article implies legal positivism. It is entirely possible that it could be developed in the form of non-positivist. On the other hand, this proposal can also be seen as a counterargument and alternative model to Dworkin's rigid and static view of convention and his account of legal conventionalism based on it. See Ronald Dworkin, "The Model of Rules II", in *Taking Rights Seriously*, Harvard University Press 1978. Ronald Dworkin, "Conventionalism", in *Law's Empire*, Hart Publishing 1998 (2003 printing).

Green, Leslie, Law and the Causes of Judicial Decisions, University of Oxford Legal Research Paper Series 14, 19.

Guastini, Riccardo, Fragments of a Theory of Legal Sources, Ratio Juris 1996.

Guastini, Riccardo, On the Theory of Legal Sources: A Continental Point of View, Ratio Juris 2007.

Guastini, Riccardo, Legal Realism as a Positivistic Theory of Law, El realism jurídico como teoría positivista del derecho 2021.

Hart, H.L.A., *The Concept of Law*, 1961, 247.

Kim, Daehwi, Theory of Critical Legal Positivism, The Journal of Jurisprudence 2024, 9.

Kim, Dokyun, Das öffentliche Interesse als Rechtsprinzip: Eine liberal-republikanische Konzeption des öffentlcihen Interesses, Seoul Law Journal, 2006, 155.

Kim, HyeonCheol, Reconsidering Critical Legal Positivism, Korean Journal of Legal Philosophy 2024, 1.

Kim, Young-Whan, The theoretical structure of legal interpretation and its practical meaning in the case of GS Caltex, Korean Journal of Legal Philosophy 2015, 5.

Kim, Young-Whan, The theory on practice of legal reasoning in Korea—especially the relation between the extensive interpretation and the analogy as well as between the restrictive interpretation and the teleological reduction, Korean Journal of Legal Philosophy 2015, 133.

Kyritsis, Dimitrios, *Shared Authority*, Hart Publishing 2015.

Lee, HyunKyung, The Distinction between 'Sources of Law' and 'Legal Norms' and Meta-Jurisprudence, Korean Journal of Legal Philosophy 2024, 495.

Lee, HyunKyung, Legal Convention Theory –Focusing on Three Dimensions of Discourse on Normativity of Convention: conceptual analysis, justification, and evaluation, Korean Journal of Legal Philosophy 2017, 7.

Lee, HyunKyung, Convention as Norm, Hanyang Law Review 2017, 263.

Lee, HyunKyung, A Dynamic Theory of Convention, KWLR 2017, 139.

Lee, HyunKyung, The Concept and Requisites of Legal Convention, CHONNAM LAW REVIEW 2017, 9.

Lee, HyunKyung, Conceptual Structure and Constitutive Elements of Coordination Convention –Reconstruction of the Concept of Convention and the Analytic Foundation for an Alternative Theory, Korean Journal of Legal Philosophy 2017, 137.

Lee, HyunKyung, Why does Custom matter in Jurisprudence? –A Fresh Understanding on the Nature and Legality of Custom?, Korean Journal of Legal Philosophy 2021, 441.

Lee, HyunKyung, The Normative Status and Validity of Conventions in Multidimensional Legal Reasoning, SungKyunKwan Law Review 2025, 1.

Lewis, David, *Convention*, Blackwell Publishing 1969.

Marmor, Andrei, *Social Conventions: From Language to Law*, Princeton University Press 2009.

Owens, David, *Bound by Convention*, Oxford University Press 2022.

Pino, Giorgio, "Sources of Law", in *Oxford Studies in Philosophy of Law* Volume 4., Gardner, John/Green, Leslie/Leiter, Brian (eds.), Oxford University Press 2021, 58.

Postema, Gerald J., Coordination and Convention at the Foundations of Law, The Journal of Legal Studies 1982, 165.

Rescorla, Michael, Convention, Stanford Encyclopedia of Philosophy 2024. (https://plato.stanford.edu/entries/convention/)

Ross, Alf, *On Law and Justice*, Holtermann, Jakob v. H. (ed.), Oxford University Press 2019.

Schauer, Frederick, "On the Relationship between Law and Legal Reasoning", in *New Essays on the Nature of Legal Reasoning*, McBride, Mark/Penner, James/Pavlakos, George (eds.), Hart Publishing 2022, 5.

Shecaira, Fábio Perin, Sources of Law Are not Legal Norms, Ratio Juris 2015, 15.

Shim, Hun-sup, Critical Legal Positivism, Collected Papers on Contemporary Legal Philosophy, Bobmun Sa, 2001.

Shiner, Roger, *Legal Institutions and the Sources of Law*, Springer 2005.

Southwood, Nicholas, "Laws as Conventional Norms", in *Dimensions of Normativity: New Essays on Metaethics and Jurisprudence*, David/Shapiro, Scott J./Toh, Kevin (eds.), Oxford University Press 2019, 23.

Tuori, Kaarlo, *Critical legal positivism*, Routledge 2016.

Waluchow, W.J., "Four Concept of Validity: Reflections on Inclusive and Exclusive Positivism", in *The Rule of Recognition and the U.S. Constitution*, Adler, Matthew/Himma, Kenneth Einar (eds.), Oxford University Press 2009, 123.

Korean Supreme Court en banc Decision, 04.23. 1998, 95Da36466

Korean Supreme Court, 12.07. 2023, 2023Do2318

In dubio pro misero: a small politics of judicial interpretation

– from Korea's perspective –

Joon-kyu Choi

> *The law, in its majestic equality, forbids the rich as well as the poor to sleep under bridges, to beg in the streets, and to steal bread.*
> (Anatole France; a French poet)
>
> *Is it OK if we eat a cow's ribs when someone is starving next to us?*
> *How about eating bulgogi instead of ribs?*
> *Then, the person next to us might eat ramen.*
> (Roh Hoe-chan; a South Korean politician)
>
> *Act in such a way that the consequences of your actions are compatible with the greatest possible avoidance of human misery.*
> (Arthur Kaufmann; a German legal philosopher)

A. Intro

How judges should interpret the law remains a complex and debated question, with no singularly correct answer. Broadly, two opposing perspectives dominate this discourse: objectivism and subjectivism. Objectivism prioritizes the identification of the law's contemporary, objective meaning, whereas subjectivism emphasizes the original intent of the legislators who enacted it.

As Raymond Saleilles observed, legal interpretation constitutes a search for social adaptation (une recherche d'adaptation sociale). Consequently, objectivist elements are inherently present in the interpretive process. Despite ongoing debates regarding the validity of subjectivism versus objectivism, neither perspective can be entirely dismissed in practice. If objectivism is accepted to some extent, it becomes essential to establish clear standards and methodologies to regulate judicial discretion and delineate the boundaries of judicial interpretation. This necessity arises from the risk that judges, under the guise of objectivism, may interpret the law arbitrarily based on personal values. Therefore, **objectivism itself must be rendered**

truly objective to mitigate judicial arbitrariness and enhance the reliability of legal interpretation.

There are multiple approaches to achieving objectification (pluralism). This article proposes the interpretive method '*in dubio pro misero*' as one such standard. This approach provides guidance to legal interpreters, serving as a concrete criterion for teleological interpretation and judicial law-making. By adopting this method, it becomes possible to introduce a sense of equity and humanism into an otherwise rigid and abstract legal framework. '*In dubio pro misero*' is neither a profound theory nor a complex doctrine; rather, it is a straightforward and practical tool for judges and litigating lawyers—functioning as a pragmatic resource for legal practitioners.

B. Basic concept

I. Explanation

1. Who is *misero*?

Misero (les misérables) refers to individuals who are marginalized or disadvantaged within the political process, facing structural barriers that hinder their ability to represent their own interests. This marginalization stems from a lack of autonomy, an underdeveloped capacity for free will, or limited political power. Examples of *misero* include social minorities and underage children.

The identification of a social minority involves both factual and normative considerations. From a factual perspective, minority status is dynamic and may shift with changes in political power. For instance, a group categorized as a minority may become the majority if a political party advocating their interests gains control of the legislative or executive branches. In contrast, normative identification is grounded in legal principles or constitutional provisions. Therefore, even if the Green Party or the Labor Party were to come to power, future generations affected by environmental degradation or contract workers could still be regarded as social minorities under normative criteria.

Fundamentally, *misero* encompasses all human beings, with its protection rooted in the constitutional guarantee of human dignity (Article 10, Constitution of the Republic of Korea). However, if necessary, the concept of *misero* may be extended analogously to include animals as "living property" under the interpretive method of '*in dubio pro animale*'. According to this approach, fundamental animal interests should not be infringed upon unless outweighed by more significant human interests.

2. When is a situation ambiguous?

The interpretive method of '*in dubio pro misero*' does not advocate for the indiscriminate protection of minorities. Rather, it serves as a tie-breaker, invoked only as a last resort when conventional interpretive methods fail to yield a clear resolution. However, no objective or universally accepted criterion exists for determining whether a situation is genuinely ambiguous and thus necessitates a tie-breaker.

Advocates for minority protection may perceive situations as maximally ambiguous, arguing for the application of '*in dubio pro misero*'. Conversely, those prioritizing conflicting interests may interpret the same situation as unambiguous, thereby resisting its application. The judiciary, serving as an impartial spectator representing the collective interests of society, must carefully balance and assess the interests of minorities against competing claims by drawing upon established interpretive methodologies. This process necessitates a principled and thorough evaluation, grounded in law and precedent, of various factors, including the identity and relative power of the parties involved (e.g., individuals, business entities, consumers, communities, public institutions, or states), the nature of the conflicting interests (such as life, bodily integrity, property, honor, privacy, freedom, or public interests), and the degree to which each interest is affected.

Following this balancing process, the judiciary must determine whether the case should be resolved by applying '*in dubio pro misero*' and, simultaneously,[1] whether the situation is indeed ambiguous ('*in dubio*'). This task represents one of the most complex challenges in legal interpretation, yet it is an integral and routine part of judicial decision-making. A parallel can be drawn to the doctrine of contra proferentem in contract interpretation, which holds that ambiguous contractual terms should be construed against the drafter. In such cases, determining the precise threshold at which a term qualifies as ambiguous remains an enduring and difficult question, much like in the application of '*in dubio pro misero*'.

1 "Die Auslegung ist das Ergebnis ihres Ergebnisses." Gustav Radbruch, Einführung in die Rechtswissenschaft, 13. Aufl. (1980), 169.

II. Justification

'*In dubio pro misero*' can be justified based on following two arguments.

1. Judges' comparative advantage & Functional separation of powers

The judiciary should actively engage in tasks where it demonstrates expertise. Judges excel in deontological reasoning, which prioritizes duties and principles over empirical outcomes. The judicial protection of minorities often aligns with deontological principles, emphasizing rights and justice rather than utilitarian calculations of overall benefit. While quantitative analysis is essential for establishing **general** rules on the distribution of public resources to minorities, the **specific application** of such general rule regarding whether an individual qualifies as '*misero*' entitled to the benefits of a given law does not require complex mathematical reasoning. A broader framework should be established democratically within constitutional boundaries, while executive branch and judiciary should handle the detailed implementation. Executive implementation may need math, whereas judicial implementation may not. '*In dubio pro misero*' is primarily connected with two judicial tasks; ① ensuring that general rules remain within constitutional limits, and ② applying general rules to specific cases by providing detailed clarification on eligibility and entitlements. These tasks involving '*misero*' are more closely aligned with deontological reasoning than with utilitarian calculations, as **human dignity** -the fundamental basis of '*in dubio pro misero*'- **cannot be quantified or assessed through numerical comparison.**

In Korea, judges are appointed based on their legal expertise, qualifications, and experience, rather than through public elections. Judicial independence is constitutionally guaranteed, enabling the judiciary to safeguard minority rights, particularly when the political process fails to do so due to majority rule dynamics. While the image of powerful, wise judges may raise concerns about elitism, which conflicts with democratic principles, a judiciary guided by moral integrity, compassion, and empathy can play a crucial role in **addressing the shortcomings of the legislature and reinforcing the functional separation of powers**, particularly in the protection of '*misero*'.

2. Commensurability & Agreement within disagreement

While contentious issues often generate deep divisions in a pluralistic society, individuals frequently converge on fundamental moral judgments, such as compassion for the vulnerable and the rejection of discriminatory practices. This shared moral foundation serves as a basis for safeguarding minority rights in the public sphere, which is essential for promoting the common good and fostering societal integration. The interpretive method of '*in dubio pro misero*' aligns with this framework, functioning as an approach akin to a social contract. While this meta-contract remains incomplete and imprecise, it nevertheless contains a hypothetical agreement on core issues, even among those who hold fundamentally opposing views on morality.[2]

The question of whether and how a '*misero*' should be protected is primarily determined through the political process. However, its scope and specific details can be further outlined or clarified by the judiciary, drawing upon a shared moral foundation that persists despite divergent perspectives on the protection of minorities. In this process, the method of '*in dubio pro misero*' seeks to **minimize minorities' suffering to the greatest extent possible.** Furthermore, this method can hold a decisive and authoritative role in judicial decision-making, as it is not merely a moral standard but a **normative legal proposition rooted in human dignity and the principle of substantial equality** guaranteed under the Korean Constitution.

C. Application: Cases & Issues

The essence of '*in dubio pro misero*' lies in assessing the ambiguity of a given situation (*in dubio*) and identifying the weaker party (*misero*). As with other forms of judicial decision-making, this process must be developed on a case-by-case basis and through the incremental categorization of various cases. The following five cases and issues will help elucidate and clarify these matters.

2 Cass Sunstein introduced the idea of "incompletely theorized agreements on particular cases" which play a significant role in legal reasoning. Sunstein, Cass R., Political Conflict and Legal Agreement (February 10, 2024). Available at SSRN: https://ssrn.com/abstract=4722248 or http://dx.doi.org/10.2139/ssrn.4722248

I. Interpreting Civil law

When interpreting civil law, the primary focus is on weighing and balancing the conflicting interests of **private individuals**. Civil law does not classify people as weak or strong, nor does it distinguish between social minorities and majorities; rather, it emphasizes individuals as abstract entities, stripped of concrete characteristics. The legal framework of civil law is founded on the premise that in a society of free individuals, **no one should be subjected to slavery, nor should a de facto caste system emerge.** If this fundamental principle is violated, the legitimacy of legal relationships based on the notion of the "free individual" is undermined. In such cases, it becomes the judiciary's responsibility to interpret the law in a manner that rectifies these injustices, ensuring that those who are oppressed or marginalized receive adequate protection and fair treatment, and are liberated from systemic subjugation. Accordingly, judges must interpret ambiguous legal provisions in favor of individuals who are treated as slaves, untouchables, or invisible members of society.

1. A Perspective in Favor of a Victim of Forced Child Marriage

Consider the following Korean Supreme Court Decision 02. 18. 2016, 2015Meu654, 651. This decision exemplifies how the judiciary can apply '*in dubio pro misero*' in the interpretation of civil law.

a) Facts and Issues
The plaintiff met the defendant, who is a Vietnamese national, through an international marriage broker. They got married and registered their marriage on April 9, 2012. Before marrying the plaintiff, the defendant had given birth to a child in Vietnam. However, the defendant did not disclose this fact to either the marriage broker or the plaintiff. As a result, at the time of the marriage, both the plaintiff and the broker believed the defendant had never given birth. After the defendant arrived in Korea to begin her married life, she was subjected to rape and assault by the plaintiff's stepfather. He was subsequently convicted of these crimes and, on May 30, 2013, was sentenced to seven years of imprisonment. Meanwhile, around August 2013, while the appeal on the said criminal case was pending, the plaintiff found out about the defendant's past childbirth in Vietnam before their marriage.

On August 28, 2013, the plaintiff filed a lawsuit seeking marriage annulment on grounds of fraud. The defendant alleged, "Around October 2003, when I was about 13 years old, I was abducted, raped, and became pregnant by a man of Thai descent, a minority ethnicity in Vietnam. As the man got frequently drunk and was violent towards me, I fled and took shelter in my parents' house around June 2004. I gave birth to a son around August 2004, but the rapist took the baby away from me." The defendant also belongs to the Thai people. Among the Thai people, there is a traditional custom of bride-kidnapping marriage called "Bắt Vợ". Following this custom, a prospective bridegroom forcibly takes a young woman to his home. After spending a few days, the prospective bridegroom visits the woman's parents to obtain permission for marriage. The defendant claimed that she was a victim of such a bride-kidnapping marriage.

The issue in this case is whether, if the defendant's assertions that she was victimized by sexual violence during a bride-kidnapping marriage, gave birth against her will, and subsequently had her relationship with her child severed are true, the failure to notify the plaintiff of such facts amounts to fraud, which is one of the grounds for annulment of marriage according to Article 816 Subparagraph 3 of the Korean Civil Code.

b) Decision of the Supreme Court

The Supreme Court held that if the defendant's assertion is true, the marriage cannot be annulled because such claims do not constitute fraud that leads to marriage annulment. The key points of the decision are as follows:

Under Article 816 Subparagraph 3 of the Civil Code, fraud encompasses not only situations where one party to the marriage or a third party affirmatively conveys false information to the other party, but also instances where a party withholds information or remains silent. However, the mere failure to disclose information or remaining silent constitutes unlawful deception only when there is a duty to provide advance notice, as established by laws and regulations, contractual obligations, customary practices, or principles of common sense. In cases where a party to a marriage failed to inform the other party of a past childbirth, a duty to notify shall not automatically arise and constitute a ground for marriage annulment under Article 816 Subparagraph 3 of the Civil Code for the mere reason that it could have influenced the other party's decision to get married. Rather, balance and harmony shall be struck between one party's honor and privacy and the other party's freedom of decision-making on marriage. The mere failure to notify the other party of one's past childbirth shall not constitute a per se ground for marriage annulment under Article 816 Subparagraph 3 of the Civil Code in cases where one became pregnant and gave birth due to child sexual assault against her will, with the relationship with the child being severed, and with neither any custody of nor any contact with the child for a considerable time. This is in view of the fact that the past childbirth belongs to the confidential sphere of an individual, constituting an essential element of her honor and privacy. Moreover, it cannot be conclusively deemed either that a notification of such a matter is expected from the party involved on grounds of social norms, or that failure to notify is culpable in light of the good faith principle.

Marriage can be dissolved through either divorce or annulment. Annulment is exceptionally granted in cases where unavoidable circumstances necessitate the invalidation of a marriage based on conditions that existed at the time of its formation. This case examines whether the non-disclosure of past childbirth resulting from sexual assault constitutes grounds for annulment. According to Article 816, Subparagraph 3 of the Korean Civil Code, an aggrieved party may seek annulment if the declaration of intent to marry was made under "fraud."

Ordinarily, if an individual enters marriage without informing their spouse of a child from a previous relationship, it is reasonable to assume that the other party may seek annulment on the grounds of fraud, as the existence of children is a significant factor in marital decision-making. However, this case presents a more complex legal and ethical dilemma.

The woman in question was a victim of grave crimes, including child abduction, forced marriage, and sexual assault. Requiring her to disclose a childbirth resulting from sexual violence risks violating her fundamental right to privacy and dignity. The core issue in this case lies in balancing the woman's right to privacy and honor with the spouse's right to make an informed marital decision, thereby creating a challenging conflict of interests.

From a legal and moral perspective, **it is unreasonable to apply modern principles of contractual freedom to individuals who have been subjected to pre-modern forms of oppression**. The woman in this case may be considered '*misero*'—an individual who, within the framework of civil law, lacks true autonomy. Judicial interpretation of the concept of "fraud" should favor such individuals. Even if the failure to disclose past childbirth infringes upon the spouse's right to make an informed marital decision, annulment should not be granted. Instead, the spouse retains the right to dissolve the marriage through divorce. Restrictions on a spouse's ability to make autonomous decision in such cases are constitutionally permissible and justified in the interests of protecting the dignity and rights of vulnerable individuals.

2. A Perspective in Favor of a Minor Inheritor

The second case concerns succession law. Under Korean succession law, a successor effectively "stands in the shoes" of the deceased, automatically assuming both ownership of the inheritance estate and responsibility for the deceased's debts. However, successors may opt out of this default rule by choosing "qualified acceptance." Under this mechanism, inheritance creditors may claim only against the deceased's estate, rather than the personal assets of the successor, thereby protecting successors from excessive inheritance debt.

However, the right to qualified acceptance is subject to a limitation period. Successors must exercise this option within three months of becoming aware of the excessive inheritance debt, provided there is no undue delay in such awareness. This raises an important legal question: if a minor inheritor's legal representative (e.g., the mother) becomes aware of excessive inheritance debt but fails to act within the prescribed three-month period, does the minor inheritor lose the right to qualified acceptance? Alternatively, can the inheritor, upon reaching the age of majority, exercise the right to qualified acceptance based on their own newly acquired awareness? This issue was addressed in the Korean Supreme Court en banc Decision, 11. 19. 2020, 2019Da232918.

The majority opinion held that the inheritor is no longer eligible to opt for qualified acceptance. According to agency law principles, the knowledge of the legal representative is imputed to the principal (the minor inheritor). As a result, once the legal representative becomes aware of the excessive inheritance debt and fails to act within the prescribed period, the minor inheritor is deemed to have fully accepted the inheritance. The effect of legally presumed full acceptance is final and irrevocable.

In contrast, the minority opinion argued that an inheritor who reaches adulthood should be given a second opportunity to choose qualified acceptance. According to this view, the limitation period should begin either (1) when the inheritor personally becomes aware of the excessive debt after reaching the age of majority or (2) upon reaching adulthood if the inheritor already had such knowledge before. The relevant statute merely states that the limitation period begins from the knowledge of the inheritor, without explicitly specifying whether this refers to the legal representative or the principal (the minor inheritor) themselves. Under this approach, a minor inheritor would effectively have two separate limitation periods: one beginning from their legal representative's awareness before the minor reaches adulthood, and another starting from the minor's own knowledge upon reaching adulthood. However, the majority opinion criticized this approach as an instance of judicial law-making without sufficient legal basis, arguing that it contradicts the statute's clear language and disrupts the stability of inheritance law.

The majority opinion further argued that allowing such an exception would undermine the fundamental principle of agency law: the knowledge of the legal representative must be attributed to the principal. If an exception were permitted in this case, it would become difficult to establish a clear boundary between permissible and impermissible exceptions, potentially eroding the attribution principle altogether.

However, the majority's concerns may be overstated. In conventional legal relationships where a legal representative acts on behalf of a principal, judicial law-making of the kind proposed by the minority opinion may indeed be problematic. When it comes to the statute of limitation for claims, granting an exception to protect a minor creditor inevitably undermines the expectations of the opposing party(=debtor) to the same extent. This presents a typical **zero-sum situation**. But the inheritance context is different. An inheritance creditor has no inherent expectation of claiming the successor's personal assets. From the creditor's perspective, the minor inheritor's assets constitute an unforeseen **windfall gain** rather than a legitimate claimable resource. Therefore, allowing an exception in favor of the minor inheritor does not infringe upon the creditor's justifiable rights. Furthermore, the law should ensure that minors are not burdened with their parents' debts upon reaching adulthood. **To start one's adult life as a 'debt slave'—forced into financial liability against one's will—is fundamentally unjust from a libertarian perspective.** Ensuring that young inheritors can begin their independent lives free from inherited debt represents the minimal standard of equal opportunity that society owes to its future generations.

'*In dubio pro misero*' is an interpretive method of favoring the weaker party in cases of legal uncertainty. It can also provide a justification for positive judicial law-making in cases where it serves to protect individuals who lack genuine autonomy in legal decision-making, such as minor heirs facing excessive debt obligations.

II. Interpretation of Administrative law: **judicial activism for *misero***

In the field of administrative law interpretation, the conflicting interests of private individuals and state or public entities must be carefully weighed and balanced. A key consideration in this process is the concept of the public interest, or common good, which transcends the mere aggregation of individual interests. When determining a just solution that upholds the common good, two opposing judicial approaches may emerge: judicial passivism and judicial activism.

Judicial passivism asserts that, because the judiciary is less equipped than the legislative or executive branches to address complex policy issues, judges should interpret the law strictly according to its literal text and refrain from engaging in judicial law-making. In contrast, judicial activism maintains that judges can and should actively interpret laws through teleological reasoning or even create judge-made law when necessary to serve the common good.

Even in cases involving minority protection, judicial passivism may sometimes be preferable when the issue is policy-driven and requires empirical analysis of various alternatives along a continuum, matters best addressed through democratic political decision-making. However, when **a single, normatively and constitutionally required outcome is necessary** to safeguard minority rights—where the legal alternative is not a spectrum but a definitive point—judicial activism may be justified. In such instances, not only is teleological interpretation warranted, but judge-made law may also be appropriate. This approach does not infringe upon legislative authority but instead aligns with the functional separation of powers. Judicial intervention can be more effective in protecting minority rights when courts directly establish legal principles, rather than waiting for the constitutional court to declare a law unconstitutional and for the legislature to subsequently enact new legislation.

A notable example of this judicial activism is the Korean Supreme Court's decision 04. 29, 2020, 2016Du41071. This ruling illustrates how the judiciary can apply the method of '*in dubio pro misero*' in the interpretation of administrative law, ensuring that vulnerable individuals receive the minimal legal protection they require.

a) Facts and Issues
The Plaintiffs are nurses who are working at Hospital X, and they were pregnant in 2009 and gave birth in 2010, but all their children had congenital heart disease. Of the nurses working at Hospital X, fifteen persons including the Plaintiffs were pregnant in 2009. Among them, only six persons gave birth to healthy babies, but the four Plaintiffs' babies were born with congenital heart disease, and the other five persons miscarried. As a result, the working conditions and environment became an issue between labor union and company management, and Hospital X commissioned an epidemiological survey to SNU R&D Foundation in accordance with the agreement between labor and management in 2011. The SNU R&D Foundation submitted an epidemiological survey report to Hospital X on February 29, 2012. According to the Industrial Accident Compensation Insurance Act (hereinafter referred to as "Industrial Accident Insurance Act"), the term "occupational accident" means any injury, disease, disability, or death of an employee that is caused by an occupational reason (Art. 5 subpara. 1), and medical care benefits shall be paid to any employee who suffers from an injury or disease caused by reason of their duties (Art. para. 1). The Plaintiffs, based on the contents of the epidemiological survey report, filed a claim for medical care benefits with the Defendant, arguing that the delivery of a child with a congenital heart disease constitutes occupational accidents as they were exposed to the elements harmful to a pregnant woman and the health of a fetus in the early stage of pregnancy, and, as a consequence, disability in the process of the formation of the heart of a fetus occurred. The case presents two key legal issues. The first concerns whether "health damage to a fetus" resulting from occupational factors affecting a pregnant female employee falls within the scope of "occupational accidents" of an employee as defined by Industrial Accident Insurance Act. The second issue, which arises only if the first question is answered affirmatively, is whether the female employee remains entitled to medical care benefits for her child's congenital disease, despite the fact that the child was born as a separate legal entity.

b) Decision of the Supreme Court

The Supreme Court answered yes to both questions. The main reasoning is as follows:

① When various interpretations are possible in respect to a certain legal provision, the court ought to choose the interpretation in line with the Constitution. Article 32 Paragraph 4 of the Korean Constitution stipulates that "Special protection shall be accorded to working women, and they shall not be subject to unjust discrimination in terms of employment, wages, and working conditions." Article 36 Paragraph 2 of the Constitution regulates that "The State shall endeavor to protect mothers." Family, society, and the State cannot continue to be sustained and maintained without pregnancy and childbirth, and thus the protection of the mother's instinctive love is also related to the continuance and maintenance of the community. Therefore, the State shall be obliged to lessen the burden of pregnancy, childbirth.

Such special provisions of the Constitution can be seen to materialize the equal right of Article 11 of the Constitution prescribing that there shall be no discrimination in political, economic, social, or cultural life on account of sex, considering the distinctiveness of the area of its application. The meaning of the aforementioned constitutional provisions in the areas of job performance of women through the provision of labor is that a pregnant female employee and her fetus ought to be fully protected from harmful occupational elements that can occur in pregnancy or childbirth, and the State shall also be obliged to provide the sufficient protection for female employees from such harmful elements.

Therefore, the health damage of a fetus caused to a pregnant female employee by her occupational reason under the interpretation of the Industrial Accident Insurance Act ought to be seen to correspond to an occupational accident of the female employee regardless of the effect that it has on the labor ability of the female employee and its degree.

② An occupational accident under the Industrial Accident Insurance Act merely requires an accident occurs to an employee due to their occupational reasons, implying a proximate causal relation between occupation and accident. It is not a requirement that the person affected or receiving benefits must be an employee at the time of the disease's onset or at the time of receiving insurance benefits. Therefore, an accident that previously qualified as an occupational accident should not be reclassified as

> non-occupational solely because the fetus's status becomes separate from the mother body by childbirth.
> When interpreting and applying the notion of occupational accidents under the Industrial Accident Insurance Act, if a female employee's entitlement to medical care benefits is admitted with regard to the health damage of her fetus by considering the fetus as a monolithic body with the mother's body during pregnancy, but then denied abruptly in regard to congenital diseases of the child after birth on the grounds that the fetus is separated from the mother's body, this is contrary to the legislative purpose of the Industrial Accident Insurance Act that intends to "contribute to the protection of employees by compensating them promptly and fairly for any occupational accident," Furthermore, such an interpretation fails to properly guarantee the fundamental rights stipulated in Article 34 Paragraph 2 and 6 of the Constitution and to correctly embody the duty to protect mothers prescribed in Article 36 Paragraph 2 of the Constitution, as well as the special protection for, and the prohibition on discrimination against, working women provided by Article 32 Paragraph 4 of the Constitution.

Korean Constitution mandates that the State provide 'special and indiscriminate' protection to female workers. The necessity of adequately protecting pregnant female workers who have suffered industrial accidents is widely recognized. However, such protective measures entail financial costs that must be covered by public resources, which are inherently limited and subject to other competing public demands. Consequently, determining the extent of such special and indiscriminate protection for the common good primarily rests with the legislative and executive branches, and the scope of this protection generally exists along a continuum. Nevertheless, there are instances where circumstances necessitate **a precise and targeted level of protection, tailored to individual cases.**

The case under consideration exemplifies this issue. During pregnancy, a pregnant female worker and her fetus are considered a single entity; after childbirth, however, they become two distinct individuals. The Industrial Accident Insurance Act was not originally designed to address this specific situation. A strictly literal interpretation of the Act might lead to the conclusion that harm to the fetus does not constitute an industrial accident affecting the female worker herself. Similarly, if the fetus is born with a work-related condition but the female worker does not exhibit any illness, she may be denied industrial accident compensation. However, such a formalistic approach fails to acknowledge and empathize with the **unique vulnerabilities of pregnant female workers**, who are entitled to special constitutional protection.

Protecting pregnant female workers and ensuring the well-being of their newborn children are intrinsically linked, and cannot be treated as separate legal concerns. A pregnant female worker occupies a uniquely vulnerable position—**she is '*misero*' in a triple sense, as a woman, as a worker, and as a mother carrying a fetus.** The Constitution mandates her special protection to prevent both discrimination and systemic under-protection within a majority-oriented framework. Accordingly, judges should interpret the definition of "occupational accident" in a manner that upholds the constitutional commitment to safeguarding a '*misero*'.

III. Interpretation of Constitutional law

The Constitution serves as the supreme legal norm and embodies a high level of abstraction. The process of constitutional interpretation is primarily undertaken by the Constitutional Court when evaluating the constitutionality of laws or legislative omissions that restrict fundamental rights. This interpretive process unfolds in two distinct stages. First, the Court determines whether the fundamental rights in question are explicitly or implicitly recognized under the Constitution. Second, if these rights are recognized, the Court assesses whether the imposed restrictions can be justified under Article 37, Paragraph 2 of the Constitution.

This second stage involves an analysis of proportionality. Article 37, Paragraph 2 of the Constitution stipulates that "The freedoms and rights of citizens may be restricted by Act only when necessary for national security, the maintenance of social order, or public welfare. Even when such a restriction is imposed, no essential aspect of freedom or right shall be violated." This provision establishes a constitutional safeguard, ensuring that any limitation on fundamental rights is subject to strict scrutiny and must not infringe upon their essential core.

1. Same-sex marriage

a. Current Legal Situation in Korea

Currently, there are no laws in Korea that permit same-sex marriage. A lower court ruling has determined that, under the Constitution and the Civil Code, marriage is defined as a union between two individuals of the opposite sex.[3] Regardless of whether a union is same-sex or heterosexual, Korean law does not provide statutory recognition for life partnerships outside of marriage. However, judicial precedents have acknowledged *de facto* marital relationships for heterosexual couples, granting them many of the legal rights and protections associated with *de jure* marriage. In contrast, a lower court has refused to recognize *de facto* marital relationships for same-sex couples.[4]

Recently Korean Supreme Court opined that a same-sex partner can be recognized as a dependent for public health insurance, like a status currently granted to spouses in *de facto* heterosexual marriages.[5] But it's not about civil status of same-sex partners.

To date, the Constitutional Court has not issued a ruling on whether the absence of legal recognition for same-sex marriage is unconstitutional.

b. Unconstitutionality of the Current Legal Framework

aa. Three Possible Positions

There are three key legal positions regarding same-sex marriage under the Korean Constitution:

① Same-sex marriage is unconstitutional.
② Same-sex marriage is permissible under the current Constitution.
③ Same-sex marriage is required under the current Constitution.

Article 36, Paragraph 1 of the Korean Constitution states: "Marriage and family life shall be entered into and sustained on the basis of individual dignity and equality of two sexes, and the State shall do everything in its power to achieve that goal." This provision is intended to emphasize gender

3 Seoul Western District Court, 05. 25, 2016, 2014Hopa1842.
4 Incheon District Court, 07. 23, 2004, 2003Deuhab292.
5 Korean Supreme Court, 07. 18, 2024, 2023Du36800 en banc Decision.

equality within marriage and the autonomy of individuals in choosing their marital partners, rather than to explicitly exclude same-sex marriage. Consequently, if the legislature were to legalize same-sex marriage, such legislation would not be unconstitutional. However, my position aligns with the third view: **same-sex marriage is not merely permissible but constitutionally required.**

bb. Constitutional Justification for Same-Sex Marriage

The primary justification for recognizing same-sex marriage is grounded in an **analogy**. The principle of equality enshrined in the Constitution necessitates an inclusive interpretation of the term "two sexes" within the context of marriage. Just as the Constitution guarantees equal treatment under the law, it must also ensure that same-sex and opposite-sex couples receive equal legal recognition. The fundamental essence of marriage—love, fidelity, devotion, sacrifice, and mutual trust—remains unchanged regardless of the gender composition of the couple. Consequently, denying same-sex couples the right to marry constitutes unjustifiable discrimination.

If same-sex unions were to be recognized only as "life partnerships" rather than "marriages," they would be relegated to an inherently inferior status compared to opposite-sex unions. **The doctrine of separate but equal has long been rejected as a valid legal principle, as it inherently perpetuates inequality**. While public opinion may be opposed to same-sex marriage, constitutional rights cannot be determined by majority sentiment. The Korean Constitution does not permit legal discrimination based on gender identity or sexual orientation.

A similar interpretive approach has been applied in other legal contexts. For instance, while certain fundamental rights are explicitly granted to citizens under the Korean Constitution, courts have recognized that, in some cases, these rights must also be extended to non-citizens (foreigners) to uphold constitutional principles of equality and human dignity.

cc. Counterarguments and Their Rebuttals

A potential counterargument asserts that because biological reproduction occurs exclusively within heterosexual unions, restricting the legal definition of "marriage" to opposite-sex couples serves the public interest by promoting societal continuity. However, this reasoning is flawed for several reasons:

Sexual orientation is an immutable characteristic. Just as race and gender are not matters of personal choice, neither is sexual orientation. Denying same-sex couples the right to marry based on reproductive potential is akin to denying marriage to infertile or elderly heterosexual couples, which would be an absurd and unconstitutional restriction.

Recognizing same-sex marriage does not hinder societal sustainability. Allowing same-sex marriage neither prevents nor discourages heterosexual unions or childbearing. If the state seeks to promote childbirth, it should do so through direct incentives rather than by restricting marriage rights. If procreation is the primary objective, legal benefits should be extended specifically to couples who choose to have children, rather than granting exclusive recognition of "marriage" to all heterosexual couples regardless of their intent or ability to procreate.

dd. The Role of the Judiciary in Protecting Minority Rights

In sum, the principle of equality demands that same-sex couples receive the same legal recognition and rights as opposite-sex couples. Denying them the right to marry constitutes unconstitutional discrimination. Gays and lesbians, as a historically marginalized minority group—'*misero*'—should not have their rights left solely to legislative discretion. The judiciary, particularly the Constitutional Court, has a duty to uphold constitutional principles by interpreting Article 36, Paragraph 1 in favor of same-sex marriage. Therefore, same-sex marriage should not only be permitted but also recognized as a constitutionally protected right under the Korean Constitution.

2. Abortion

a. Backgrounds

Article 269, Paragraph 1 of the former Korean Criminal Code criminalized women who procured their own miscarriage through drugs or other means. Additionally, Article 270, Paragraph 1 imposed criminal penalties on medical practitioners who performed abortions at the request or with the consent of the pregnant woman. However, Articles 14 and 28 of the Mother and

Child Health Act provided specific exceptions to these prohibitions. Under these provisions, abortion was not subject to criminal punishment in cases where: ① the woman or her spouse had a genetic or contagious disease, ② the pregnancy resulted from rape or quasi-rape, ③ the pregnancy occurred between close relatives who were legally prohibited from marrying, or ④ the pregnancy posed a serious risk of injury or the likelihood of severe harm to the woman's health.

Notably, abortion on socioeconomic grounds was not included within these exceptions, thereby maintaining a strict legal framework that limited access to abortion.

In 2019, the Constitutional Court of Korea ruled that the aforementioned provisions of the Criminal Code criminalizing abortion were unconformable to the Constitution.[6] The Court set a deadline of December 31, 2020, for the legislature to amend the law to bring it into compliance with constitutional principles. However, the legislature failed to enact the required revisions by the specified deadline. Consequently, as of January 1, 2021, the provisions of the Criminal Act criminalizing abortion became invalid. Currently, abortion in South Korea is no longer subject to criminal penalties for either women or medical practitioners, regardless of the reason for or stage of the pregnancy.

b. Key points of the 2019 Constitutional Court Decision

Among the nine judges of the Constitutional Court, the decision was divided as follows:

① Four justices determined that the provisions were unconformable to the Constitution and should remain in effect only temporarily until revised by the legislature.

② Three justices found the provisions to be outright unconstitutional and advocated for their immediate repeal.

③ Two justices upheld the provisions as constitutional.

The following sections will analyze the primary reasoning behind the decisions of nonconformity and outright unconstitutionality.

6 Korean Constitutional Court, 04. 11, 2019, 2017Hunba127.

aa. Reasoning Behind the Constitutional Nonconformity Opinion

(1) The Right to Abortion as an Extension of the Right to Self-Determination

The first sentence of Article 10 of the Korean Constitution states, "All citizens shall be assured of human worth and dignity and have the right to the pursuit of happiness." From this provision, the general right to personality is derived as an expression of human dignity, and the right to self-determination emerges as a key aspect of this general right to personality. The right to self-determination encompasses a woman's ability to shape her private sphere of life with dignity, including the right to decide whether to continue or terminate a pregnancy. This decision involves complex personal considerations, including physical, psychological, social, and economic factors. Given its profound impact on a woman's life and well-being, the choice to continue or terminate a pregnancy constitutes a fundamental aspect of personal dignity and autonomy.

(2) The State's Duty to Protect Fetal Life

While the state has an obligation to protect fetal life, this duty does not necessitate uniform legal protection at all stages of fetal development. Within the Korean legal framework, the state may provide varying degrees of legal protection to the fetus depending on its stage of development. This flexibility allows for a nuanced approach that balances fetal protection with competing constitutional rights.

(3) Balancing Pro-Choice and Pro-Life Interests

The existing abortion provisions impose a blanket prohibition on abortion throughout the entirety of pregnancy, compelling women to carry pregnancies to term and subjecting them to criminal penalties for seeking abortion services. However, fetal viability is generally considered to begin at approximately 22 weeks of gestation, at which point the fetus is capable of surviving independently outside the womb. Before this threshold, the fetus is not viable, and the pregnant woman's right to self-determination should take precedence. A viable fetus, capable of independent existence, possesses a qualitatively different status compared to a non-viable fetus in earlier stages of development.

In recognition of the significance of a pregnant woman's right to self-determination, the state must ensure that women have a sufficient period—prior to the viability threshold (approximately 22 weeks)—to make an informed and comprehensive decision regarding the continuation of pregnancy. Furthermore, the current abortion prohibition fails to effectively safeguard fetal life and lacks empathy for pregnant women facing significant socioeconomic hardships. It does not employ the least restrictive means to achieve its legislative objectives and inadequately reconciles the public interest in protecting fetal life with the private interest in preserving a woman's right to self-determination.

(4) Scope of Unconstitutionality

The opinion advocating for constitutional nonconformity asserted that pregnant women should be granted the legal right to freely decide on abortion within the first 22 weeks of gestation. However, the legislature retains discretion in determining the precise timeframe and may impose additional requirements, such as socioeconomic justification or mandatory consultation with a medical professional, as part of the legal framework governing abortion access.

bb. Reasoning Behind the Simple Unconstitutionality Opinion

The opinion advocating for simple unconstitutionality largely concurred with the constitutional nonconformity opinion, emphasizing that the abortion provisions disproportionately infringed upon a pregnant woman's right to self-determination. This violation stemmed from the absolute prohibition of abortion before fetal viability and the imposition of criminal penalties on women seeking abortions, even in cases of significant socioeconomic hardship.

However, the simple unconstitutionality opinion went further, arguing that abortion should be permitted without restriction as to reason and should be left to the deliberation and judgment of the pregnant woman during the first trimester of pregnancy (approximately 14 weeks from the first day of the last menstrual period). The justifications for this position were as follows:

① Respect for a Woman's Autonomous Decision-Making: a pregnant woman's decision to terminate a pregnancy, as an expression of her dignity and autonomy, should be fundamentally respected throughout the entirety of pregnancy.

② Increased Health Risks Associated with Second-Trimester Abortions: abortions performed after the first trimester involve more complex medical procedures and pose greater health risks to the pregnant woman. Consequently, the state's interest in both protecting fetal life and safeguarding maternal health may justify increased regulation beyond this point.

③ Concerns Regarding Selective Abortions: after the first trimester, the risk of selective abortion based on fetal sex or potential disabilities increases. This concern provides a further justification for imposing certain restrictions beyond the initial 14-week period.

c. Constitutionality of Laws Criminalizing Abortion: A Perspective in Favor of Fetal Rights

aa. Incommensurability of Abortion Issue, and the Scope of Constitutional Right to Self-Determination

The abortion debate remains one of the most complex and contentious issues in contemporary society. This discussion encompasses ethical, religious, scientific, medical, sociological, and legal dimensions, all of which are shaped by individual values, experiences, and attitudes toward human life. Given these diverse perspectives, the issue remains highly polarized, with no clear consensus. In the 2019 decision, even among the judges who deemed the abortion provisions unconstitutional, there was significant disagreement regarding the permissible extent of abortion under the Constitution. Three justices argued that permitting abortion during the first trimester solely for socioeconomic reasons was unconstitutional, as it unduly restricted the right to self-determination. In contrast, four justices, in their constitutional nonconformity opinion, suggested that such an approach could be constitutionally acceptable.

The inherent complexity of the abortion debate—characterized by **its incommensurability and the wide range of possible legal approaches**—suggests that this issue should primarily be addressed through legislation rather than judicial rulings. The legislative process allows for broader public deliberation, ensuring that abortion laws reflect a democratic consensus. Legislators, as elected representatives, are better positioned to consider the evolving social, scientific, and ethical factors that inform abortion policy. Moreover, legislation can be more adaptable to societal changes than judicial pronouncements.

Additionally, the Constitution does not explicitly define key criteria such as the "first trimester of pregnancy" or the "point of fetal viability," which were central to the Constitutional Court's 2019 decision in determining the extent of a pregnant woman's right to self-determination. **The Constitution does not expressly recognize a right to abortion**[7]; rather, any such right is derived from the broader right to self-determination, which itself stems from the general right to personality. However, **under the principle of private autonomy, self-determination is inherently linked to self-responsibility.** Fault-based liability is a fundamental aspect of private autonomy, meaning that **self-determination without corresponding accountability cannot be justified within this framework.**

From this perspective, legislation that prohibits abortion in cases where a woman has exercised her right to self-determination by choosing to engage in sexual intercourse, yet permits abortion where this choice was absent (e.g., in cases of rape),[8] still affords a degree of protection to a woman's autonomy. **Fault-based liability can be justified through the principle of autonomy**, which underpins the right to self-determination. If abortion is prohibited when a woman becomes pregnant as a result of her own voluntary actions, despite a failed contraceptive plan, her right to self-determination is not entirely negated but merely limited. In other words, it cannot be definitively concluded that a woman's right to self-determination is **constitutionally protected only if** abortion is permitted up to the 22nd week of pregnancy. The viability of a fetus can serve as a criterion for distinguishing abortion from infanticide, yet it **cannot be the sole determinant for constitutional permissibility** of abortion. If the

7 The French Constitution Art. 34 revised on March 4, 2024, added the following sentence; "La loi détermine les conditions dans lesquelles s'exerce la liberté garantie à la femme d'avoir recours à une interruption volontaire de grossesse." (The law determines the conditions under which the freedom guaranteed to a woman to have recourse to a voluntary termination of pregnancy is exercised).

8 In cases of rape, a woman is entirely deprived of her right to self-determination. Conversely, when a woman attempts to use contraception but it fails, she may be regarded as having exercised some degree of self-determination in her effort to control whether or not to become pregnant.

ability of the fetus to feel pain or a reasonable timeframe for a mother to decide on abortion emerges as an alternative standard—such as the 20th or 15th week of gestation—there is no clear constitutional basis for deeming a law that criminalizes abortion beyond this point unconstitutional. The Korean Constitution does not provide explicit guidance for establishing such a threshold, thereby leaving the determination of abortion regulations primarily within the purview of the legislature.

While laws that prohibit abortion in cases of rape or where pregnancy endangers the life or health of the mother may be unconstitutional due to violations of fundamental rights, the broader question of abortion's permissibility remains a matter for the legislature. The extent to which abortion should be permitted, beyond these extreme cases, is ultimately a legislative decision that must balance competing rights and interests within a constitutional framework.[9]

bb. Constitutional Interpretation in Favor of Those who Cannot Speak for Themselves

People who support the 2019 decision might argue two key points:

① **Proportionality**: The law serves as a minimum standard of morality, and criminal law should be a measure of last resort. A fetus does not receive the same constitutional protection as human life. A woman's decision to terminate a pregnancy is deeply personal, encompassing ethical, religious, and holistic considerations that impact her entire life. Criminalizing abortion throughout all stages of pregnancy would be an excessive legal response.

---

9 If we accept the following premises—① there is no fundamental difference between a fetus and a newborn in terms of human dignity or the need for life protection, and ② at least once an embryo is implanted in the uterus, it should be afforded human dignity as a life with intrinsic human value regardless of gestational age—then the provision allowing early abortion on socioeconomic grounds **should** be declared unconstitutional. However, this argument lacks explicit constitutional support, too. The Constitution does not mandate the protection of fetal life to the same extent as that of a person. In a similar vein, I find the dissenting opinion in the 2019 decision questionable. The dissenting view appears to suggest that allowing abortion to some extent may be unconstitutional, yet there is no clear constitutional basis for treating fetal life as equivalent to human life.

② **Judicial activism**: Although the Constitution does not explicitly or directly guarantee the right to abortion, the conclusion reached in the 2019 Constitutional Court decision can be justified through judicial activism. The prohibition of abortion poses a significant threat to a woman's life and well-being, particularly for those facing social and economic hardships. It would be inappropriate for the state to impose official, collective moral convictions on deeply personal, ethical and religious matters. Forcing women to endure severe hardship based on metaphysical beliefs about the nature or inherent value of life—beliefs they may not share—constitutes an undue infringement on individual autonomy.[10]

These two interrelated arguments, which may initially appear somewhat compelling, ultimately revolve around **balancing conflicting interests**. I'd like to present three counterarguments;

① **Fetal Status and Human Dignity**
While a fetus is not constitutionally recognized as a human being, it does not imply that its protection is unrelated to its own interests or that it is merely an objective public value upheld by community, akin to the protection of cultural assets or animals.[11] Although fetuses and future generations are not yet complete human beings, they possess the potential for full personhood. Their interests should, therefore, be considered and weighed in legal deliberations. The notion that fetal dignity constitutes only **20–30 % of full human dignity**, does not negate the presence of human dignity altogether. Once the fetus is acknowledged within the realm of human dignity, the interpretive

---

10 Ronald Dworkin, Freedom's Law, (1996), 120–121.

11 Dworkin distinguishes between "derivative value" and "detached and intrinsic value" in relation to the value of a fetus. He emphasizes that a fetus's potential life can only possess the latter, as a fetus is not constitutionally a human being whose life holds derivative value based on the rights and interest of an individual. According to Dworkin, **a fetus itself does not possess independent rights or interest**; rather **only the state's interests in protecting the fetus exists.** This interest, he argues, is rooted in religious beliefs that "the value of human life transcends its value for the creature whose life it is." Such beliefs, he contends, should not be imposed on pregnant women. Ronald Dworkin, Freedom's Law, (1996), 87–104.
However, it remains unclear why the interests of the fetus should not be considered independently when balancing conflicting interests. The conclusion that a fetus lacks independent rights does not necessarily follow from the premise that it is not a human being.

method of protecting the weaker party becomes applicable. Consequently, the 20–30 % human dignity of the fetus must be weighed against the pregnant individual's right to self-determination, particularly in cases where abortion has profound and lasting implications for the woman's life.

② **Judicial Activism: Whom Should It Protect?**
From an empirical perspective, both Christian groups opposing abortion and civic groups advocating for abortion rights hold significant influence, making it difficult to determine whether the fetus or the pregnant woman is the more vulnerable party in the political process. However, from a normative standpoint, the fetus is clearly the weaker party. Firstly, self-representation is a fundamental aspect of advocacy; no one can represent their own interests better than themselves. In this respect, the fetus is structurally disadvantaged compared to the pregnant woman. The judiciary has a role in representing those who cannot speak for themselves. Secondly, the fetus is entirely dependent on the pregnant woman, whose choice determine its fate. This inherent asymmetry justifies the imposition of certain obligations on the pregnant woman toward the fetus. Judicial activism in abortion cases can therefore be justified only if it serves the interests of the fetus, rather than those of the pregnant woman.[12]

③ **Less Restrictive Measure?**
Given the inherent dignity of life, including fetal life, ensuring its unconditional protection is constitutionally permissible, though not necessarily mandated, despite potential policy or utilitarian objections. While the Constitution does not require fetal life to be protected to the same degree as an individual's life, once legislation opts to extend protection to the fetus, the criminal prohibition of abortion represents **one of the reasonable enforcement mechanisms.** Decriminalizing

---

12 John Hart Ely argued that the Court should prioritize the protection of interests that, **in comparison to the dominant interests they are subordinated to**, belong to minorities uniquely incapable of defending themselves. Ely suggested that the fetus might constitute such a minority relative to women. In this context, legislation restricting abortion could have been enacted by a highly motivated minority and may not necessarily reflect the will of the broader legislative majority. However, Ely emphasized that even if this were the case, it is not the Court's role to invalidate such legislation. The Court's declaration of unconstitutionality should be based on **more than mere speculation regarding the extent and intensity of public support for the law.** John Hart Ely, The Wages of Crying Wolf: A Comment on Roe v. Wade, Yale L.J. 920, 933–935 (1973).

> abortion may prove insufficient or inappropriate, as alternative measure such as administrative fines could be ineffective, and allowing fetuses to pursue civil claims for damages is impractical.

Compassion for beings unable to articulate their own interests – even if those beings possess only 20–30 % of full human dignity- should be able to take precedence over the right to the self-determination of those who already enjoy autonomy. At the very least, this consideration should serve as the foundation for constitutional interpretation. The argument is not that the state should impose a singular moral view that life holds absolute value regardless of circumstances. Rather, it asserts that the partial human dignity of the fetus deserves constitutional recognition as a legal principle. Pregnant individuals should, in turn, be open to acknowledge and respect this principle, even if their own rights are affected to some extent.

Therefore, the previous Criminal Code, which criminalized abortion, should have been upheld as constitutional. However, the ethical and policy implications of compelling women facing socioeconomic difficulties to give birth and subjecting them to criminal penalties if they fail to do so, remain open to debate.[13] Personally, I believe that permitting early-stage abortions following medical consultation represents a desirable legislative direction. Nonetheless, the present discussion pertains to constitutional interpretation, and the most appropriate judicial reasoning does not always align with the most desirable policy decision.

13 From a comparative legal perspective, Korea's previous abortion law was excessively strict, particularly in relation to other OECD countries. The Constitutional Court's 2019 decision declaring the law unconstitutional can be seen as a positive step toward aligning with global standards on reproductive rights. However, the responsibility for such legislative changes lies with the National Assembly, not the Constitutional Court. If the Korean National Assembly fails to act or demonstrates incompetence in this regard, the ultimate responsibility falls on the electorate. In a democracy, citizens who elect their representatives must also bear the consequences of their representatives' actions or inactions. This principle is fundamental to democratic governance.

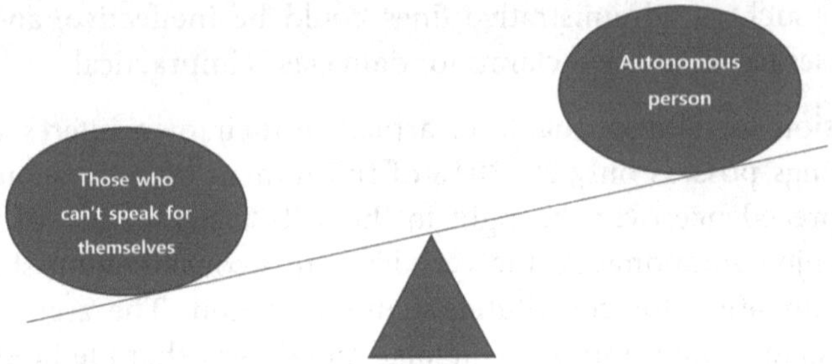

the Lever of Constitutional Interpretation: *in dubio pro misero*

d. The Unconstitutionality of Current Legal Situation

According to the interpretive method '*in dubio pro misero*', the current legal framework, which permits abortion without any restrictions regarding gestational period or cause, should be considered unconstitutional. This is because it fails to demonstrate any respect for the life of the fetus who is unable to advocate for itself.

Some may ask, "In your opinion, from what point should abortion be constitutionally criminalized?" My response is that the court does not need to determine an exact point, as this is a multifaceted, policy-driven matter. The court's role is simply to adjudicate the specific case at hand and decide whether the law in question is constitutional or unconstitutional. "If it is not necessary to decide more to dispose of a case, then it is necessary not to decide more."[14]

Furthermore, one might pose the subsequent question; "You argue that criminalizing throughout the entire pregnancy is constitutional, while decriminalizing it during the same period is unconstitutional. Is this distinction justifiable?" My response is that this distinction is totally reasonable. The former aligns more closely with **regulatory law**, whereas the latter pertains to a **significant constitutional matter**, as it concerns the **fundamental right** of a fetus to life. Judges, therefore, should interpret the Constitution in accordance with the method '*in dubio pro misero*'.

14 ROBERTS, C. J., concurring in judgment of Dobbs v. Jackson women's health organization 597 U.S. 215 (2022).

e. The Strategic Aspect of the Constitutional Court's Decision

From a strategic perspective, the Constitutional Court's decision may be seen as a calculated move to prompt legislative action. The legislative branch has been reluctant to address the issue of abortion, fearing political backlash from pro-life advocates. By issuing its ruling, the Court placed pressure on lawmakers to enact a more balanced, moderate abortion law, one that would improve upon the previous restrictive provisions. However, legislators have not responded as expected; instead, they have remained inactive. As a result, the situation has become more serious than before, creating a **legal vacuum** in which abortion is now unrestricted at all stages of pregnancy. Recently, a hospital's termination of a 36-week pregnancy became a subject of public controversy in Korea. Although such cases may be rare, the absence of any legal framework regulating abortion is clearly problematic.

While strategy can sometimes influence judicial decisions, the **essence of legal and democratic principles must remain paramount.** Ends do not always justify means. In a pluralistic and open society, the means by which decisions are made are just as important as the outcomes. Even when the results are undesirable, they must be accepted if they arise from a just and democratic process. This is a fundamental condition of pluralism and democratic governance. Courts can serve as catalysts for change, but they cannot guarantee it. A well-intended judicial strategy cannot, by itself, justify a court's decision. Ultimately, the Court must remain committed to legal principles and the integrity of the law rather than a result-oriented approach.

D. Conclusion

Legal interpretation takes place within the framework of norms. The interpretive method of '*in dubio pro misero*' which operates affirmatively within this normative sphere, serves not to grant disproportionate advantage to the '*misero*' in the real world, but to prevent real-world outcome from disproportionately disadvantaging the '*misero*.' Such an inclusive and protective approach constitutes the minimal necessary condition for maintaining and fostering a just and cohesive community.[15]

Therefore, *'in dubio pro misero'* does not infringe upon the constitutional boundaries governing the freedom of the opposing party in a conflict with the '*misero*'. Rather, from a communitarian perspective, it ultimately enhances collective freedom. Judges who, despite careful balancing, remain unable to reach a satisfactory conclusion should actively rule in favor of the '*misero*' and, if necessary, urge that the legislative and executive branches to give a greater consideration to the interests of the '*misero*'. In this limited context, judges must assume a role resembling that of politicians. This is the idea conveyed by the phrase **"a small politics of judicial interpretation"** in the title of this article.

15 Arthur Kaufmann emphasized the significance of tolerance in modern society, which is characterized by risk and complexity. He proposed the **categorical imperative of tolerance**, stating; "Act in such a way that the consequences of your actions are compatible with the greatest possible avoidance of human misery."("Handle so, daß die Folgen deiner Handlungen verträglich sind mit der größt- möglichen Vermeidung menschlichen Elends"). Arthur Kaufmann, Rechtsphilosophie, (1997), S.344. This Principle aligns with the concept of '**negative utilitarianism**', and is also consistent with the interpretive method of '***in dubio pro misero***'.

Der Koreanische Oberste Gerichtshof und juristische Methodik: Ein Blick auf die jüngsten Entscheidungen des gesamten Senats*

Kye Il Lee

I. Einleitung

In den jüngsten Entscheidungen des Obersten Gerichtshofs Koreas lässt sich eine zunehmende methodische Gründlichkeit in den Argumentationen feststellen. Diese Entwicklung ist zum einen auf ein gewachsenes methodisches Bewusstsein innerhalb der Gerichte zurückzuführen, zum anderen auf den produktiven Einfluss jener Rechtswissenschaftler, die stets die Bedeutung der Methodenlehre hervorgehoben haben.[1] Diese Tendenzen dienen prima facie der Stärkung der Rechtsstaatlichkeit, sofern das Hauptziel

---

* Dieser Beitrag basiert auf einer Reihe von Arbeiten, die der Verfasser im Rahmen seiner Forschung zur Auslegungsmethodik des koreanischen Obersten Gerichtshofs verfasst und in der koreanischen Rechtswissenschaft veröffentlicht hat. Diese Studien wurden mehrfach überarbeitet und erheblich erweitert, sodass sie ihre aktuelle Form erhielten. Ein Teil davon wurde auf dem Special Workshop „The Legal Methodology in Korea" des Weltkongresses für Rechts- und Sozialphilosophie (IVR) 2024 präsentiert.

1 Eine komprimierte Darstellung der bisherigen Diskussionen bietet *Y.-H. Kim*, Die gegenwärtige Lage der juristischen Methodenlehre in Korea, in: ders., Rechtsphilosophie und Strafrecht in Deutschland und Korea, Baden-Baden, 2017, S. 114 ff. m.w.N. Eine Sammlung zentraler methodologischer Studien und einschlägiger Debatten innerhalb der koreanischen Rechtswissenschaft findet sich in D.-K. Kim (Hrsg.), Rechtsordnung und Gesetzesauslegung in Korea (Kor.), Seoul, 2013, sowie in K.-I. Lee (Hrsg.), Juristische Methodenlehre (Kor.), Seoul, 2017. Im Folgenden wird die in koreanischer Sprache verfasste Literatur am Ende des Titels mit „(Kor.)" gekennzeichnet. In diesem Zusammenhang sei auch eine ergänzende Erläuterung zur Schreibweise von Autorennamen in koreanischen Quellen gegeben. Üblicherweise besteht ein koreanischer Name aus einem einsilbigen Familiennamen und einem zweisilbigen Vornamen. Bei der Umschrift in das lateinische Alphabet werden die beiden Silben des Vornamens auf verschiedene Weisen wiedergegeben: teils zusammenhängend als ein Wort, teils mit einem Bindestrich oder mit Leerzeichen geschrieben. Wird der Vorname abgekürzt, kann es häufig schwierig sein, die Autoren eindeutig zu identifizieren, insbesondere wenn nur der Anfangsbuchstabe der ersten Silbe angegeben wird. Daher wird in diesem Beitrag einheitlich die erste Initiale jeder Silbe des Vornamens angegeben und beide Initialen durch einen Bindestrich verbunden. So lautet der offizielle englische Name des Verfassers dieses Beitrags „Kye Il Lee"; in den Fußnoten wird er jedoch einheitlich als „K.-I. Lee" angegeben.

der juristischen Methodenlehre darin besteht, richterliche Entscheidungen einer rationalen Kontrolle zu unterziehen.

An diesem Punkt sieht sich die Rechtsphilosophie Koreas mit zwei zentralen Herausforderungen konfrontiert: Erstens gilt es, die methodischen Ansätze in der Rechtspraxis analytisch nachzuvollziehen, und zweitens, darauf aufbauend Perspektiven für ihre normative Weiterentwicklung aufzuzeigen sowie deren kritische Implikationen zu erforschen. Um sich diesen Aufgaben zu nähern, konzentriert sich die vorliegende Studie insbesondere auf die Entscheidungen des gesamten Senats des Obersten Gerichtshofs Koreas aus den letzten vier bis fünf Jahren. Denn in diesen Urteilen werden methodische Begründungen deutlicher herausgearbeitet als in der Vergangenheit, und die Differenzen zwischen den Richtermeinungen treten klarer zutage.

Die Analyse knüpft an die herkömmliche Struktur der Methodenlehre an. Zunächst werden diejenigen Urteile untersucht, die die Auffassungen der Richter zum ‚Auslegungsziel' verdeutlichen, insbesondere im Hinblick auf das Spannungsverhältnis zwischen objektiver und subjektiver Auslegungslehre. Im Anschluss erfolgt die Analyse der ‚Auslegungskriterien': Hierbei werden zunächst die vier Hauptkriterien betrachtet, gefolgt von ergänzenden Kriterien wie der folgenorientierten und präjudizienorientierten Auslegung. Darauf aufbauend wird die Argumentation im Bereich der richterlichen Rechtsfortbildung analysiert, wobei der Fokus insbesondere auf der ‚lückenfüllenden Rechtsfortbildung' und der ‚richterlichen Gesetzeskorrektur' liegt. Diese Untersuchung bezieht zudem die richterlichen Auffassungen zum Vorrangverhältnis der Auslegungskriterien ein.

Im Anschluss an diese detaillierte Analyse werden die rechtstheoretischen Implikationen sowohl in normativer als auch in strukturkritischer Hinsicht herausgearbeitet. Ziel ist es nicht nur, mögliche Wege für methodischen Fortschritt aufzuzeigen, sondern auch die strukturellen Ressourcen argumentativer Gegensätze, die in der Methodenlehre selbst immanent angelegt sind, sichtbar zu machen.

II. Das Ziel der Auslegung in den jüngsten Entscheidungen

Zunächst werden die Urteile analysiert, die das *Auslegungsziel* – insbesondere im Spannungsfeld zwischen objektiver und subjektiver Auslegungslehre – offenlegen.

1. Methodische Diskussionslage

In der rechtswissenschaftlichen Diskussion zum Auslegungsziel wurde im kontinentalen Rechtssystem die Debatte traditionell entlang der Gegenüberstellung von subjektiver und objektiver Auslegungslehre geführt und darauf aufbauend weiterentwickelt. Im angloamerikanischen Rechtskreis hingegen stehen Begriffe wie ‚Textualism', ‚Intentionalism' und ‚Purposivism' im Zentrum der methodischen Auseinandersetzung.[2]

Die subjektive Auslegungslehre zielt darauf ab, die Vorstellungen oder Absichten des historischen Gesetzgebers zum Zeitpunkt der Formulierung des Gesetzestextes zu ermitteln. Demgegenüber verfolgt die objektive Auslegungslehre das Ziel, die objektiv gültige Bedeutung des Gesetzestextes zum Zeitpunkt seiner Anwendung zu bestimmen.[3]

Es wurde darauf hingewiesen, dass die Position der koreanischen Gerichte zum Auslegungsziel in der Vergangenheit nicht eindeutig war.[4] In jüngsten Diskussionen lässt sich jedoch ein gewisser methodischer Fortschritt erkennen. Ein besonders aufschlussreiches Beispiel hierfür ist das Urteil zur Militärdienstverweigerung. In diesem Fall formuliert die ergänzende Meinung der Mehrheitsrichter eine klassisch objektive Auslegungslehre, um die Straflosigkeit der Militärdienstverweigerung zu begründen:

> „Zwar sollte bei der Auslegung die Absicht des Gesetzgebers berücksichtigt werden, jedoch ohne daran gebunden zu sein. Vielmehr soll das Gesetz selbst bindend sein. Genau dieses Gesetz bestimmt ‚die legitimen

2 Bekanntlich wird im Kontext der Verfassungsinterpretation im angloamerikanischen Rechtskreis eher die Diskussion um Konzepte wie ‚Originalism' oder ‚Living Constitutionalism' geführt, jedoch wird auf eine weiterführende Erläuterung hier verzichtet.

3 Zur aktuellen Diskussion über das Auslegungsziel in Korea siehe *Y.-H. Kim*, Das Auslegungsziel: Zur Auseinandersetzung zwischen der subjektiven und der objektiven Auslegungslehre (Kor.), Koreanische Zeitschrift für Rechtsphilosophie, Bd. 21, H. 1 (2018), 367 (375 ff.); *J.-O. Kim* [u.a.], Rechtsphilosophie: Theorie und Problemstellungen, 3. Aufl., Seoul, 2022, S. 297 ff. Zu diesem Thema in der deutschen Literatur siehe nur *Engisch*, Einführung in das juristische Denken, 13. Aufl., Stuttgart, 2024, S. 131 ff.; *Larenz/Canaris*, Methodenlehre der Rechtswissenschaft, Berlin [u. a.], 1995, S. 137 ff. m.w.N.

4 Etwa *S.-H. Oh*, Eine kritische Überprüfung der Methode der richterlichen Auslegung – mit Fokus auf die Prioritäten zwischen den Methoden der Gesetzesauslegung – (Kor.), Chungang Law Review, Bd. 22, H. 3 (2020), 121 (131).

> Gründe' ... *Das Gesetz ist klüger als die Gesetzgeber selbst.*"[5] (Hervor. i. Orig.)

Dieser Teil zitiert den berühmten Gustav Radbruch: „Der Ausleger kann das Gesetz besser verstehen, als es seine Schöpfer verstanden haben, das Gesetz kann klüger sein als sein Verfasser – es *muß* sogar klüger sein als seine Verfasser."[6] (Hervor. i. Orig.)

Die objektive Auslegungslehre wurde jedoch von der Minderheit (Kim So-young, Jo Hee-de, Park Sang-ok, Lee Ki-taek) scharf kritisiert. Sie führen folgendes Argument an:

> „Wenn man – wie die Mehrheitsmeinung – interpretiert, überschreitet man die Prinzipien und Grenzen der Gesetzesauslegung, die auf Wortlaut, Logik und System des Gesetzes basieren und sich im Rahmen seines Zwecks bewegen müssen."

Im Folgenden geht es um ein Urteil zu Arbeitsunfällen. In diesem Urteil stützt sich die Mindermeinung wie folgt auf die objektive Auslegungslehre:

> „Der Wortlaut des Gesetzes ist das wichtigste Indiz dafür, den Willen des Gesetzgebers zu erkennen. Weicht der im Gesetz formulierte Inhalt von der subjektiven Absicht oder der ursprünglichen Intention des Gesetzgebers ab, so ist die objektive Absicht, die im Wortlaut des Gesetzes zum Ausdruck kommt, vorrangig auszulegen."[7]

Ähnliche Ausführungen finden sich auch im jüngsten Urteil zu sexuellem Missbrauch in militärischen Einrichtungen.[8] Im Urteil zur künstlichen Befruchtung vertritt die Mehrheitsmeinung ebenfalls die objektive Auslegungslehre und führt dazu aus:

> „Die Bedeutung des Gesetzeswortlauts ist nicht starr. Sie kann sich mit sozioökonomischen Veränderungen sowie mit dem Fortschritt von Wissenschaft und Technologie wandeln. Sachverhalte, die zuvor nicht unter

---

5 Oberster Gerichtshof, Urteil des gesamten Senats vom 1. November 2018, Az. 2016do10912.

6 *G. Radbruch*, Rechtsphilosophie, hrsg. von E. Wolf und H.-P. Schneider, 8. Aufl., Stuttgart, 1973, S. 207.

7 Oberster Gerichtshof, Urteil des gesamten Senats vom 9. September 2021, Az. 2017-du45933 (Mindermeinung von Richter Kim Jae-hyung, Park Jeong-hwa, Kim Seon-soo, Lee Heung-koo).

8 Oberster Gerichtshof, Urteil des gesamten Senats vom 21. April 2022, Az. 2019do3047.

> den Regelungsbereich des Gesetzes fielen, können je nach gesellschaftlichem und zeitlichem Wandel in diesen einbezogen werden."[9]

Im Gegensatz zu den oben genannten Fällen gibt es jedoch auch Urteile, in denen die Mehrheitsmeinung die subjektive Auslegungslehre deutlich betont. Ein Beispiel dafür ist das Urteil zur Feiertagsvergütung.

> „Im früheren Arbeitsstandardgesetz könnte die Auslegung von ‚eine Woche' als ‚sieben Tage einschließlich Feiertagen' der üblichen Wortbedeutung entsprechen. Allerdings hat der Gesetzgeber im geänderten Arbeitsstandardgesetz durch Definitions- und Übergangsbestimmungen unmissverständlich klargestellt, dass die Arbeitszeit an Feiertagen nicht zur wöchentlichen Arbeitszeit zählt. Wenn ein Gericht eine Gesetzesbestimmung entgegen dem ausdrücklich festgelegten Willen des Gesetzgebers auslegt, könnte dies als Verstoß gegen das Prinzip der Gewaltenteilung gewertet werden."[10]

2. Das strukturelle Potenzial der argumentativen Gegensätze

Ein weiterer wichtiger Punkt ist, dass jede Auslegungslehre - unabhängig davon, welche übernommen wird - zwangsläufig die „Grenzen der Auslegung" festlegen muss. Dies wiederum kann ein entscheidender Faktor für Meinungsdivergenzen sein.

Ein exemplarisches Beispiel hierfür ist das Urteil zur treuhänderischen Übereignung von Immobilien.[11] Die Mehrheitsmeinung lehnt es ab, die Bestimmung zur Leistung für einen illegalen Grund (§ 746 KBGB) auf Fälle der nichtigen treuhänderischen Übereignung anzuwenden. Stattdessen betont sie die Notwendigkeit, „die grundlegende Entscheidung des Gesetzgebers" bei der Gesetzesauslegung zu respektieren.

---

9 Oberster Gerichtshof, Urteil des gesamten Senats vom 23. Oktober 2019, Az. 2016me2510.

10 Oberster Gerichtshof, Urteil des gesamten Senats vom 21. Juni 2018, 2011da112391.

11 Oberster Gerichtshof, Urteil des gesamten Senats vom 20. Juni 2019, Az. 2013da218156. § 4 Absatz 1 *des Gesetzes über die Registrierung von Immobilien im Namen des tatsächlichen Eigentümers* in Südkorea regelt, dass die treuhänderische Übereignung von Immobilien null und nichtig ist, und Absatz 2 regelt, dass die Änderung der dinglichen Rechte an einer Immobilie, die durch eine Registrierung im Rahmen der treuhänderischen Übereignung erfolgt, ebenfalls null und nichtig ist.

> „Da das Gericht als Organ mit der Aufgabe betraut ist, Gesetze auszulegen und anzuwenden, ist es geboten, die grundlegenden Entscheidungen des Gesetzgebers zu achten."

Jedoch hebt die Mindermeinung eher die ‚Notwendigkeit judikativer Intervention' hervor und befürwortet, die Bestimmung zur rechtswidrigen Leistung auf diesen Fall anzuwenden.

> „Es ist nun an der Zeit, dass judikative Maßnahmen, von den legislativen Maßnahmen unterschieden, erforderlich sind, um das Problem der treuhänderischen Übereignung von Immobilien effektiv zu bewältigen."

Die Kontroverse um die Festlegung der Auslegungsgrenze kann auch eng mit der Frage verknüpft sein, wie die Kompetenzbereiche von Gesetzgebung und Justiz abgegrenzt werden sollen. Ein exemplarisches Beispiel hierfür ist das Urteil zur besonderen beschränkten Annahme im Erbrecht.[12] Die Mehrheitsmeinung betont, dass die grundsätzliche Trennung von Gesetzgebung und Justiz als Grenze der Gesetzesauslegung zu respektieren ist. Einige bezeichnen dies als „Bereichstheorie". Die Kritik der Mindermeinung daran ist jedoch bemerkenswert.

> „Viele Präjudizien zeigen, dass die Frage, ob und wann das Parlament Gesetze erlässt und wie gesetzliche Abhilfe geschaffen wird, ein rein politischer Prozess ist, der völlig unabhängig davon abläuft, welche Ansicht das Oberste Gericht in Bezug auf diese Fragen vertritt. Folglich ist die Ansicht des Obersten Gerichts, dass ‚es [nicht durch das Gericht, sondern] durch den Gesetzgeber geschehen muss', nicht nur inhaltsleer, weil sie den betroffenen Parteien keine Abhilfe bietet, sondern auch keine rechtlichen Grundsätze für ähnliche zukünftige Fälle aufstellt."

Die Grenzen der Auslegung können somit unterschiedlich festgelegt werden, je nachdem, wie man den Charakter gesetzgeberischer oder gerichtlicher Entscheidungen versteht und wie die Zuständigkeiten zwischen Gesetzgebung und Justiz verteilt sind. Darüber hinaus wird auf das Phänomen hingewiesen, dass die Ansichten der Richter bezüglich des Auslegungsziels oft fallabhängig schwanken, was auf eine gewisse Inkonsistenz hindeutet. Zu diesem Punkt wird es später noch Gelegenheit geben, ausführlicher darauf einzugehen.

---

12 Oberster Gerichtshof, Urteil des gesamten Senats vom 19. November 2020, Az. 2019da232918.

Tabelle 1: Methodologische Struktur bezüglich des Ziels der Auslegung und das strukturelle Potenzial argumentativer Gegensätze

<table>
<tr><td rowspan="4">Ziel der Auslegung</td><td colspan="3">Objektive Ausleung</td><td rowspan="4">↔</td><td colspan="3">Subjektive Auslegung</td></tr>
<tr><td colspan="3">·Erforschung der gültigen Bedeutung des Textes zum Zeitpunkt der Anwendung
·Versuch einer normativen Erfassung des legislativen Zwecks, nicht der tatsächlichen Absicht zum Zeitpunkt der Gesetzgebung</td><td colspan="3">·Erforschung der Absicht des historischen Gesetzgebers zum Zeitpunkt der Gesetzgebung
·Erforschung einer tatsächlichen Absicht zum Zeitpunkt der Gesetzgebung</td></tr>
<tr><td rowspan="2">·Die Absicht des historischen Gesetzgebers wird nur insoweit berücksichtigt, wie sie sich aus dem Gesetzestext ergibt.</td><td rowspan="2">↔</td><td>Versuch, die Grenzen der objektiven Auslegung festzulegen</td><td rowspan="2">·Warnung vor dem Missbrauch der teleologischen Auslegung in der gegenwärtigen Zeit</td><td rowspan="2">↔</td><td>Gewährleistung der Möglichkeit, die subjektive Auslegung zu lockern</td></tr>
<tr><td>·Wenn die Absicht des historischen Gesetzgebers im Gesetzestext ausgedrückt oder angedeutet ist, wird die Notwendigkeit, diese Absicht zu respektieren, eher verstärkt behauptet, um die objektive Auslegung einzuschränken.
· Betonung der Trennung der Zuständigkeiten von Gesetzgebung und Rechtsprechung als Mittel zur Einschränkung der objektiven Auslegung.</td><td>· Versuch, die Trennung zwischen Gesetzgebung und Rechtsprechung flexibler auszulegen oder neu zu definieren</td></tr>
</table>

Die obenstehende Tabelle verdeutlicht die potenzielle Struktur der argumentativen Gegensätze, die in Diskussionen über das Ziel der Auslegung auftreten. Sie zeigt nicht nur die typischen gegensätzlichen Positionen zum Auslegungsziel, sondern macht auch deutlich, dass diese Gegensätze innerhalb jeder Position strukturell wiederkehren. Dieses Potenzial ergibt sich daraus, dass innerhalb jeder Position Mittel identifiziert werden können, um die Ideen und Absichten der jeweils gegensätzlichen Position zu berücksichtigen.

III. Klassische Auslegungskriterien in den jüngsten Entscheidungen

1. Wortlautauslegung

In diesem Abschnitt werden jüngste Entscheidungen untersucht, bei denen die Wortlautauslegung eine zentrale Rolle spielt.

a) Methodische Fortschritte in der Wortlautauslegung

In jüngsten Entscheidungen des Obersten Gerichtshofs zeigt sich eine Tendenz, dass die Gerichte ihre Interpretation zunächst auf die Wortlautauslegung stützen. Ein bekanntes Beispiel, bei dem die Wortlautauslegung intensiv diskutiert wurde, ist das Urteil zur „Flugumkehr".[13] Ebenso von Bedeutung ist das Urteil zum „Vermieter", in dem das Gericht die Begriffe „eindeutige Bedeutung", „übliche Bedeutung" und „mögliche Bedeutung" des Wortlauts differenziert analysiert hat.

> „Das Ziel der Gesetzesauslegung sollte darin bestehen, innerhalb der Grenzen, die die Rechtssicherheit nicht gefährden, eine Fallgerechtigkeit zu finden. In diesem Prozess gilt der Grundsatz, dass die Auslegung *so treu wie möglich der üblichen Bedeutung* der in den Gesetzen verwendeten Begriffe entsprechen sollte. Darüber hinaus sollten die gesetzgeberische Absicht und der Zweck, die Entstehungs- und Änderungsgeschichte, die Harmonie mit dem gesamten Rechtssystem sowie die Beziehung zu anderen Rechtsvorschriften, die zu einer systematischen und logischen Auslegungsmethode führt, berücksichtigt werden. Auf diese Weise sollte den Anforderungen des Grundsatzes der Gesetzesauslegung entsprochen werden. Ist hingegen der Wortlaut eines Gesetzes relativ *eindeutig*, besteht grundsätzlich entweder kein Bedarf an anderen Auslegungsmethoden oder deren Anwendung ist daher zwangsläufig eingeschränkt. Selbst wenn versucht wird, Begriffe in Gesetzesvorschriften entgegen ihrer üblichen Bedeutung auszulegen, gibt es hierfür gewisse Grenzen, da die systematische Beziehung innerhalb des betreffenden Gesetzes, im gesamten Rechtssystem sowie zu anderen Gesetzen berücksichtigt werden muss." (Hervor. d. Verf.)[14]

---

13 Oberster Gerichtshof, Urteil des gesamten Senats vom 21. Dezember 2017, Az. 2015do8335.

14 Oberster Gerichtshof, Urteil vom 23. April 2009, Az. 2006da81035.

Der Oberste Gerichtshof vertritt grundsätzlich die Auffassung, dass die übliche Bedeutung eines Begriffs zu beachten ist. Allerdings kann in Situationen, in denen durch eine systematische oder teleologische Auslegung eine andere Bedeutung hinreichend gestützt werden kann, auch die mögliche Bedeutung des Wortlauts die übliche Bedeutung überwiegen.

Gleichzeitig fordert der oberste Gerichtshof in Korea, dass im Bereich des Strafrechts, das dem Grundsatz ‚nulla poena sine lege' unterliegt, sowie im Bereich des Steuerrechts, das dem Grundsatz der Steuerbestimmtheit unterliegt, und im Bereich der gesetzlichen Grundlagen für belastende Verwaltungsakte nicht nur eine Analogie, sondern auch eine extensive Auslegung zurückgehalten werden soll.

Früher wurde angenommen, dass der Oberste Gerichtshof in Korea eine teleologische Auslegung der Wortlautauslegung vorzieht.[15] In jüngeren Entscheidungen finden sich jedoch einzelne Richter, die eine deutliche Präferenz für die Wortlautauslegung gegenüber der teleologischen Auslegung zeigen. Die folgende Äußerung von Richter Jo Hee-de kann als exemplarisches Beispiel hierfür gelten:

> „*Die Auslegung des Gesetzes muss dem Wortlaut treu bleiben und darf diesen keinesfalls überschreiten.* Bei der Auslegung sind Begriffsdefinitionen, die im Gesetz ausdrücklich geregelt sind, verbindlich. In allen anderen Fällen ist *der Wortlaut nach der Bedeutung auszulegen, die im allgemeinen Sprachgebrauch von der Bevölkerung verwendet und verstanden wird,* und zwar auf der Grundlage vernünftiger Überlegungen. *Nur eine solche Auslegung kann allgemein als verpflichtend und überzeugend anerkannt werden.* Wenn aus dem logischen Bedeutungszusammenhang zwischen den einzelnen Bestimmungen und aus der allgemeinen Bedeutung der Sprache eine eindeutige Auslegung abgeleitet werden kann, ist jede andere Auslegung nicht erlaubt, selbst wenn die klare Auslegung nicht in jeder Hinsicht zu einem befriedigenden Ergebnis führt. *Eine Auslegung, die vom Wortlaut abweicht, ist nicht mehr eine Auslegung der bestehenden Norm, sondern schafft unter dem Deckmantel der Auslegung eine neue*

15 Ein Beispiel für die Auffassung, dass unser Gericht eine teleologische Auslegung bevorzugt, findet sich bei: *S.-H. Oh*, Methode der richterlichen Auslegung (Fn. 4), 201 f. Ein Beispiel für die Auffassung, dass unser Gericht eine wortlautzentrierte Auslegung bevorzugt, bietet: *B.-C. Choi*, Eine Kritik des traditionellen semantischen Modells der Gesetzesauslegung, in: D.-K. Kim, Gesetzesauslegung in Korea (Fn. 1), S. 33 (35).

Norm und übt somit auch die Befugnisse des Gesetzgebers aus." (Hervorhebung d. Verf.)[16]

b) Strukturelles Potenzial argumentativer Gegensätze in der Wortlautauslegung

Jedoch treten diese Prinzipien in vielen Fällen in den Hintergrund. Oft wird festgestellt, dass teleologische Auslegungen ohne ausreichende Begründung die „übliche Bedeutung des Wortlauts" übergehen. Selbst in Bereichen des Straf- oder Steuerrechts bildet dies keine Ausnahme. Dies wird häufig mit Argumenten gerechtfertigt, die die Vermeidung unvernünftiger Ergebnisse oder eine angemessene und gerechte Steuererhebung befürworten.

Das „Auto-Bumper-Urteil",[17] das „Sewolho-Urteil"[18] und das „eBay-Urteil"[19] sind bekannte Beispiele hierfür. In solchen Fällen überwiegt oft die mögliche Bedeutung gegenüber der üblichen Bedeutung, und sogar eine „extrem weit gefasste mögliche Bedeutung" kann sich durchsetzen. Darüber hinaus lässt sich feststellen, dass die „Rechtsfortbildung über den Wortlaut hinaus" mitunter als Auslegung innerhalb des „Wortlauts" gerechtfertigt wird.

In stark umstrittenen Urteilen des Obersten Gerichtshofs stellt die „mögliche Bedeutung des Wortlauts" oft einen typischen Punkt dar, an dem sich die Standpunkte der Mehrheits- und der Minderheitsmeinung scheiden. Das „Sewolho-Urteil" oder das „Urteil zur fahrlässigen Brandstiftung"[20] können als exemplarische Beispiele hierfür gelten.

Insgesamt könnte es als Fortschritt in der juristischen Argumentation betrachtet werden, dass unser Gericht die Bedeutungsebenen des Wortlauts sorgfältig zu unterscheiden versucht. Dennoch ist kaum zu leugnen, dass dies gleichzeitig ein strukturelles Potenzial für argumentative Gegensätze birgt.

---

16 Oberster Gerichtshof, Urteil des gesamten Senats vom 20. November 2014, Az. 2013다64908 (Ergänzung der Mindermeinung von Richter Jo Hee-de).

17 Oberster Gerichtshof, Urteil des gesamten Senats vom 30. Mai 1997, Az. 97do597.

18 Oberster Gerichtshof, Urteil vom 12. November 2015, Az. 2015do6809.

19 Oberster Gerichtshof, Entscheidung vom 10. September 2019, Az. 2019ma5464.

20 Oberster Gerichtshof, Urteil des gesamten Senats vom 20. Dezember 1994, Az. 94-mo32.

2. Historische Auslegung

a) Methodologischer Fortschritt der historischen Auslegung

In den Entscheidungen des Obersten Gerichtshofs zeigt sich die historische Auslegung häufig in Form der Berücksichtigung der Entstehungsgeschichte oder des legislativen Werdegangs. Allerdings dienen diese Argumente meist lediglich als ergänzende Unterstützung für andere Auslegungsmethoden.

Früher wurde oft darauf hingewiesen, dass die Rolle der historischen Auslegung begrenzt sei, da der Gesetzgebungsprozess nicht immer sorgfältig und professionell verlief. In jüngster Zeit hat jedoch die Digitalisierung historischer Materialien aus dem Gesetzgebungsverfahren erhebliche Fortschritte gemacht, wodurch die historische Auslegung zunehmend an Bedeutung gewinnt.

Mit der wachsenden Geschichte des koreanischen Rechtssystems nimmt auch die Berücksichtigung des legislativen Werdegangs stetig zu. Zudem spielt der Vergleich mit Rechtssystemen aus der Kolonialzeit, insbesondere im Zivilrecht, nach wie vor eine gewisse Rolle. Daher lässt sich sagen, dass die historische Auslegung einen eigenständigen Stellenwert besitzt.

b) Strukturelles Potenzial argumentativer Gegensätze in der historischen Auslegung

Bei der Analyse der Argumentationen des Gerichts zeigt sich häufig, dass die historische Auslegung eher eine ergänzende als eine zentrale Rolle spielt. In Fällen, in denen die historische Auslegung im Zentrum der Argumentation steht, finden sich einerseits Fälle, in denen sie durch ihre Verbindung mit der üblichen Bedeutung des Wortlauts die teleologische Auslegung überwindet,[21] andererseits aber auch Fälle, in denen sie durch ihre Verbindung mit der teleologischen Auslegung die übliche Bedeutung des Wortlauts überwindet.[22]

Bei der Anwendung der historischen Auslegung unter Bezugnahme auf den Begriff der „Legislativabsicht“ ist es nicht ungewöhnlich, dass sie sich

---

21 Zum Beispiel die Mehrheitsmeinung im „Kolben-Urteil“ (Oberster Gerichtshof, Entscheidung des gesamten Senats vom 18. November 2004, Az. 2004Do1228) oder die Minderheitsmeinung im „Geschlechtsänderungs-Urteil“ (Oberster Gerichtshof, Beschluss des gesamten Senats vom 22. Juni 2006, Az. 2004Su42).

22 Zum Beispiel die zuvor erwähnte ‚Feiertagsvergütungs-Urteil‘ sowie das ‚Missbrauch von öffentlichen Mitteln-Urteil‘ (Oberster Gerichtshof, Entscheidung vom 22. No-

in der Tat einer objektiven teleologischen Auslegung annähert, die auf den Zweck der Norm gerichtet ist. In dieser Hinsicht zeigt sich, dass die historische Auslegung des koreanischen Gerichts in manchen Aspekten mit der teleologischen Auslegung überschneidet.

3. Systematische Auslegung

a) Erscheinungsformen der systematischen Auslegung

Mit der Weiterentwicklung der Auslegungsmethoden wird die systematische Auslegung vom koreanischen Obersten Gerichtshof ebenso gewichtig eingesetzt wie die Wortlautauslegung. Häufig wird der Begriff „logisch-systematische Auslegung“ verwendet. Diese dient jedoch nicht nur dazu, mögliche Bedeutungsoptionen durch Logik und Systematik einzugrenzen, sondern auch dazu, aus ihr die historische Absicht des Gesetzgebers oder das objektive Ziel des Gesetzestextes abzuleiten. Dabei wird besonders auf die Konsistenz mit benachbarten Rechtsvorschriften sowie auf eine kohärente Auslegung innerhalb des betreffenden Gesetzes geachtet. In jüngster Zeit hat sich der Fokus jedoch verstärkt auf die grundlegenden Prinzipien des jeweiligen Rechtsgebiets gerichtet, wodurch die Bedeutung einer Auslegung, die mit diesen Prinzipien im Einklang steht, zunehmend an Gewicht gewinnt. Zudem wird die Beziehung zu anderen Gesetzen, insbesondere zu übergeordneten Normen wie der Verfassung, immer bedeutsamer. Angesichts der entscheidenden Rolle der verfassungskonformen Auslegung in den jüngsten Entscheidungen des Obersten Gerichtshofs wird diese spezielle Erscheinungsform in einem separaten Abschnitt (unten Abschnitt IV.) vertieft behandelt.

b) Strukturelles Potenzial argumentativer Gegensätze in der systematischen Auslegung

Die argumentativen Gegensätze in der systematischen Auslegung ergeben sich daraus, dass die normativen Einheiten, die einer systematischen Auslegung unterliegen, mehrschichtig sind. In jüngsten Entscheidungen des Obersten Gerichtshofs wird zunehmend deutlich, dass die argumentativen

vember 2018, Az. 2018Du48601) und das ‚eBay-Urteil‘ (Oberster Gerichtshof, Beschluss vom 10. September 2019, Az. 2019Ma5464).

Konflikte um die systematische Auslegung nicht nur aus unterschiedlichen Verständnissen der relevanten Vorschriften resultieren, sondern auch aus der Divergenz zwischen einer systematischen Auslegung einzelner konkreter Vorschriften und einer systematischen Auslegung, die versucht, mit den grundlegenden Prinzipien des jeweiligen Gesetzes in Einklang zu stehen. Ein typisches Beispiel sind Fälle im Strafrecht, in denen eine „Auslegung, die besser mit benachbarten konkreten Vorschriften vereinbar ist", durch eine „Auslegung, die mit dem Prinzip der Verhältnismäßigkeit von Strafe und Schuld übereinstimmt", abgelehnt wird (zum Beispiel das Urteil zur Brandstiftung). Zudem kommt es häufig zu Konflikten zwischen einer systematischen Auslegung, die mit den Verfassungsprinzipien übereinstimmt, und einer systematischen Auslegung, die mit den benachbarten Vorschriften besser vereinbar ist. Genau an diesen Punkten gehen die Mehrheits- und Minderheitsmeinungen in vielen Urteilen auseinander (zum Beispiel im bereits erwähnten Wehrdienstverweigerungs-Urteil).

4. Teleologische Auslegung

a) Erscheinungsformen der teleologischen Auslegung

In den Urteilen des Obersten Gerichtshofs nimmt die teleologische Auslegung oft eine zentrale Rolle ein, sei es explizit oder implizit. Formulierungen wie „Regelungsabsicht und -zweck" sowie „Gesetzesintention" sind typische Ausdrucksformen dieser Auslegungsmethode und fungieren zugleich als Brücke zwischen teleologischer und historischer Auslegung. Ein weiteres Beispiel für die teleologische Auslegung findet sich in der strafrechtlichen Diskussion über „Schutzgüter". Auch eine „Auslegung, die die Funktion des Regelungsbereichs adäquat erfüllt", stellt eine Erscheinungsform der teleologischen Auslegung dar.

Überlegungen zu den „Grundprinzipien des betreffenden Rechtsgebiets" oder zur „Rechtsidee" können im weiteren Sinne als Bestandteil der teleologischen Auslegung betrachtet werden. Allerdings überschneiden sie sich teilweise mit Bereichen, die der „systematischen Auslegung" oder der „verfassungskonformen Auslegung" zuzuordnen sind. Einige vertreten die Auffassung, dass die teleologische Auslegung einer klaren Abgrenzung bedarf, und plädieren dafür, Auslegungen, die sich an Rechtsprinzipien oder

Rechtsideen orientieren, von der teleologischen Auslegung zu unterscheiden.[23]

Die Frage, wie die teleologische Auslegung rationalisiert und kontrollierbar gestaltet werden kann, ist auch in der koreanischen Rechtswissenschaft ein zentrales Thema. Das wachsende Interesse an der „folgenorientierten Auslegung“ in jüngster Zeit steht ebenfalls im Zusammenhang mit dem Bestreben, die teleologische Auslegung methodisch stringenter zu gestalten. Vor diesem Hintergrund wird die folgenorientierte Auslegung in dieser Arbeit in separaten Kapiteln vertieft behandelt. Dies trägt auch dem wachsenden Problembewusstsein des Obersten Gerichtshofs Koreas sowie der zunehmenden Zahl einschlägiger Urteile Rechnung.

b) Strukturelles Potenzial argumentativer Gegensätze bei der teleologischen Auslegung

Der Versuch des koreanischen Obersten Gerichtshofs, die teleologische Auslegung zu kontrollieren, zeigt sich insbesondere in den Argumentationen, die die „übliche Bedeutung des Wortlauts“ bei der Auslegung betonen. Im Gegensatz dazu misst die Position, die in dem betreffenden Fall an der teleologischen Auslegung festhalten möchte, der „möglichen Bedeutung“ des Wortlauts größeres Gewicht bei als seiner üblichen Bedeutung.

Im Strafrecht wird eine Position, die der teleologischen Auslegung besondere Bedeutung beimisst, von der Gegenposition häufig als „verbotene Rechtsfortbildung über die Grenzen des Wortlauts hinaus“ kritisiert. Das „Sewolho-Urteil“ oder das „Brandstiftungs-Urteil“ sind hierfür typische Beispiele. Ähnliche Tendenzen lassen sich auch im Steuer- und Verwaltungsrecht beobachten. Eine verstärkte teleologische Auslegung kann in diesen Bereichen das Prinzip der strikten Auslegung steuerrechtlicher Vorschriften oder das Prinzip der strikten Auslegung einer gesetzlichen Grundlage für belastende Verwaltungsakte umgehen, woran unser Gericht ausdrücklich festgehalten hat. Dieser Punkt bildet häufig einen kontroversen Meinungsstrang, der Argumentationskonflikte nach sich zieht.

In der Rechtsprechung führt die aktive Berücksichtigung des Gesetzeszwecks teils zu einer Erweiterung der möglichen Grenzen der Auslegung und teils zu einer Ausweitung der rechtfertigungsfähigen Rechtsfortbil-

23 Etwa *D.-H. Kong*, Modelle der Gesetzesauslegung im Koreanischen Obersten Gerichtshof: Rechtspositivismus, Rechtsrealismus und die Theorie der Rechtsprinzipien (Kor.), Koreanische Zeitschrift für Rechtsphilosophie, Bd. 22, H. 2 (2019), 185 (195 f.).

dung. Sie wird jedoch häufig von der Gegenposition kritisiert, da sie in den Bereich des Gesetzgebers eingreift. Oft wird dies als eine dem Wortlaut widersprechende Gesetzeskorrektur betrachtet. Wenn versucht wird, die Lückenausfüllung mit dem Gesetzeszweck zu rechtfertigen, betont die Gegenposition, dass solche Lücken nicht anerkannt werden können, weil sie vielmehr als Folge einer gesetzgeberischen Entscheidung zu betrachten sind.

Zusammenfassend lässt sich feststellen, dass die teleologische Auslegung in den jüngsten Urteilen des koreanischen Obersten Gerichtshofs in vielfältigen Formen Anwendung findet, während zugleich verschiedene Versuche erkennbar sind, sie zu begrenzen. Dies kann jedoch auch als strukturelle Quelle für argumentative Gegensätze betrachtet werden.

Tabelle 2: Methodische Struktur der klassischen Auslegungskriterien und das strukturelle Potenzial argumentativer Gegensätze

Methodische Struktur der klassischen Auslegungskriterien und das strukturelle Potenzial argumentativer Gegensätze			
	Strengere Position bei der Wortlautauslegung		Flexible Position bei der Wortlautauslegung
Wortlautauslegung	·Wenn der Wortlaut eine eindeutige Bedeutung hat, ist eine davon abweichende Auslegung unzulässig. ·Die übliche Bedeutung des Wortlauts wird vorrangig berücksichtigt und nach Möglichkeit befolgt. ·Im Strafrecht gilt eine über die übliche Bedeutung hinausgehende Auslegung als unzulässig. ·Gesetze im Strafrecht, Steuerrecht und als Grundlage für belastende Verwaltungsakte müssen strikt ausgelegt werden.	↔	·Die Eindeutigkeit des Wortlauts wird nicht als von vornherein gegeben betrachtet. Sie gerät in Zweifel, sobald das Ergebnis einer Auslegung im konkreten Fall keine angemessene Lösung bietet. ·Es ist auch möglich, eine Bedeutung auszuwählen, die nicht der eindeutigen oder üblichen Bedeutung des Wortlauts entspricht, sofern diese durch andere Auslegungskriterien gestützt wird und innerhalb des möglichen Bedeutungsrahmens liegt. ·Im Strafrecht wird eine Auslegung zwar als unzulässig betrachtet, die den möglichen Bedeutungsrahmen überschreitet; jedoch wird eine Auslegung anerkannt, die den möglichen Bedeutungsrahmen des Wortlauts möglichst weit auslegt und dabei den normativen Zweck sowie die Intention der Regelung in den Vordergrund stellt. ·Eine flexiblere Auslegung wird in folgenden Fällen als zulässig angesehen: wenn unverhältnismäßige Strafen vermieden, faire und gerechte Steuern erhoben oder Ergebnisse verhindert werden sollen, die dem normativen Zweck widersprechen oder die Normen aushöhlen.
	Position, die der eigenständigen Rolle der historischen Auslegung mehr Beachtung schenkt		Position, die der ergänzenden Rolle der historischen Auslegung mehr Beachtung schenkt.
Historische Auslegung	·Die Entstehungsgeschichte oder der legislative Werdegang wird unabhängig vom Bedeutungsrahmen einer Regelung berücksichtigt. ·Die gesetzgeberische Absicht wird vom teleologischen Zweck unterschieden und als eigenständiger Aspekt herangezogen.	↔	·Die Entstehungsgeschichte oder der legislative Werdegang wird nur innerhalb des möglichen Bedeutungsrahmens des Gesetzes berücksichtigt. ·Der gesetzgeberische Zweck wird weit gefasst und überschneidet sich häufig mit dem teleologischen Zweckverständnis. ·Die historische Auslegung dient hauptsächlich als ergänzendes Kriterium zu anderen Auslegungsmethoden.

	·Die historische Auslegung wird häufig unabhängig von anderen Auslegungskriterien angewendet.		
Systematische Auslegung	**Position, die den Bereich der systematischen Auslegung relativ eng fasst**		**Position, die den Bereich der systematischen Auslegung relativ weit fasst**
	·Betonung der systematischen Auslegung hinsichtlich der konkreten Bestimmungen und ihrer Zusammenhänge ·Zurückhaltung bei der systematischen Auslegung, die darauf abzielt, mit den Prinzipien oder Idealen des betreffenden Bereichs in Einklang zu stehen. ·Im Strafrecht wird der systematischen Auslegung, die die Wortlautauslegung unterstützt, mehr Beachtung geschenkt.	↔	·Die systematische Auslegung wird nicht nur innerhalb des betreffenden Gesetzes, sondern auch im Einklang mit anderen Gesetzen und höherrangigen Rechtsnormen vorgenommen. ·Aktive Berücksichtigung der systematischen Auslegung, die darauf abzielt, mit den Prinzipien oder Idealen des betreffenden Bereichs in Einklang zu stehen ·Im Strafrecht zeigt sich die Rolle der systematischen Auslegung oft darin, unvernünftige Auslegungsergebnisse relevanter Vorschriften zu vermeiden.
Teleologische Auslegung	**Zurückhaltende Position beim Einsatz der teleologischen Auslegung**		**Aktive Position beim Einsatz der teleologischen Auslegung**
	·Sie wird möglichst nachrangig im Verhältnis zu anderen Auslegungskriterien berücksichtigt. ·Es wird nur der Zweck berücksichtigt, der eindeutig aus den gesetzlichen Bestimmungen abgeleitet werden kann. ·Jedoch sind die Zumutbarkeit und die politische Angemessenheit der sich aus der Auslegung ergebenden Folgen nicht zu berücksichtigen. ·Einschränkung der teleologischen Auslegung im Strafrecht oder Steuerrecht.	↔	·Sie wird möglichst vorrangig in Bezug auf andere Auslegungskriterien berücksichtigt. ·In den Zweck werden nicht nur die konkrete Regelungsabsicht, sondern auch die Prinzipien und Ideale des betreffenden Bereichs sowie verfassungsrechtliche Grundsätze einbezogen. ·Die Zumutbarkeit und die politische Angemessenheit der sich aus der Auslegung ergebenden Folgen sind zu berücksichtigen. ·Auch im Strafrecht oder Steuerrecht wird eine aktive Berücksichtigung der teleologischen Auslegung für möglich gehalten..

Die obige Tabelle veranschaulicht die potenzielle Struktur der argumentativen Gegensätze, die in Diskussionen über die klassischen Auslegungskriterien auftreten. Da bei der Auslegung von Gesetzestexten mehrere Kriterien kombiniert werden, ist Folgendes möglich: Selbst wenn man sich bei der Anwendung eines bestimmten Kriteriums für eine der gegensätzlichen Positionen entscheidet, kann man bei der Anwendung eines anderen Kriteriums eine entgegengesetzte Entscheidung treffen, indem man die Ideen oder Intentionen berücksichtigt, die der jeweils anderen Position zugrunde liegen.[24]

IV. Insbesondere: Verfassungskonforme Auslegung in den jüngsten Entscheidungen

1. Methodischer Fortschritt der verfassungskonformen Auslegung

Im Folgenden befassen wir uns mit der verfassungskonformen Auslegung, die in den jüngsten Urteilen eine zunehmend wichtigere Rolle spielt. Aufgrund der Ausstrahlungswirkung der Grundrechte gewinnt diese Auslegungsmethode stetig an Bedeutung.[25] In letzter Zeit lässt sich zudem ein methodischer Fortschritt beim Einsatz der verfassungskonformen Auslegung feststellen. Besonders bemerkenswert ist dabei die Unterscheidung zwischen „verfassungskonformer Auslegung“ und „verfassungsorientierter Auslegung“.

Ein kürzlich ergangenes Urteil zum sexuellen Missbrauch im Militär führt dazu aus:

> „Wenn verschiedene Auslegungen eines Gesetzestextes möglich sind, sollte zunächst diejenige gewählt werden, die potenzielle Verfassungswidrigkeiten beseitigt (verfassungskonforme Auslegung). Innerhalb der verfassungskonformen Auslegungen sollte weiterhin diejenige bevorzugt

24 Dieser Punkt steht auch im Zusammenhang mit einem der traditionellen Probleme der Auslegungslehre, nämlich der Frage, ob es eine Vorrangrelation zwischen den Auslegungskriterien geben kann. Weitere Ausführungen dazu finden sich im folgenden Abschnitt VII.

25 Zur allgemeinen Diskussionslage siehe *K.-I. Lee*, Eine methodologische Studie über verfassungskonforme Entscheidung (Kor.), Korean Journal of Law & Society, Bd. 60 (2019), 271 (276 ff.).

> werden, die die Prinzipien und Werte der Verfassung am besten verkörpert (verfassungsorientierte Auslegung)."[26]

Darüber hinaus finden sich verschiedene Ansätze, die die Grenzen der verfassungskonformen Auslegung präzisieren. Ein Beispiel hierfür lautet:

> „Auch bei der verfassungskonformen Auslegung müssen die Grenzen der Gesetzesauslegung beachtet werden. Die Lösung von Problemen durch verfassungskonforme Auslegung ist nur in dem Rahmen zulässig, das den Prinzipien der Auslegungslehre entspricht."[27]

Bestehen Zweifel an der Verfassungsmäßigkeit einer Regelung, ist das Gericht verpflichtet, diese dem Verfassungsgericht zur Prüfung vorzulegen. Diese Passagen können als exemplarische Beispiele für die Grenzen der verfassungskonformen Auslegung angesehen werden.

> „Wenn eine gesetzliche Regelung, die der Gesetzgeber erlassen hat, offenkundig gegen die Gerechtigkeitsvorstellung der Gesellschaft verstößt, äußerst unfair ist und eine verfassungskonforme Auslegung die Verfassungswidrigkeit nicht vollständig beseitigen kann, ist der Richter verpflichtet, eine Vorlage beim Verfassungsgericht einzureichen. Auch in einem solchen Fall darf, wie bereits erwähnt, eine gesetzgeberische Entscheidung nicht durch eine richterliche ersetzt werden."[28]

2. Das strukturelle Potenzial der argumentativen Gegensätze bei der verfassungskonformen Auslegung

Dennoch lassen sich auch bei der Anwendung der verfassungskonformen Auslegung Inkonsistenzen feststellen. Ein typisches Beispiel hierfür lautet: „Wie weit erstreckt sich der mögliche Umfang der verfassungskonformen Auslegung?"

In einem Urteil zum „Steuerausgleich" führt eine Mindermeinung die Möglichkeit an, Gesetzeslücken durch verfassungskonforme Auslegung zu schließen.

26 Oberster Gerichtshof, Urteil des gesamten Senats vom 21. April 2022, Az. 2019do3047 (Die Ergänzung der Mehrheitsmeinung von Richter Kim Jae-hyung, Roh Jeong-hee, Cheon Dae-yeop, Oh Kyoung-mi).

27 Oberster Gerichtshof, Urteil des gesamten Senats Az. 2013da 218156 (Die Ergänzung der Mehrheitsmeinung von Richter Kim Jae-hyung).

28 siehe oben Fn. 11.

> „Die Schließung von Gesetzeslücken durch verfassungskonforme Auslegung ist Teil der richterlichen Rechtsfortbildung."[29]

Dies wird jedoch von der Mehrheitsmeinung kritisiert.

> „In Fällen, in denen eine Lücke in der gesetzlichen Regelung besteht, sollten auch verfassungskonforme Auslegung, Analogie oder teleologische Erweiterung stets im Einklang mit dem Wortlaut und dem Zweck des Gesetzes bleiben. Es sollte vermieden werden, den möglichen Sinn eines Gesetzestextes zu überschreiten oder ihn in einer Weise auszulegen, die dem eindeutigen Willen und Zweck des Gesetzgebers widerspricht."[30]

Hier zeigt sich ein typischer Gegensatz: Während die eine Seite die verfassungskonforme Rechtsfortbildung befürwortet, kritisiert die andere Seite, dass solche Auslegungen die Grenzen des Textes und des Zwecks des Gesetzes überschreiten und daher nicht gerechtfertigt sind. Kürzlich wurde auch die Frage diskutiert, ob eine verfassungskonforme Auslegung, die eher die Grundrechte schwächt, zu rechtfertigen ist. Ein Beispiel aus einem Urteil lautet:

> „Eine verfassungskonforme Gesetzesauslegung, die nicht dazu dient, die Grundrechte der Bürger zu stärken, sondern diese zu schwächen, ist fehlerhaft"[31]

29 Oberster Gerichtshof, Urteil des gesamten Senats vom 9. September 2021, Az. 2019-du53464 (Mindermeinung von Richter Kim Jae-hyung).

30 Oberster Gerichtshof, Urteil des gesamten Senats vom 9. September 2021, Az. 2019-du53464 (Mehrheitsmeinung).

31 Oberster Gerichtshof, Urteil des gesamten Senats vom 18. Februar 2021, Az. 2017-du38959 (Mindermeinung von Richter Lee Ki-taek, Kim Jae-hyung, Park Jeong-hwa, Ahn Cheol-sang und Roh Jeong-hee).

Tabelle 3: Methodologische Struktur in Bezug auf die verfassungskonforme Auslegung und das strukturelle Potenzial argumentativer Gegensätze

<table>
<tr><td rowspan="4">Verfassungskonforme Auslegung</td><td colspan="3">Festlegung weniger strenger Bedingungen für die verfassungskonforme Auslegung</td><td rowspan="2"></td><td colspan="3">Festlegung strengerer Bedingungen für die verfassungskonforme Auslegung</td></tr>
<tr><td colspan="3">·Festlegung der Grenze ausschließlich nach dem Wortlaut (ohne kumulative Erwähnung des legislativen Zwecks)
·Anerkennung einer verfassungskonformen Auslegung, die eher die Grundrechte schwächt
·Aktive Anerkennung der verfassungskonformen Rechtsfortbildung</td><td colspan="3">·Festlegung der Grenze sowohl nach dem Wortlaut als auch nach dem legislativen Zweck
·Ablehnung einer verfassungskonformen Auslegung, die eher die Grundrechte schwächt
·zurückhaltende Anerkennung der verfassungskonformen Rechtsfortbildung</td></tr>
<tr><td>Gelockerte Bedingungen für eine verfassungskonforme Rechtsfortbildung</td><td rowspan="2">↔</td><td>Methoden zur Stärkung der gelockerten Bedingungen</td><td rowspan="2">↔</td><td>Verschärfte Bedingungen für eine verfassungskonforme Rechtsfortbildung</td><td rowspan="2">↔</td><td>Methoden zur Lockerung der strengen Bedingungen</td></tr>
<tr><td>·Erleichterung der Rechtfertigungsbedingungen für eine verfassungskonforme Analogie.
·Anerkennung der Möglichkeit einer verfassungskonformen Gesetzeskorrektur.</td><td>·Hervorhebung der getrennten Zuständigkeiten von Gesetzgebung und Rechtsprechung sowie der Vorlagepflicht beim Verfassungsgericht
·Betonung der Absicht des historischen Gesetzgebers als Instrument zur Begrenzung der verfassungskonformen Auslegung</td><td>·Strikte Festlegung der Rechtfertigungsbedingungen für eine verfassungskonforme Analogie
·Verneinung der Möglichkeit einer verfassungskonformen Gesetzeskorrektur</td><td>·Flexibilisierung der Wortlautgrenze
·Ein lockeres Verständnis der Absichten des historischen Gesetzgebers (gegenwärtige Auffassung der Absichten des historischen Gesetzgebers)
·Ein lockeres Verständnis der Trennung von Gesetzgebung und Rechtsprechung</td></tr>
</table>

Die obenstehende Tabelle veranschaulicht die potenzielle Struktur der argumentativen Gegensätze, die in Diskussionen über die verfassungskonforme Auslegung auftreten. Sie zeigt nicht nur die typischen gegensätzlichen Positionen zur verfassungskonformen Auslegung auf, sondern macht auch deutlich, dass diese Gegensätze innerhalb jeder Position strukturell wiederkehren. Dieses Potenzial ergibt sich aus der Möglichkeit, innerhalb jeder Position Elemente zu identifizieren, die es erlauben, die Ideen und Absichten der jeweils gegensätzlichen Position zu berücksichtigen.

V. Ergänzende Auslegungskriterien in den jüngsten Entscheidungen

Im Folgenden betrachten wir exemplarische Fälle zu den „ergänzenden Auslegungskriterien". Aufgrund des begrenzten Rahmens werden dabei nur die „folgenorientierte Auslegung" und die „präjudizienorientierte Auslegung" kurz behandelt.

1. Folgenorientierte Auslegung – ihr methodischer Fortschritt und das strukturelle Potenzial der argumentativen Gegensätze

Bei der folgenorientierten Auslegung können verschiedene Arten von Folgen berücksichtigt werden. Daher ist es entscheidend, unter welchen Bedingungen welche Folgentypen in Betracht gezogen werden können.[32] Eine bedeutende Unterscheidung im Rahmen der Rechtfertigung der Folgenberücksichtigung ist die zwischen rechtlichen und empirischen Folgen. Ein einfaches Beispiel für rechtliche Folgen sind harte Sanktionen wie hohe Strafen oder Schadenersatz, die eintreten können, wenn eine bestimmte Auslegung gewählt wird.

Im Gegensatz zu rechtlichen Folgen gibt es oft Kontroversen darüber, ob und inwieweit die Berücksichtigung empirischer Folgen gerechtfertigt werden kann. Wenn jedoch die Berücksichtigung empirischer Folgen im Rahmen einer teleologischen oder systematischen Auslegung erfolgt, wird

---

32 Zu den verschiedenen Diskussionen über die Art der Folgen und die Rechtfertigungsmöglichkeiten der folgenorientierten Auslegung siehe *K.-I. Lee*, Eine kritische Studie über die Struktur juristischer Folgenberücksichtigung (Kor.)., Koreanische Zeitschrift für Rechtsphilosophie, Bd. 23, H. 2 (2020), 109 (123 ff.). Zur Diskussion in Deutschland vgl. etwa *M. R. Deckert*, Folgenorientierung in der Rechtsanwendung, München, 1995; *Q. Zhang*, Juristische Argumentation durch Folgenorientierung, Baden-Baden, 2010.

die Rechtfertigungsbelastung verringert. Ein exemplarisches Beispiel, bei dem sich die folgenorientierte Auslegung mit der teleologischen Auslegung überschneidet, ist der eBay-Fall. Der Oberste Gerichtshof betont in diesem Urteil:

> „Eine Auslegung, die die ‚Verkäufer von Publikationen' (§ 22 Verlagsgesetz [Festlegung und Verkauf des Ladenpreises von Publikationen]) auf ‚Verkäufer' [im engeren Sinne] beschränkt und Betreiber von Open-Markets wie eBay ausschließt, könnte dazu führen, dass Beteiligte im Vertrieb den rechtlichen Rahmen missbrauchen und die Buchpreisbindung untergraben. Daher sollte eine Auslegung angestrebt werden, die unvernünftige Ergebnisse vermeidet."[33]

Jedoch gibt es auch Einwände gegen dieses Urteil. Es könnte im Widerspruch zu einem früheren Grundsatz des Obersten Gerichtshofs stehen, der besagt, dass bei der rechtlichen Grundlage für belastende Verwaltungsakte nicht nur ihre Analogie, sondern auch ihre erweiternde Auslegung zurückhaltend erfolgen sollte.

In jüngsten Entscheidungen des Obersten Gerichtshofs wurden auch Fälle gefunden, in denen versucht wurde, den Eintritt unangemessener ‚Adoptionsfolgen' in der Auslegung zu verhindern. Unter ‚Adoptionsfolgen' versteht man hier die Folgen, die eintreten könnten, wenn eine bestimmte Auslegung des Gerichts die Normadressaten dazu veranlasst, ihr zukünftiges Verhalten entsprechend anzupassen. Ein Beispiel dafür ist das Urteil über die Taxifahrerabgabe. Eine exemplarische Passage lautet wie folgt:

> „Es muss betont werden, dass eine Auslegung, wonach die Vereinbarung zur Verkürzung der regelmäßigen Arbeitszeit als wirksam gilt, die Besorgnis nahelegt, dass damit Handlungen weiterhin begünstigt werden, die darauf abzielen, die besondere Ausnahmeregelung zum Mindestlohn zu umgehen."[34]

Jedoch können verschiedene Variablen in die Entstehung der Adoptionsfolgen eingreifen, was wiederum unterschiedliche Möglichkeiten für deren Vorhersage eröffnet. Daher gibt es auch die Ansicht, dass die Berücksichtigung der Adoptionsfolgen die argumentativen Gegensätze eher verstärken könnte.

---

33 Oberster Gerichtshof, Entscheidung vom 10. September 2019, Az. 2019ma5464.

34 Oberster Gerichtshof, Urteil des gesamten Senats vom 18. April 2019, Az. 2016da2451.

Tabelle 4: Methodologische Struktur in Bezug auf die folgenorientierte Auslegung und das strukturelle Potenzial argumentativer Gegensätze

	Lockerere Festlegung der Bedingungen für die folgenorientierte Auslegung				Strengere Festlegung der Bedingungen für die folgenorientierte Auslegung		
Folgenorientierte Auslegung	·Weitergehende Anerkennung der Möglichkeit, neben den rechtlichen Folgen auch empirische Folgen zu berücksichtigen.				·Ablehnung oder stark eingeschränkte Anerkennung der Möglichkeit, neben den rechtlichen Folgen auch empirische Folgen zu berücksichtigen.		
	Bedingungen der Folgenorientierung		Methoden zur Verschärfung der Bedingungen für die Folgenorientierung		Bedingungen der Folgenorientierung		Methoden zur Lockerung der Bedingungen für die Folgenorientierung
	·Erfordernis der Begründung für die folgenden Punkte: –Möglichkeit des Eintritts der Folgen –Abwägung der eintretenden Folgen gegeneinander –Rechtliche Vertretbarkeit der angenommenen Folgen ·Erfordernis der Erfüllung der Bedingungen für die Lückenergänzung oder Gesetzeskorrektur, wenn die Grenze des Wortlauts überschritten wird.	↔	·Verschärfung der Begründung für das Auftreten von Folgen ·Verschärfung der Begründung für die Abwägung der eintretenden Folgen gegeneinander ·Verschärfung der Begründung für die rechtliche Vertretbarkeit der angenommenen Folgen ·Verschärfung der Bedingungen für die Lückenergänzung oder Gesetzeskorrektur, wenn die Wortlautgrenze überschritten wird	↔	·Erfordernis, dass die Folgenorientierung nur als ergänzendes Argument für die systematische oder teleologische Auslegung dienen soll. ·Verstärkung der Bedingungen für die richterliche Rechtsfortbildung, wenn die Wortlautgrenze überschritten wird	↔	·Erweiterung der Folgenberücksichtigung durch eine umfassende Erfassung der Reichweite der teleologischen und systematischen Auslegung ·Breitere Erfassung der Wortlautgrenze oder Lockerung der Bedingungen für Lückenergänzung oder Gesetzeskorrektur

Die obige Tabelle veranschaulicht die potenzielle Struktur der argumentativen Gegensätze, die in Diskussionen über die folgenorientierte Auslegung auftreten. Sie zeigt nicht nur die typischen konträren Positionen zur folgenorientierten Auslegung auf, sondern macht auch deutlich, dass diese Gegensätze innerhalb jeder Position strukturell wiederkehren. Dieses Potenzial ergibt sich aus der Möglichkeit, innerhalb jeder Position Elemente zu identifizieren, die es erlauben, die Ideen und Absichten der jeweils gegensätzlichen Position zu berücksichtigen.

2. Präjudizienorientierte Auslegung – ihr methodischer Fortschritt und das strukturelle Potenzial der argumentativen Gegensätze

Im Folgenden wird auf die Urteile eingegangen, die durch eine präjudizienorientierte Auslegung geprägt sind. Die Rechtfertigung dieser Auslegung wirft zugleich die Frage nach den Bedingungen und Grenzen von Präjudizienänderungen auf. Die Beantwortung dieser Frage ist komplex, da sie mit der grundlegenden Problematik verbunden ist, ob Präjudizien als Rechtsquelle anzusehen sind und wie weit der Geltungsbereich geänderter Präjudizien reicht.

a) Methodologischer Fortschritt bei der Argumentation über die Bedingungen von Präjudizienänderungen und das strukturelle Potenzial der argumentativen Gegensätze

In den jüngsten Urteilen des Obersten Gerichts lässt sich eine Weiterentwicklung des methodischen Bewusstseins für die Bedingungen von Präjudizienänderungen beobachten. Dennoch gibt es häufig Meinungsverschiedenheiten über diese Änderungsbedingungen.[35] Die Diskussion darüber birgt daher auch das strukturelle Potenzial für argumentative Konflikte.

Ein prägnantes Beispiel, bei dem intensiv über die Bedingungen für Präjudizienänderungen diskutiert wird und scharfe Meinungsgegensätze zutage treten, ist das „Verlinken-Urteil".[36] In diesem Fall stellte sich die

35 Zu den einschlägigen wissenschaftlichen Diskussionen siehe nur *K.-I. Lee*, Eine Studie über den Anwendungsbereich und die normative Kraft des Richterrechtes (Kor.), Yonsei Law Review, Bd. 26, H. 3 (2016), 209 (243 ff.) m.w.N.

36 Oberster Gerichtshof, Urteil des gesamten Senats vom 9. September 2021, Az. 2017do19025.

Frage, ob das regelmäßige und gewinnbringende Setzen von Links zu urheberrechtsverletzenden audiovisuellen Werken durch den Betreiber einer Website als Beihilfe zur Straftat der Urheberrechtsverletzung gewertet werden kann, insbesondere wenn der Website-Betreiber diese Links in vollem Bewusstsein der Urheberrechtsverletzung des Täters platzierte. Die bisherige Rechtsprechung des Obersten Gerichts vertrat die Auffassung, dass das Setzen eines Links zu anderen Webseiten, die urheberrechtsverletzende Inhalte bereitstellen, allein nicht als Beihilfe zur Urheberrechtsverletzung angesehen werden kann.[37] Die neue Entscheidung versuchte jedoch, diese Auffassung zu ändern.

Dies wird jedoch von der Mindermeinung kritisiert, mit der Begründung, dass Änderungen der bisherigen Präjudizien die Rechtssicherheit ernsthaft gefährden könnten. Gleichzeitig führt sie die Bedingungen für Präjudizienänderungen wie folgt aus:

> „Eine Präjudizienänderung, die den Anwendungsbereich des Strafrechts erweitert, kann nur in Ausnahmefällen zugelassen werden, nämlich wenn Widersprüche in der Rechtsprechung oder Verstöße gegen Präzedenzfälle nur so beseitigt werden können oder wenn sich die sozialen Bedingungen so grundlegend geändert haben, dass das Festhalten an früheren Ansichten offensichtlich dem Recht widerspricht."[38]

Bei der Ergänzung der Mindermeinung konkretisiert Richter Jo Jae-yeon die Bedingungen für Präjudizienänderungen weiter, durch die sich der Anwendungsbereich des Strafrechts erweitert, wie folgt:[39]

(1) Wenn nachgewiesen werden kann, dass frühere Präjudizien eindeutige Fehler enthalten und das betreffende Verhalten offensichtlich gesellschaftswidrig sowie strafwürdig ist,
(2) wenn die bisherigen Präjudizien keine konsistenten Entscheidungen des Obersten Gerichts darstellen und daher keine verbindliche Kraft für die Bevölkerung besitzen, und

37 Oberster Gerichtshof, Urteil des Obersten Gerichtshofs vom 12. März 2015, Az. 2012do13748.

38 Oberster Gerichtshof, Urteil des gesamten Senats vom 9. September 2021, Az. 2017do19025 (Mindermeinung von Richter Jo Jae-yeon, Kim Seon-soo und Roh Tae-Ak).

39 Oberster Gerichtshof, Urteil des gesamten Senats vom 9. September 2021, Az. 2017do19025 (Ergänzung der Mindermeinung von Richter Jo Jae-yeon).

(3) wenn ein gesetzgeberisches Eingreifen nicht zu erwarten ist oder die gesellschaftlichen Schäden zu schwerwiegend sind, um auf gesetzgeberische Maßnahmen zu warten.

Im Gegensatz dazu vertreten die Ergänzungen der Mehrheitsmeinung (Kim Jae-hyung, Cheon Dae-yeop) die Ansicht,

> „die Bedingungen für Präjudizienänderungen sollten weniger streng sein als in der Mindermeinung. Auch Urteile des Obersten Gerichts sollten möglichst schnell korrigiert werden, wenn sie sich als unrichtig erweisen.“[40]

In Bezug auf die Frage, ob Präjudizienänderungen die Rechtssicherheit untergraben, vertreten sie eine andere Auffassung als die Mindermeinung.

> „Präjudizien, die durch eine fehlerhafte Auslegung und Anwendung des Gesetzes entstanden sind, unkorrigiert zu lassen, könnte die Gerechtigkeit eher verzerren und sowohl die Rechtssicherheit als auch die Sachgerechtigkeit beeinträchtigen.“

Insbesondere wird darauf hingewiesen, „dass das bisherige Präjudiz allein das Urteil vom 21. März 2015 ist und somit keine langfristig gefestigte Rechtsprechung des Obersten Gerichts darstellt. Daher entfaltet es noch keine allgemeine Verbindlichkeit für die Bevölkerung.“ Darüber hinaus wird betont, dass auch der Umstand, dass in der Legislative Änderungen an einem bereits als unangemessen empfundenen Gesetz vorbereitet werden, als Rechtfertigungsgrund für Präjudizienänderungen dienen kann.

Natürlich berücksichtigt die Mehrheitsmeinung auch die Möglichkeit einer Beeinträchtigung der Rechtssicherheit durch Präjudizienänderungen. Es ist jedoch zu beachten, dass sie dieses Problem auf ihre eigene Weise angeht. Dies zeigt sich daran, dass die Ergänzungen der Mehrheitsmeinung versuchen, Beeinträchtigungen der Rechtssicherheit im Strafrecht durch die Lehre vom „Verbotsirrtum“ zu kompensieren.

40 Oberster Gerichtshof, Urteil des gesamten Senats vom 9. September 2021, Az. 2017do19025 (Ergänzung der Mehrheitsmeinung von Richter Kim Jae-hyung, Cheon Dae-yeop).

b) Die methodischen Fortschritte und das strukturelle Potenzial der argumentativen Gegensätze bei der Bestimmung des zeitlichen Geltungsbereichs von Präjudizienänderungen

In jüngster Zeit lassen sich methodologische Fortschritte sowie potenzielle Konflikte in den Argumentationen des Obersten Gerichtshofs in Bezug auf den zeitlichen Geltungsbereich von Präjudizienänderungen beobachten. Traditionell hat der Oberste Gerichtshof die „prinzipielle Rückwirkung der Präjudizienänderung" vertreten, jedoch in bestimmten Fällen auch Ausnahmen wie die „rein prospektive Veränderung" oder die „selektiv prospektive Veränderung" anerkannt.[41]

Als aktuelles Beispiel dient das Urteil zur treuhänderischen Übereignung.[42] Dabei stellte sich die Frage, ob die Regelung über die Leistung aufgrund eines illegalen Grundes (§ 746 KBGB) auf Fälle der treuhänderischen Übereignung von Immobilien angewendet werden kann. Die Mindermeinung befürwortet eine Änderung der Präjudizien und erkennt zugleich im Interesse der Rechtssicherheit ausdrücklich die Möglichkeit einer prospektiven Änderung an.

> „Wenn ernsthafte Bedenken hinsichtlich einer Verletzung des verfassungsrechtlichen Eigentumsrechts bestehen, ... wäre es auch möglich, die Rückwirkung der Präjudizienänderung zu begrenzen. Auf diese Weise könnte ... das Vertrauen des Treuhänders in die bisherige Rechtsprechung geschützt werden, sodass die Bedenken hinsichtlich einer Verletzung des Eigentumsrechts des Treuhänders ausreichend ausgeräumt werden könnten."[43]

Die Mehrheitsmeinung lehnt jedoch diese Lösung ab. Sie besagt,

> „Die Mindermeinung schlägt eine kontroverse Lösung vor, die versucht, ... die Rückwirkung der Präjudizienänderung einzuschränken. Dieses Problem könnte jedoch viel einfacher durch eine Übergangsre-

---

41 Zu den einschlägigen wissenschaftlichen Diskussionen siehe nur *K.-I. Lee*, Eine kritische Studie über zeitliche Geltungsbereiche der Rechtsprechungsänderung (Kor.), Zeitschrift für Rechtsphilosophie, Bd. 24, H. 1 (2021), 149 (155 ff.) m.w.N.

42 Oberster Gerichtshof, Urteil des gesamten Senats vom 20. Juni 2019, Az. 2013da218156.

43 Oberster Gerichtshof, Urteil des gesamten Senats vom 20. Juni 2019, Az. 2013da218156 (Mindermeinung von Richter Jo Hee-dae, Park Sang-ok, Kim Seon-soo, Kim Sanghwan).

gelung im Rahmen der Gesetzgebung gelöst werden. Nicht alle gesellschaftlichen Probleme müssen von Gerichten gelöst werden. Wenn das Gericht versucht, auch solche Probleme zu lösen, die eigentlich in den Zuständigkeitsbereich der Legislative fallen, könnte dies die Funktionen der Gesetzgebung und der Rechtsprechung durcheinanderbringen und letztlich zu Misstrauen gegenüber dem Gesetz führen."[44]

44 Oberster Gerichtshof, Urteil des gesamten Senats vom 20. Juni 2019, Az. 2013da218156 (Ergänzung der Mehrheitsmeinung von Richter Kim Jae-hyung).

Tabelle 5: Methodologische Struktur der Bedingungen für Präjudizienänderungen und das Potenzial für argumentative Gegensätze

	Position für lockerere Bedingungen bei Präjudizienänderungen				Position für strengere Bedingungen bei Präjudizienänderungen		
			Methode zur Verschärfung der lockeren Bedingungen für Präjudizienänderungen				Methode zur Lockerung der strengen Bedingungen für Präjudizienänderungen
Bedingungen für Präjudizienänderungen	·Erfordernis einer schnellen Änderung im Falle eines fehlerhaften Präjudiz oder ·Vorbereitung einer Gesetzesänderung als Anlass für Präjudizienänderung	↔	·Erhöhung der Hürden für Präjudizienänderungen, wenn ein Präzedenzfall über längere Zeit als verbindlich für die allgemeine Öffentlichkeit etabliert wurde oder ·Erfordernis alternativer Ansätze zum Schutz des Vertrauens in bestehende Präzedenzfälle (wie etwa der „Verbotsirrtum" oder „Grundsatz von Treu und Glauben" usw.)	↔	·Nur in Ausnahmefällen zulässig, wenn es notwendig ist, um Widersprüche oder Konflikte zwischen Präjudizien zu beseitigen, oder wenn sich die gesellschaftlichen Bedingungen grundlegend geändert haben, sodass das Festhalten an früheren Ansichten offensichtlich der Gerechtigkeit widerspricht.[45]	↔	·Lockerung der Änderungsbedingungen in Fällen, in denen der Schutz des Vertrauens in bestehende Präzedenzfälle oder die Rechtssicherheit durch „Allgemeinklauseln" oder „eine prospektive Veränderung" gewährleistet werden kann.

Tabelle 6: Methodologische Struktur zur Bestimmung des Geltungsbereichs von Präjudizienänderungen und das Potenzial für argumentative Gegensätze

	Position, die rückwirkende Wirkung von Präjudizienänderungen unterstützt			Position, die prospektive Wirkung von Präjudizienänderungen unterstützt	
Geltungsbereich von Präjudizienänderungen	In Konflikten zwischen der prinzipiellen Durchsetzung einer richtigeren neuen Rechtsauffassung und dem Vertrauensschutz in die bestehende Rechtsauffassung sowie der Rechtssicherheit wird die erstere bevorzugt.	Ausgleichsmethoden zum Schutz des Vertrauens der unterlegenen Partei	↔	Im Konflikt zwischen der prinzipiellen Durchsetzung einer richtigeren neuen Rechtsauffassung und dem Vertrauensschutz in die bestehende Rechtsauffassung sowie der Rechtssicherheit wird die zweitere bevorzugt.	Ausgleichsmethoden für die unterlegene Partei, die nicht von der geänderten Rechtsauffassung profitiert
		Einsatz von Verbotsirrtum oder dem Grundsatz von Treu und Glauben			Einsatz von allgemeinen Klauseln oder Festlegung der Grenzen der prospektiven Wirkung

45 Alternativ finden sich auch Argumente für folgende strengere Bedingungen: (1) Wenn ein offensichtlicher Fehler im früheren Präzedenzfall nachgewiesen werden kann und die asoziale oder strafbare Natur der Handlung klar erkennbar ist, (2) Wenn der frühere Präzedenzfall über einen bestimmten Zeitraum hinweg noch nicht als etablierte Rechtsprechung des Obersten Gerichtshofs anerkannt wurde, die für die allgemeine Bevölkerung verbindlich ist, (3) Nur in Ausnahmefällen, wenn keine legislative Verbesserung zu erwarten ist oder die gesellschaftlichen Schäden so groß sind, dass auf gesetzgeberische Maßnahmen nicht mehr gewartet werden kann.

Die obenstehende Tabelle veranschaulicht die potenzielle Struktur der argumentativen Gegensätze, die in Diskussionen über die präjudizienorientierte Auslegung auftreten. Sie zeigt nicht nur die typischen gegensätzlichen Positionen zur präjudizienorientierte Auslegung auf, sondern verdeutlicht auch, dass diese Gegensätze innerhalb jeder Position strukturell wiederkehren. Dieses Potenzial ergibt sich aus der Möglichkeit, innerhalb jeder Position Elemente zu identifizieren, die es erlauben, die Ideen und Absichten der jeweils gegensätzlichen Position zu berücksichtigen.

VI. Richterliche Rechtsfortbildung in den jüngsten Entscheidungen – ihr methodischer Fortschritt und das strukturelle Potenzial der argumentativen Gegensätze

Die richterliche Rechtsfortbildung kann in „lückenfüllende Rechtsfortbildung" und „richterliche Gesetzeskorrektur" unterteilt werden.[46] Zunächst werden die Fälle untersucht, in denen die Lückenfüllung intensiv behandelt wurde.

1. Lückenfüllende Rechtsfortbildung

Das Oberste Gericht nennt als zentrale Mittel der richterlichen Lückenfüllung insbesondere die „Analogie". In jüngster Zeit sind auch Fälle aufgefallen, in denen relativ ausführlich über „teleologische Reduktion" oder „teleologische Erweiterung" argumentiert wurde.

Die Bedingungen für die Analogie konkretisiert das Oberste Gericht im Urteil 123do 345 wie folgt:

> „Für eine Analogie ist es erforderlich, dass zwischen einem nicht gesetzlich geregelten Sachverhalt und einem gesetzlich geregelten Gemein-

46 Richterliche Rechtsfortbildung, insbesondere die Arten der Lücken und die Möglichkeit der Rechtfertigung einer richterlichen Gesetzeskorrektur, sind auch in der deutschen Rechtswissenschaft seit Langem Gegenstand zahlreicher Diskussionen und bleiben bis heute umstritten. So bestehen beispielsweise Unterschiede hinsichtlich der Möglichkeit einer gesetzesübersteigenden Rechtsfortbildung und des Umfangs von Lücken zwischen dem allein von *Karl Larenz* verfassten Lehrbuch zur *Methodenlehre der Rechtswissenschaft* und dem gemeinsam mit *Klaus-Wilhelm Canaris* veröffentlichten Lehrbuch zur *Methodenlehre der Rechtswissenschaft*. Zu den verschiedenen Klassifikationen der Untertypen richterlicher Rechtsfortbildung vgl. *K.-I. Lee*, Eine Studie über richterliche Rechtsfortbildung (Kor.), Korean Journal of Law & Society, Bd. 56 (2017), 297 (298 ff.).

samkeiten oder Ähnlichkeiten bestehen. Jedoch reicht dies allein nicht aus, um eine Analogie zu begründen. Eine Analogie kann nur dann gerechtfertigt werden, wenn eine *wesentliche Ähnlichkeit* im Hinblick auf die Systematik der Rechtsnormen sowie auf den Willen und Zweck des Gesetzgebers vorliegt."(Hervor. d. Verf.)

Daher gibt es häufig Streitfälle darüber, ob eine „wesentliche Ähnlichkeit" für die Analogie gegeben ist oder nicht. Ein exemplarisches Beispiel ist das Urteil zur Untersuchungshaft im Ausland. In diesem Fall stellte sich die Frage, ob die Zeit der Untersuchungshaft im Ausland in analoger Anwendung von § 7 KStGB auf eine inländische Strafe angerechnet werden kann. Diese Vorschrift regelt jedoch nur die Anrechnung von im Ausland vollstreckten Strafen. Die Mehrheitsmeinung des Obersten Gerichts lehnte die analoge Anwendung ab. Im Gegensatz dazu befürwortete die Mindermeinung sie mit der Begründung, dass sich die Analogie auf den Gesetzeszweck, die Grundrechte und rationalitätsbezogene Argumente stützen könne.[47]

Auch die Frage, ob im Gesetz eine Lücke besteht oder nicht, ist häufig umstritten. Ein anschauliches Beispiel ist das Urteil zum Anwaltshonorarsvertrag, in dem es darum ging, ob das Honorar eines Anwalts ohne ausdrückliche gesetzliche Grundlage auf Basis der Generalklausel, also des Grundsatzes von Treu und Glauben, reduziert werden kann. Die Mehrheitsmeinung bejahte diese Möglichkeit und berief sich auf den Grundsatz von Treu und Glauben als Kriterium für die Feststellung und Ausfüllung von Gesetzeslücken. Die Mindermeinung hingegen vertrat die Ansicht, „die fehlende gesetzliche Regelung dieser Möglichkeit solle nicht als eine Lücke, sondern als eine bewusste Entscheidung des Gesetzgebers betrachtet werden".[48]

47 Oberster Gerichtshof, Urteil des gesamten Senats vom 24. August 2017, Az. 2017do5977.

48 Oberster Gerichtshof, Urteil des gesamten Senats vom 17. Mai 2018, Az. 2016da35833.

Tabelle 7: Methodologische Struktur in Bezug auf die lückenfüllende Rechtsfortbildung und das strukturelle Potenzial argumentativer Gegensätze

	Lockerere Bedingungen für die lückenfüllende Rechtsfortbildung				Strengere Bedingungen für die lückenfüllende Rechtsfortbildung		
	·Wichtige Berücksichtigung des objektiven Regelungszwecks sowie der innerhalb der Rechtsordnung geltenden Rechtsprinzipien und Rechtsideen bei der Feststellung und Ausfüllung von Lücken ·Flexible Erfassung der Regelungsabsicht des historischen Gesetzgebers				·Wichtige Berücksichtigung und strenge Erfassung der Regelungsabsicht des historischen Gesetzgebers bei der Feststellung und Ausfüllung von Lücken ·Es gibt auch die Ansicht, dass die Möglichkeit der Lückenfüllung grundsätzlich abzulehnen ist.		
	Einzelnen Bedingungen der Lückenfüllung		Verstärkung der lockeren Bedingungen für die Lückenfüllung		Einzelnen Bedingungen der Lückenfüllung		Abmilderung der strengen Bedingungen für die Lückenfüllung
Lückenfüllende Rechtsfortbildung	·Das Vorhandensein einer Lücke im Gesetz ·Die Begründung der Lückenfüllung durch Analogie, teleologische Reduktion und allgemeine Rechtsprinzipien ·Die Lückenfüllung sollte nicht in Bereichen erfolgen, in denen die Rechtsfortbildung verboten ist.	↔	·Ausweitung der Rolle des Wortlauts durch verstärkte Anwendung des *Argumentum e contrario* ·Strenge Anwendung des Maßstabs wesentlicher Ähnlichkeiten, insbesondere durch ein enges Verständnis normativer Ziele oder zugrundeliegender Rechtsprinzipien ·Erweiterung der Bereiche, in denen eine Rechtsfortbildung unzulässig ist.	↔	·Restriktive Anerkennung des Umfangs von Lücken (Beharren auf einem engen Verständnis von Lücken). ·Teleologische Reduktion wird ebenfalls als Rechtsfortbildung *contra legem* angesehen. ·Erweiterung der Bereiche, in denen eine Lückenfüllung unzulässig ist.	↔	·Situativ flexible Bestimmung der Wortlautgrenze. ·Gelegentliche Aufweichung der gesetzgeberischen Absicht zugunsten einer objektivierenden statt subjektiven Auslegung. ·Teilweise Einschränkung der Bereiche, in denen eine Rechtsfortbildung unzulässig ist.

Die obenstehende Tabelle veranschaulicht die potenzielle Struktur der argumentativen Gegensätze, die in Diskussionen über die lückenfüllende Rechtsfortbildung auftreten. Sie zeigt nicht nur die typischen gegensätzlichen Positionen zur lückenfüllenden Rechtsfortbildung auf, sondern verdeutlicht auch, dass diese Gegensätze innerhalb jeder Position strukturell wiederkehren. Dieses Potenzial ergibt sich aus der Möglichkeit, innerhalb jeder Position Elemente zu identifizieren, die es erlauben, die Ideen und Absichten der jeweils gegensätzlichen Position zu berücksichtigen.

2. Richterliche Gesetzeskorrektur

In diesem Abschnitt werden die Fälle betrachtet, in denen eine richterliche Gesetzeskorrektur gewagt und ihre Begründung versucht wurde. Für einige Zeit wurden häufig das „Urteil zur Höchstgrenze der Geldstrafe“[49] aus dem Jahr 1978 oder das „Urteil zum Wechsel ohne Angabe des Ausstellungsortes“[50] aus dem Jahr 1998 als exemplarische Beispiele angeführt.[51] Nach einer gewissen Ruhephase haben kürzlich eine Reihe neuer Entscheidungen das Interesse an diesem Thema wiederbelebt – insbesondere das „Urteil zum Nationalen Lehrergewerkschaftsverband“, bei dem die Mindermeinung von Richter Kim Jae-hyung besondere Beachtung fand. Bekannte Argumentation von Richter Kim lautet wie folgt:

> „Bei der Auslegung und Anwendung des Gesetzes müssen auch die Folgen berücksichtigt werden. Wenn die Folge einer bestimmten Auslegung als äußerst unvernünftig oder ungerecht erscheint, sollte versucht werden, diese Auslegung auszuschließen. Zu diesem Zweck werden übliche Kriterien wie grammatische, logische/systematische, historische und teleologische Auslegungen herangezogen. Wenn jedoch trotz dieser Bemühungen unvernünftige und ungerechte Folgen nicht vermieden werden können, muss das Gericht eine Interpretation vornehmen, die den Wortlaut des Gesetzes übergeht – in Ausnahmefällen sogar eine gerechte Auslegung gegen den Wortlaut des Gesetzes wagen.“[52]

---

49 Oberster Gerichtshof, Urteil des gesamten Senats vom 25. April 1978, Az. 78do246.

50 Oberster Gerichtshof, Urteil des gesamten Senats vom 23. April 1998, Az. 95da36466.

51 Etwa *D.-H. Kim*, Einführung in die Rechtsphilosophie und Rechtstheorie, Seoul, 2021, S. 281.

52 Oberster Gerichtshof, Urteil des gesamten Senats vom 3. September 2020, Az. 2016-du32992 (Mindermeinung von Richter Kim Jae-hyung).

Solche Rechtsfortbildungen seien zu rechtfertigen, weil das Gericht dazu verpflichtet sei, „nicht das Gesetz, sondern das Recht" zu erklären.

Fälle, in denen die Grenzen der richterlichen Rechtsfortbildung kürzlich aufgezeigt wurden, wurden bereits oben erwähnt – insbesondere das „Urteil zur treuhänderischen Übereignung von Immobilien",[53] das „Urteil zur besonderen beschränkten Annahme im Erbrecht"[54] und das „Urteil zum Anwaltshonorarvertrag".[55] Eine richterliche Gesetzeskorrektur kann demnach typischerweise unter folgenden Bedingungen gerechtfertigt sein:

- wenn eine Entscheidung nach dem Gesetz erheblich mit der Verfassung unvereinbar ist,
- wenn eine Entscheidung nach dem Gesetz stark gegen die in der Gesellschaft vorherrschenden Gerechtigkeitsvorstellungen verstößt,
- wenn eine richterliche Gesetzeskorrektur erforderlich ist, um ein unerträgliches Maß an Ungerechtigkeit zu verhindern.

Diese Bedingungen sind jedoch vergleichsweise abstrakt, sodass sich oft die Frage stellt, ob sie im konkreten Fall tatsächlich erfüllt sind. Daher bilden sie selbst ein strukturelles Potenzial für argumentative Gegensätze: Während die eine Seite die Erfüllung dieser Voraussetzungen bejaht, kritisiert die andere häufig, dass ein solcher Ansatz die Kompetenzen der Justiz überschreite.

53 Oberster Gerichtshof, Urteil des gesamten Senats vom 20. Juni 2019, Az. 2013da18156.
54 Oberster Gerichtshof, Urteil des gesamten Senats vom 19. November 2020, Az. 2019da232918.
55 Oberster Gerichtshof, Urteil des gesamten Senats vom 17. Mai 2018, Az. 2016da35833.

Tabelle 8: Methodologische Struktur in Bezug auf die richterliche Gesetzeskorrektur und strukturelles Potenzial argumentativer Gegensätze

<table>
<tr><td rowspan="2"></td><td colspan="3">Position, die die Möglichkeit der richterlichen Gesetzeskorrektur relativ weit fasst</td><td rowspan="2"></td><td colspan="3">Position, die die Möglichkeit der richterlichen Gesetzeskorrektur leugnet oder sie relativ eng fasst</td></tr>
<tr><td colspan="3">·Aktive Berücksichtigung grundlegender oder verfassungsrechtlicher Rechtsgüter zur Rechtfertigung richterlicher Gesetzeskorrektur im gewaltenteilenden Rechtsstaat</td><td colspan="3">·Keine oder nur äußerst begrenzte Berücksichtigung grundlegender oder verfassungsrechtlicher Rechtsgüter zur Rechtfertigung richterlicher Gesetzeskorrektur im gewaltenteilenden Rechtsstaat</td></tr>
<tr><td rowspan="2">Richterliche Gesetzeskorrektur</td><td>Relativ lockere Bedingungen für die richterliche Gesetzeskorrektur</td><td></td><td>Verschärfung der relativ lockeren Bedingungen der richterlichen Gesetzeskorrektur</td><td></td><td>Relativ strenge Bedingungen für die richterliche Gesetzeskorrektur</td><td></td><td>Lockerung der relativ strengen Bedingungen der richterlichen Gesetzeskorrektur</td></tr>
<tr><td>Die folgenden Bedingungen gelten nicht kumulativ, sondern alternativ:
·wenn erforderlich, um die Verfassungskonformität sicherzustellen
·wenn erforderlich, um extremen Verstößen gegen die Idee der Gerechtigkeit vorzubeugen
·wenn erforderlich, um die Sicherheit im Geschäftsverkehr gewährleisten</td><td>↔</td><td>Der Wegfall der Möglichkeit der richterlichen Gesetzeskorrektur, sofern folgende Bedingungen erfüllt sind:
·sofern die richterliche Gesetzeskorrektur eine erhebliche rechtliche Unsicherheit oder eine Verletzung der Rechte Dritter verursachen würde,
·sofern eine alternative Lösungsmöglichkeit durch das Verfassungsgericht oder das Parlament besteht,
·sofern der Inhalt der Korrektur außerhalb des durch das Gericht beurteilbaren Rahmens liegt,
·sofern sie dem klaren Willen des historischen Gesetzgebers widerspricht.</td><td>↔</td><td>Die folgenden Bedingungen gelten kumulativ:
·soweit sie nicht dem klaren Willen des historischen Gesetzgebers widerspricht,
·und nur, wenn es erforderlich ist, um die Verfassungskonformität sicherzustellen oder um extremen Verstößen gegen die Idee der Gerechtigkeit vorzubeugen.</td><td>↔</td><td>·Rechtfertigung durch Auslegung oder Lückenergänzung statt durch Gesetzeskorrektur, basierend auf der Erweiterung der Wortlautgrenze oder der Reichweite der Lücke
·Rechtfertigung durch objektive Erfassung des gesetzgeberischen Willens zum aktuellen Zeitpunkt</td></tr>
</table>

Die obenstehende Tabelle veranschaulicht die potenzielle Struktur der argumentativen Gegensätze, die in Diskussionen über die richterliche Gesetzeskorrektur auftreten. Sie zeigt nicht nur die typischen gegensätzlichen Positionen zur richterlichen Gesetzeskorrektur auf, sondern verdeutlicht auch, dass diese Gegensätze innerhalb jeder Position strukturell wiederkehren. Dieses Potenzial ergibt sich aus der Möglichkeit, innerhalb jeder Position Elemente zu identifizieren, die es ermöglichen, die Ideen und Absichten der jeweils gegensätzlichen Position zu berücksichtigen.

VII. Methodensynkretismus oder Vorrangsrelationen unter den Auslegungskriterien?

1. Gelegentlich auftretende Inkonsistenzen in der angewandten Auslegungslehre je nach Fall

Bislang wurden die Erscheinungsformen der Auslegungskriterien und ihre argumentativen Gegensätze in jüngsten Entscheidungen des koreanischen Obersten Gerichtshofs untersucht. Eine weitere Fragestellung, die in diesem Abschnitt behandelt werden soll, ist, ob die Auslegungskriterien in verschiedenen Urteilen konsistent und kohärent angewendet wurden.

Richter wie Kim Jae-hyung und Min Yoo-suk haben in einigen Fällen – etwa im Urteil zur Verweigerung des Militärdienstes, im Urteil zur künstlichen Befruchtung oder im Urteil zum Nationalen Lehrergewerkschaftsverband – eine aktive Auslegung vorgenommen, während sie in anderen Fällen – wie im Urteil zur treuhänderischen Übereignung von Immobilien oder im Urteil zur besonderen beschränkten Annahme im Erbrecht – eine zurückhaltende Auslegung bevorzugt haben. Demgegenüber haben Richter Jo Hee-de und Park Sang-ok in den erstgenannten Fällen eine zurückhaltende, in den letztgenannten Fällen hingegen eine aktive Auslegung angewendet.

Tabelle 9: Gelegentlich auftretende Inkonsistenzen in der Anwendung der Auslegungslehre je nach Fall

Gegensätzliche Ansichten im Urteil zur Verweigerung des Militärdienstes[56]	
Die aktive Auslegung von Kim Jae-hyung, Min Yoo-suk	Die zurückhaltende Auslegung von Jo Hee-de, Park Sang-ok
„Die Absichten der Gesetzgeber – also, welche Gründe sie tatsächlich als legitim angesehen und erwartet haben – sind nicht entscheidend. Zwar sollte bei der Auslegung die Absicht des Gesetzgebers berücksichtigt werden, jedoch ohne daran gebunden zu sein. Vielmehr soll das Gesetz selbst bindend sein. Genau dieses Gesetz bestimmt ‚die legitimen Gründe', wie oben beschrieben. *Das Gesetz ist klüger als die Gesetzgeber selbst.*" „Bei der Auslegung des Gesetzes muss das Ergebnis berücksichtigt werden. Auch wenn der Gesetzestext verschiedene Auslegungsmöglichkeiten zulässt und eine bestimmte Interpretation äußerlich betrachtet mit dem Wortlaut, der Logik und der Systematik vereinbar erscheint, *sollte man dennoch innehalten, wenn das Ergebnis als offensichtlich untragbar erscheint – insbesondere dann, wenn es fundamentalen Werten höherrangigen Rechts wie der Verfassung widerspricht.* Eine verfassungskonforme Auslegung bedeutet, diese Prinzipien zu berücksichtigen und die Verfassung als Maßstab heranzuziehen..." (Hervorh. d. Verf.)	„Es besteht die Befürchtung, dass die Auffassung der Mehrheitsmeinung, die eine Änderung der bestehenden Rechtsprechung vorschlägt, wesentliche rechtliche Werte wie die Rechtssicherheit erheblich beeinträchtigen könnte. Dies könnte nicht nur den gesetzgeberischen Zweck des Wehrpflichtgesetzes grundlegend untergraben, sondern auch zu einem unverhältnismäßigen Privileg bei der Erfüllung der Wehrpflicht führen. Darüber hinaus würde dies gegen das normative Gebot der Gleichbehandlung bei der Wehrpflicht verstoßen und deutlich von den Erwartungen der Bevölkerung abweichen, was zu gesellschaftlicher Unruhe und Spannungen führen könnte. *Ferner könnte die Interpretation der Mehrheitsmeinung den Eindruck erwecken, dass die Gerichte über die Grenzen der Justiz hinaus in den Bereich der Gesetzgebungspolitik eingreifen, was Missverständnisse und Kritik hervorrufen könnte.* Selbst wenn die ausnahmslose Anwendung des Wehrpflichtgesetzes auf gewissenhafte Militärdienstverweigerer und andere Wehrpflichtige in einigen Fällen als unfair oder unverhältnismäßig empfunden wird, sollte eine Korrektur durch den Gesetzgebungsprozess des Parlaments erfolgen – nicht durch eine gerichtliche Auslegung, die dem Zweck oder der Funktion des Wehrpflichtgesetzes widerspricht. Diese Schlussfolgerung beruht auf den grundlegenden Prinzipien und Pflichten, die Richter bei der Gesetzesauslegung und der Ausübung der rechtsprechenden Gewalt zwingend zu beachten haben." (Herv. d. Verf.)
Umgekehrte gegensätzliche Ansichten im Urteil zur treuhänderischen Übereignung von Immobilien[57]	

56 Oberster Gerichtshof, Urteil des gesamten Senats vom 1. November 2018, Az. 2016do10912.

57 Oberster Gerichtshof, Urteil des gesamten Senats vom 20. Juni 2019, Az. 2013da218156.

Die aktive Auslegung von Jo Hee-de, Park Sang-ok	Die zurückhaltende Auslegung von Kim Jae-hyung, Min Yoo-suk
„Die illegale Leistung bezeichnet eine Handlung, die gegen die guten Sitten und die soziale Ordnung verstößt, und stellt daher eine flexible Konzeption dar, die je nach Zeit und Ort unterschiedlich konkretisiert werden kann. Die Wahrnehmung von Treuhandvereinbarungen im Immobilienbereich zum Zeitpunkt der Einführung des Immobilienrealnamengesetzes,[58] als ihre Wirksamkeit noch durch die Rechtsprechung anerkannt wurde, unterscheidet sich zwangsläufig von der heutigen Sichtweise nach über zwanzig Jahren, in denen das Immobilienrealnamengesetz solche Vereinbarungen verboten, unter Strafe gestellt und als unwirksam eingestuft hat. *Ob eine treuhänderische Übereignung von Immobilien eine illegale Leistung darstellt, ist aus heutiger Perspektive zu beurteilen – nicht nach Maßstäben von vor zwanzig Jahren.* Angesichts der festen Etablierung des Realnamensystems im Finanzwesen seit der Einführung des Finanzrealnamengesetzes besteht heute kein Zweifel mehr an der Notwendigkeit und Dringlichkeit, das Realnamensystem auch im Bereich der Immobiliengeschäfte durchzusetzen. Eine Auslegung, wonach Treuhandvereinbarungen über Immobilien, die gegen das Immobilienrealnamengesetz verstoßen, nicht gegen die guten Sitten und die soziale Ordnung verstoßen, würde bedeuten, dass *man das veränderte Normenbewusstsein und die zeitgenössischen Anforderungen der allgemeinen Gesellschaft vernachlässigt.*" (Herv. d. Verf.)	„Entsprechend der Mehrheitsmeinung ist es weder als verfassungswidrig noch als gravierender Verstoß gegen das gesellschaftliche Gerechtigkeitsempfinden anzusehen, das Immobilienrealnamengesetz entsprechend seinem klaren Wortlaut dahingehend auszulegen, dass die Eigentumsrechte an Treuhandimmobilien dem Treugeber zustehen. *Daher ist es für die Judikative als das für die Gesetzesauslegung und -anwendung zuständige Organ geboten, solche grundlegenden Entscheidungen des Gesetzgebers zu respektieren.* Das Immobilienrealnamengesetz sieht sogar vor, dass die Verwaltung Maßnahmen ergreifen kann, um dem Treugeber die Wiedererlangung seines Eintragungsanspruchs als tatsächlicher Eigentümer zu ermöglichen. Es bleibt unklar, auf welcher rechtlichen Grundlage der Oberste Gerichtshof nun plötzlich die bisher gesetzestreu handelnden Beamten, die die Treugeber sanktioniert haben, als Rechtsbrecher bezeichnet." (Herv. d. Verf.)

Daher könnte man sich fragen, ob die Auslegungslehre der Richter nicht von Urteil zu Urteil inkonsistent ist.

58 „Immobilienrealnamengesetz" ist die Abkürzung für das „Gesetz über die Registrierung von Immobilien im Namen des tatsächlichen Eigentümers". Die relevanten Bestimmungen dieses Gesetzes finden sich in Fußnote 11 oben.

2. Eine Entwicklungslinie von einer „ganzheitlichen und holistischen Auslegungslehre„ hin zu einer „schwachen Form der Vorrangsrelationen unter den Kriterien„

Diese aktuelle Lage führt einerseits zur Frage: Ist der Methodensynkretismus unvermeidlich, oder ist auch eine gemilderte Vorrangsrelation der Auslegungskriterien noch möglich? Andererseits stellt sich die Frage, ob die Bemühungen nicht weiter vorangetrieben werden sollten, um eine konsistente und verfeinerte Auslegungslehre zu entwickeln.

Bezogen auf die erstgenannte Frage zeigt die Entscheidung des Obersten Gerichts eine Entwicklung von einer „ganzheitlichen und holistischen Auslegungslehre“ (als eine Form des Methodensynkretismus) hin zu einer „schwachen Form der Vorrangsrelationen unter den Auslegungskriterien“.[59] Ein exemplarisches Beispiel für die ganzheitliche Auslegungslehre ist das Urteil zur „Fahrlässigen Brandstiftung“ aus dem Jahr 1998.

> “... die Methode der ganzheitlichen und holistischen Auslegung der einschlägigen Bestimmungen...”[60]

Ebenso in einem Urteil aus dem Jahr 2014,

> „Die Bedeutung einer Rechtsnorm wird durch eine Auslegung konkretisiert, die nicht nur ihren Wortlaut, sondern auch den Gesetzeszweck, die gesetzgeberische Absicht, den legislativen Werdegang und die systematische Struktur der Rechtsnorm *insgesamt* berücksichtigt.“(Hervor. d. Verf.)[61]

Gelegentlich wurde auch darauf hingewiesen, dass diese Auslegungslehre eine Affinität zur problemorientierten, topischen Denkweise und zur ostasiatischen Relationsphilosophie aufweist. Im Gegensatz dazu dient das Urteil zum „Vermieter“ aus dem Jahr 2008 als ein exemplarisches Urteil, das eine Form von Vorrangsrelationen unter den Auslegungskriterien zeigt.[62]

---

59 Hierzu siehe *J.-O. Kim* [u.a], Rechtsphilosophie: Theorie und Problemstellungen (Kor.), 3. Auflage, Seoul, 2022, Kap. 13: „Die gesetzliche Auslegungslehre in Korea“, S. 292 ff. m.w.N.

60 Oberster Gerichtshof, Entscheidung des gesamten Senats vom 20. Dezember 1994, Az. 94mo32.

61 Oberster Gerichtshof, Urteil vom 29. Januar 2014, Az. 2013do12939.

62 Oberster Gerichtshof, Urteil vom 23. April 2009, Az. 2006da81035. Eine Analyse der in diesem Urteil offengelegten Auslegungslehre findet sich bei *K.-I. Lee*, Eine kritische Studie über Vorrangsrelationen der Auslegungskriterien (Kor.), Koreanische Zeitschrift für Rechtsphilosophie, Bd. 18, H. 3 (2015), 125 (129 f.) m.w.N. Siehe außer-

- Grundsätzlich sollte die Auslegung, die auf der „üblichen Bedeutung der Worte“ basiert, als vorrangig angesehen werden.
- Natürlich gibt es Fälle, in denen man durch die Berücksichtigung des „Zwecks und der Absicht der Regelung“ über die übliche Bedeutung hinausgehen kann.
- Selbst bei einer solchen teleologischen Auslegung fungiert jedoch das „System der einschlägigen Bestimmungen und Gesetze“ als Einschränkung.
- Bei „eindeutiger Bedeutung einer gesetzlichen Bestimmung“ sollte jedoch die Anwendung anderer Auslegungsmethoden als unnötig oder eingeschränkt angesehen werden.

Es sollte jedoch beachtet werden, dass diese vorgeschlagenen Vorrangsrelationen noch als „schwach“ gelten. In den nachfolgenden Entscheidungen des Obersten Gerichtshofs zeigt sich, dass die Gewichtung der einzelnen Kriterien innerhalb der Vorrangsrelationen je nach Fall unterschiedlich konkretisiert wurde. Dies liegt daran, dass die Stärke, mit der die Kriterien auf den jeweiligen Fall zutreffen, zwangsläufig variiert. Daher dienen auch diese Vorrangsrelationen als strukturelles Potenzial für argumentative Gegensätze.

VIII. Rechtstheoretische Implikationen aus analytisch-kritischer Sicht

1. Die kristalline Struktur argumentativer Gegensätze

Bislang haben wir in den jüngsten Urteilen des Obersten Gerichtshofs die Erscheinungsformen der Auslegungskriterien untersucht. Diese Analyse zeigt, dass die Auslegungslehre eine innere Mehrschichtigkeit aufweisen kann, die gleichzeitig als strukturelles Potenzial für argumentative Gegensätze dient. Dieses Potenzial haben wir für jedes einzelne Auslegungskriterium grafisch dargestellt. Die Gesamtkombination dieser Darstellungen macht dieses Potenzial noch deutlicher sichtbar. Wegen des beschränkten Raums, der diesem Artikel zur Verfügung steht, möchten wir uns nur auf eine kurze Erörterung der daraus resultierenden Implikationen beschränken. Folgende Punkte:

---

dem *J.-H. Kim*, Pracht der herbstlichen goldenen Felder: Ein Aspekt der Gesetzesauslegung – Die Auslegung des Mieters im Mietwohnungsgesetz – (Kor.), SNU Law Review, Bd. 1 (2010), 200 (235 ff.).

Wenn eine der methodisch gegenüberstehenden Positionen ausgewählt und konkretisiert wird, können innerhalb dieser Position implizite Bedingungen zu ihrer Begrenzung oder Relativierung festgelegt werden. Dies betrifft sowohl das Auslegungsziel als auch einzelne Auslegungskriterien sowie die richterliche Rechtsfortbildung. Strukturell liegt dies daran, dass die Konflikte zwischen grundlegenden Prinzipien des Rechtsstaats, die häufig in Gegensatzpaaren auftreten, sich auch in der Struktur der Methodenlehre widerspiegeln. Beispielsweise:

- Rechtssicherheit vs. Fallgerechtigkeit
- Primat der Legislative vs. Primat der Judikative
- Textorientierung vs. Zweckorientierung
- Stabilität des Geschäftsverkehrs vs. Rechtsschutz der Prozessparteien
- Regelorientierung vs. Verfassungsorientierung.

Selbst wenn in diesen Gegensatzpaaren zugunsten einer Seite entschieden wird, wird die Berücksichtigung der Gegenseite innerhalb dieser Entscheidung methodisch nicht vernachlässigt. Die methodische Argumentation nimmt daher eine Struktur an, die der eines Kristalls sehr ähnelt. Selbst wenn ein Kristall in kleine Stücke zerbricht, enthalten diese Teile intern wieder gegensätzliche Ideen.[63]

Diese kristalline Struktur erklärt auch, warum ein Richter seine Auslegungslehre in unterschiedlichen Fällen unterschiedlich konkretisiert oder sogar anscheinend inkonsistent anwendet, obwohl er einer bestimmten Lehre treu bleibt. Wenn ein Richter in einem Fall zu einem Urteil gelangt, bei dem auch Perspektiven von methodisch ihm gegenüberstehenden Ansätzen berücksichtigt werden müssen, wird er (bewusst oder unbewusst) von dieser Struktur Gebrauch machen. Die teils aktive, teils passive Position eines Richters wird somit verständlich.

63 Rechtssemiotische Studien haben diese Form als „kristalline Struktur juristischer Argumentation" bezeichnet. So beispielsweise *Jack M. Balkin* in „The Crystalline Structure of Legal Thought", 39 Rutgers Law Review 1 (1986). Auch in Korea bezieht sich *Jeong-Oh Kim* auf diese Struktur in „Die Struktur juristischer Argumentation an der Schnittstelle von Genderdiskurs und Rechtsdiskurs"(Kor.), in: Koreanische Vereinigung für Rechtsphilosophie (Hrsg.), Angewandte Rechtsphilosophie, Seoul, 2002, S. 49 ff.

2. Der unvermeidliche Spielraum der Urteilskraft und die begrenzte Rationalität der normativen Methodik

Die strukturelle Wiederkehr gegensätzlicher Wahlmöglichkeiten untergräbt jedoch nicht die gesamte Bedeutung der methodischen Bemühungen. Die juristische Methodik übt zweifellos einen Druck auf den Richter aus, innerhalb seiner eigenen Auslegungslehre eine einigermaßen konsistente Argumentation zu entwickeln, wodurch sie eine gewisse „Kontrollmacht" ausübt. Dennoch sollte der verbleibende, unvermeidliche Spielraum, in dem Urteilskraft erforderlich ist, nicht übersehen werden. Dies bekräftigt, dass die angestrebte Rationalität der normativen Methodik letztlich nur eine „begrenzte Rationalität" darstellt, die als eine Art „Filterfunktion" fungiert.

Die begrenzte Leistungsfähigkeit der juristischen Methodik zeigt sich auch deutlich in der Haltung der koreanischen Gerichte zum Vorrangsverhältnis der Auslegungskriterien. Ihre frühere Position der „ganzheitlichen und holistischen Auslegung" hat sich inzwischen zu einer „geschwächten Form des Vorrangverhältnisses" entwickelt, wie bereits oben dargestellt wurde. In einigen späteren Entscheidungen lässt sich jedoch erkennen, dass diese Position erneut abgeschwächt wird, indem Raum geschaffen wird, das Gewicht der einzelnen Kriterien subtil und je nach Fall unterschiedlich zu gewichten. Gelegentlich wurde dieses Vorrangsverhältnis sogar als rhetorisches Mittel verwendet.[64]

3. Die Kluft zwischen Rechtsherstellung und Rechtsdarstellung sowie die Notwendigkeit des Methodenpluralismus

Die begrenzte Rationalität der normativen Methodik kann ein Hinweis auf die Kluft zwischen Rechtsherstellung und Rechtsdarstellung sein. Die Kontrolle richterlicher Macht sollte daher nicht nur durch methodologische, sondern auch durch andere Mechanismen ergänzt werden. Dies führt insbesondere zur Notwendigkeit, bei der Untersuchung richterlicher Entscheidungen auch institutionelle und machtbezogene Elemente zu berücksichtigen. Natürlich kann keine einzelne Rechtstheorie all diese Aspekte

64 Zum Beispiel Oberster Gerichtshof, Urteil des gesamten Senats vom 17. Januar 2013, Az. 2011da83431; Oberster Gerichtshof, Urteil vom 23. Dezember 2010, Az. 2010da81254; Ostseoul Bezirksgericht, Urteil vom 15. Februar 2012, Az. 2011gahap20056.

vollständig erfassen. In diesem Zusammenhang lässt sich die Implikation des Methodenpluralismus nach wie vor als gültig betrachten.[65]

65 Als Beispiel für die Diskussionen in Korea siehe *H.-S. Shim*, Recht und Methodenpluralismus (Kor.), in: Festschrift für Professor Kim Ji-su, Seoul, 2003, S. 177 ff.; *Y.-M. Jang*, Die Methode der Rechtswissenschaft: Eine Skizze (Kor.), ebenda, S. 262 ff.

Einbeziehung rechtsethischer Argumente in die Gesetzesauslegung

Seongbum Lee

A. Einleitung

Das Gesetz legt seinen Inhalt nicht vollständig selbst dar. Die primäre und wichtigste Aufgabe der Gesetzesauslegung besteht darin, den Inhalt des Gesetzes und seine normative Bedeutung zu erfassen. Selbst wenn der Gesetzesinhalt aus einer wörtlichen oder auf Gesetzgebungsmaterialien basierenden Perspektive relativ klar erkannt werden kann, bleibt die Auslegungsmöglichkeit als impliziter und potenzieller Gesetzesinhalt bestehen und wird immer wieder hinterfragt. Dies ist auf die „Schriftlichkeit" des Gesetzestextes zurückzuführen, die mit einer Differenz „zwischen Geschriebenem und Gemeintem"[1] einhergeht.[2] Diese Differenz führt dazu, dass verschiedene Auslegungsmöglichkeiten in Betracht gezogen werden, die auf dem gegebenen Gesetzestext basieren. Es zeigt sich, dass das Verhältnis zwischen dem Geschriebenen und dem Gemeinten asymmetrisch sein kann.[3] Somit bezieht sich das im Gesetz Geschriebene nicht ausschließlich auf das, was explizit formuliert wurde. Die Gesetzesauslegung sieht sich daher unmittelbar mit dieser Asymmetrie konfrontiert.[4]

In der Regel entspricht der geschriebene Gesetzesinhalt dem Wortlaut des Gesetzes oder lässt sich aus öffentlichen Gesetzgebungsmaterialien ableiten. Dies könnte als formeller und expliziter Gesetzesinhalt bezeichnet werden. Daneben ist auch an den materiellen und impliziten Gesetzesinhalt zu denken, dessen Erfassung zwangsläufig das innerlich Beabsichtigte und Gedachte zum Gegenstand hat. Hierbei spielen der Gesetzeszweck

---

1 *M. Auer*, Zum Erkenntnisziel der Rechtstheorie, Nomos, 2018, S. 66; vgl. *P. Legendre* (übersetzt von *P. Mattern*), Die Kinder des Textes, Verlag Turia+Kant 2011, S. 72; *D. Barck*, De Legum interpretatione, Duncker & Humblot, 2020, S. 21 f., 118 f.

2 Vgl. *N. Luhmann*, Soziale Systeme, Suhrkamp, 1987, S. 111.

3 Vgl. *C. Bohn*, Schriftlichkeit und Gesellschaft, Westdeutscher Verlag, 1999, S. 36; *V. Hösle*, Kritik der verstehenden Vernunft, C.H.Beck, 2018, S. 262.

4 *S. Lee*, Rechtsethische Auslegung im Schadensrecht, Duncker & Humblot, 2020, S. 13.

sowie rechtsethische Prinzipien eine entscheidende Rolle.[5] Dadurch verschmilzt die Perspektive des Rechts, die eng mit dem Gerechtigkeitsgedanken verbunden ist, mit dem objektiven Zweck des Gesetzes und den rechtsethischen Wertungen. Dies gilt insbesondere für rechtliche Prinzipien oder abstrakte, wertgebundene Begriffe im Gesetz, wobei es um den potenziellen Gesetzesinhalt geht.

Der explizite Gesetzesinhalt und der potenzielle, implizite Gesetzesinhalt können übereinstimmen, aber auch voneinander abweichen. Daraus ergibt sich die Frage, wie der potenzielle, implizite Gesetzesinhalt durch Gesetzesauslegung erkannt werden kann und in welchem Umfang der explizite Gesetzesinhalt aufrechterhalten werden kann. Dadurch entsteht ein Spannungsverhältnis zwischen den normativen Inhalten möglicher Gesetzesauslegungen.[6] Dies verdeutlicht, was als Gesetzesinhalt verstanden werden kann. Selbst wenn die Ermittlung des impliziten Gesetzesinhalts den expliziten in den Hintergrund drängt, kann die Materialisierung des Gesetzesverständnisses nicht uneingeschränkt erfolgen. Aus methodologischer Perspektive der Gesetzesauslegung besteht stets die Gefahr, das Prinzip der Gesetzesbindung zu gefährden. Daher ist es von größter Bedeutung, wie und inwieweit der implizite Gesetzesinhalt innerhalb des genannten Spannungsverhältnisses erkannt werden kann. Die Erkenntnis des impliziten Gesetzesinhalts steht dabei in engem Zusammenhang mit rechtsethischen Wertungen, die einzelne Gesetzesinhalte entweder rechtfertigen oder ihnen zuwiderlaufen können. Zur Erfassung der im Gesetz enthaltenen rechtsethischen Wertungen wurde im bestehenden methodologischen System der Gesetzesauslegung seit langem die sogenannte objektiv-teleologische Gesetzesauslegung herangezogen.[7]

5 *K. Larenz/C.-W. Canaris*, Methodenlehre der Rechtswissenschaft, 3. Aufl., Springer, 1995, S. 177.

6 *J. Froese*, Die Grenze des Rechts als Herausforderung der Auslegung, oder: Interpretation als Flexibilitätsreserve der Rechtsordnung, Rechtstheorie 2015, 481, 483 f.; *J. Gardner*, Law as a Leap of Faith, Oxford University Press, 2012, S. 46; vgl. auch *D. Looschelders/W. Roth*, Juristische Methodik im Prozeß der Rechtsanwendung, Duncker & Humblot, 1996, S. 23 ff.; *E. Bulygin*, Essays in Legal Philosophy, Oxford University Press, 2015, S. 222 f.; *R. Guastini*, Defeasibility, Axiological Gaps, and Interpretation, in: *J. Beltrán/G. Ratti* (eds.), The Logic of Legal Requirements, Oxford University Press, 2012, S. 192.

7 Vgl. *T. Henninger*, Europäisches Privatrecht und Methode, Mohr Siebeck, 2009, S. 106 ff.

B. Die bestehende Auslegungsmethode für rechtsethische Argumente

In der koreanischen juristischen Methodenlehre zeigt sich ein erheblicher Einfluss der deutschen Auslegungslehre, insbesondere der objektiv-teleologischen Auslegung. Der Zweck (*telos*) ist ein weitreichendes und umfassendes Konzept. Dementsprechend ist auch das methodologische Spektrum der teleologischen Auslegung breit gefächert. Innerhalb dieses Spektrums rückt die objektiv-teleologische Auslegung die normative Bedeutung des Gesetzesinhalts in den Fokus, wobei die Rolle der *ratio legis* besonders hervorgehoben wird. Vor allem wird davon ausgegangen, dass das Gesetz darauf abzielt, eine vernünftige, gerechte und zweckmäßige Ordnung zu schaffen.[8] Die Objektivität des Gesetzeszwecks kann dabei unter Berücksichtigung der Umstände nach der Gesetzgebung – insbesondere in der gegenwärtigen rechtlichen Situation – konstruktiv ermittelt werden.[9]

Damit stellt die objektiv-teleologische Gesetzesauslegung zwei wesentliche Kriterien zur Erfassung des Gesetzesinhalts auf.[10] Das erste Kriterium ist der objektive Gesetzeszweck, der zugleich als Zweck des Rechts verstanden werden kann – nämlich die Gewährleistung der Rechtssicherheit, die gerechte Lösung von Streitigkeiten sowie die Optimierung der Berücksichtigung der jeweiligen Interessen im Sinne einer harmonischen rechtlichen Ordnung. Das zweite Kriterium ist das Bemühen, für jedes Gesetz eine sachgerechte Lösung zu finden. Diese Kriterien können insbesondere dann entscheidend sein, wenn andere Auslegungsmethoden keine eindeutige Antwort liefern. Innerhalb dieses auf dem objektiven Gesetzeszweck beruhenden Verständnisses lässt sich ein Auslegungsergebnis erzielen, welches die jeweiligen Interessenslagen angemessen berücksichtigt.

Bei der objektiv-teleologischen Auslegung stehen einerseits die Struktur des gegebenen Regelungsgegenstands und andererseits die dahinterstehenden rechtsethischen Prinzipien im Vordergrund – also jene Prinzipien, die für die Ideale und Bedeutungen des Rechts relevant sind.[11] Der objektive Gesetzeszweck wird nicht empirisch festgestellt, sondern normativ konstruiert bzw. deklariert. Aufgrund seiner normativen Struktur lässt er sich leicht

---

8 Staudinger/*Honsell*, Einleitung zum BGB, Rn. 134, 149; *J. Neuner*, Allgemeiner Teil des Bürgerlichen Rechts, 13. Aufl., C.H.Beck, 2023, § 4, Rn. 40; *T. Möllers*, Juristische Methodenlehre, 5. Aufl., C.H.Beck, 2023, § 5, Rn. 2.

9 Vgl. *E. A. Kramer*, Juristische Methodenlehre, 6. Aufl., Stämpfi Verlag, 2019, S. 173; *F. Kerschner*, Juristische Methodenlehre, facultas, 2022, S. 33.

10 *Larenz/Canaris*, Methodenlehre (Fn. 5), S. 153.

11 *Larenz/Canaris*, Methodenlehre (Fn. 5), S. 154.

mit Prinzipienargumenten in Verbindung bringen.[12] Innerhalb dieses objektiv-teleologischen Auslegungskriteriums können Bewertungswidersprüche zwischen den betroffenen Wertungen bestehen. Die objektiv-teleologische Auslegung zielt darauf ab, solche Widersprüche so weit wie möglich zu vermeiden.[13] Letztlich wird - aus der gegenwärtigen Perspektive und im Lichte des objektiven Gesetzeszwecks - das Auslegungsergebnis als das verstanden, was im Gesetz intendiert oder mitgedacht ist.

C. Kritik

Wird die objektiv-teleologische Auslegung herangezogen, kann der objektive Gesetzeszweck selbst als zu abstrakt und unklar wahrgenommen werden. Es stellt sich die Frage, ob die Berufung auf den objektiven Gesetzeszweck bei der Gesetzesauslegung möglicherweise zu normativen Aussagen führt, die über den eigentlichen inhaltlichen Rahmen des Gesetzes hinausgehen. Die objektiv-teleologische Auslegung betrachtet beispielsweise die harmonische Lösung von Interessenkonflikten als Teil des objektiven Gesetzeszwecks.[14] Dabei können verschiedene methodologische Ansätze mit ihren jeweiligen Charakteristika unterschiedslos in die Ermittlung des Gesetzeszwecks einfließen. Ein Beispiel dafür ist, dass auch rechtspolitische oder folgenorientierte Argumente im objektiven Gesetzeszweck berücksichtigt werden.[15]

In dieser Hinsicht lässt sich die objektiv-teleologische Auslegung dahingehend bewerten, dass sie sich weniger darauf konzentriert, die dem gege-

---

12 Vgl. *R. Alexy*, Theorie der juristischen Argumentation, Suhrkamp, 1983, S. 296 f., 299; vgl. auch *J.-R. Sieckmann*, Regelmodelle und Prinzipienmodelle des Rechtssystems, Nomos, 1990, S. 78 f.

13 *Larenz/Canaris*, Methodenlehre (Fn. 5), S. 155; vgl. *Kerschner*, Methodenlehre (Fn. 9), S. 42.

14 *Larenz/Canaris*, Methodenlehre (Fn. 5), S. 153; vgl. *L. Pajunk*, Die Einbindung von Folgenberücksichtigungen in den deutschen Auslegungskanon, in: *D. Sliwiok-Born/B. Steinrötter* (Hg.), Intra- und interdisziplinäre Einflüsse auf die Rechtsanwendung, Mohr Siebeck, 2017, S. 163 f.

15 Dazu vgl. *Neuner*, Allgemeiner Teil (Fn. 8), § 4, Rn. 41; *F. Leal*, Ziele und Autorität, Nomos, 2014, S. 53 ff., 182 f.; *B. Schünemann*, Die Gesetzesinterpretation im Schnittfeld von Sprachphilosophie, Staatsverfassung und juristischer Methodenlehre, in: *G. Kohlmann* (Hg.), Festschrift für Ulrich Klug zum 70. Geburtstag, Bd. I , Deubner, 1983, S. 185; *E. Picker*, Richterrecht und Rechtsdogmatik, in: *C. Bumke* (Hg.), Richterrecht zwischen Gesetzesrecht und Rechtsgestaltung, Mohr Siebeck, 2012, S. 88 f.

benen Gesetzestext innewohnenden potenziellen Bedeutungen unmittelbar zu erfassen, sondern vielmehr darauf abzielt, bestimmte Rechtsgedanken zu klären.[16] Daher stellt sich die Frage, ob das Prinzip der Gesetzesbindung durch eine solche Auslegungsmethode willkürlich beeinträchtigt wird oder ob die Leistungsfähigkeit des Gesetzes lediglich aufgrund praktischer Notwendigkeiten unangemessen erweitert wird.[17] Es besteht also die Gefahr einer Bedeutungsüberladung. Wird der objektive Gesetzeszweck zu frei und abstrakt betrachtet, kann dies letztlich zu einer uferlosen Ethisierung des Gesetzesinhalts führen. Darüber hinaus kann auch eine sorgfältige Begründung des Verständnisses des Gesetzeszwecks verschleiert werden.[18] Der objektive Gesetzeszweck verwischt somit die Grenzen des Gesetzes und vernachlässigt die Existenz seines Außenbereichs.

Die objektiv-teleologische Auslegung birgt die Gefahr, dass der Interpretationsprozess anstelle der Erfassung des tatsächlichen Gesetzesinhalts dazu führt, den objektiven Gesetzeszweck zur Rechtfertigung einer bereits vorgefassten Schlussfolgerung des Interpreten heranzuziehen. Unter dem Einfluss reflexiver Vorstellungen über den Gesetzeszweck könnte leicht angenommen werden, dass sich jeder entsprechende Inhalt aus dem Gesetz ableiten lässt. In Wirklichkeit kann es sich dabei jedoch lediglich um eine subjektive Sinngebung des Interpreten handeln.[19] In gewisser Hinsicht ist der Zweck seinem Wesen nach untrennbar mit dem Menschen verbunden, da nur der Mensch handelt und über eine solche Zwecksetzung verfügt. Es erscheint daher fraglich, ob ein Gesetzestext selbst einen Zweck innehaben kann.[20] Dabei könnte der objektive Gesetzeszweck, der auf der Prämisse

---

16 Vgl. *J. Braun*, Deduktion und Invention, Mohr Siebeck, 2016, S. 69.

17 Vgl. *W. Fikentscher*, Methoden des Rechts, Bd. III, Mohr Siebeck, 1976, S. 677 f.; *M. Auer*, Methodenkritik und Interessenjurisprudenz Philipp Heck zum 150. Geburtstag, ZEuP 2008, 517, 529; *F. Reimer*, Gerechtigkeit als Methodenfrage, Mohr Siebeck, 2020, S. 27; *Looschelders/Roth*, Juristische Methodik (Fn. 6), S. 33 ff.; *E. Holzleithner*, Gerechtigkeit, facultas, 2009, S. 96 f.

18 *A. Aarnio*, Denkweisen der Rechtswissenschaft, Springer, 1979, S. 135.

19 *Kerschner*, Methodenlehre (Fn. 9), S. 34 f.; *A. Lefebvre*, The Image of Law, Stanford University Press, 2008, S. 26; *C. Höpfner*, Die Gesetzesauslegung, in: *J. Eisfeld* u. a. (Hg.), Zivilrechtswissenschaft, Mohr Siebeck, 2024, S. 327; vgl. *I. Puppe*, Kleine Schule des juristischen Denkens, 5. Aufl., Vandenhoeck & Ruprecht, 2023, S. 162; *M. Kriele*, Theorie der Rechtsgewinnung, 2. Aufl., Duncker & Humblot, 1976, S. 173.

20 Vgl. *Puppe*, Kleine Schule (Fn. 19). 162; *M. Reichelt*, Die Absicherung teleologischer Argumente in der Zivilrechtsprechung des Bundesgerichtshofes, Duncker & Humblot, 2011, S. 41; *Looschelders/Roth*, Juristische Methodik (Fn. 6), S. 38; vgl. auch *A. Badiou/J.-L. Nancy* (übersetzt von *J. Völker*), Deutsche Philosophie, Matthes & Seitz,

einer gerechten und zweckmäßigen Ordnung beruht, ein übersteigertes Produkt des „Anthropomorphismus“[21] sein. Tatsächlich könnte es sich um einen vom Interpreten auferlegten Zweck handeln. Der Inhalt des Gesetzes sollte als etwas verstanden werden, das aus dem Gesetz selbst hervorgeht und an uns herantritt. Wird diese Richtung jedoch umgekehrt, besteht die Gefahr, dass subjektive Werturteile des Interpreten – unter dem Deckmantel des objektiven Gesetzeszwecks, wonach das Gesetz auf Gerechtigkeit oder eine rationale Interessenabwägung abzielt – in das Gesetz eingeführt werden.[22] In diesem Zusammenhang erinnert auch die traditionelle Kritik am teleologischen Denkansatz daran, dass er die Ergebnisse vor die Ursachen stellt und anstelle der Prämissen, aus denen Schlussfolgerungen abgeleitet werden sollen, diese Schlussfolgerungen selbst setzt. Der Zweck konstituiert sich so, dass er das Ergebnis einschließt, das noch als ein Anderes innerhalb seiner selbst erscheint; auf diese Weise bewahrt der Zweck die Eigenschaft, sich selbst zu erhalten und allein aus sich selbst hervorgehen zu können.[23] Letztlich wäre die objektiv-teleologische Auslegung keine Gesetzesauslegung, sondern vielmehr eine selbstrechtfertigende Suche nach normativen Ergebnissen, die der praktischen Vernunft entspringen.[24] Dadurch wird auch die methodologische Intransparenz[25] zu einem Problem.

Die objektiv-teleologische Auslegung, die eine uneingeschränkte Verbindung zwischen nicht-positiven Rechtsprinzipien und dem objektiven Gesetzeszweck stillschweigend zulässt,[26] überschreitet somit den methodologischen Rahmen der Gesetzesauslegung. Das Gesetz – im Gegensatz zum

---

2017, S. 32 f.; *M. Greenberg*, Legal Interpretation, in: Stanford Encyclopedia of Philosophy (Fall 2021 Edition), S. 36 f.

21 *Puppe*, Kleine Schule (Fn. 19). 162; vgl. *R. Spaemann/R. Löw*, Die Frage Wozu?, Piper, 1985, S. 279.

22 In diesem Sinne kann die objektiv-teleologische Auslegung in Wirklichkeit als subjektiv angesehen werden. Vgl. *U. Wesel*, Juristische Weltkunde, 8. Aufl., Suhrkamp, 2000, S. 182.

23 Dazu vgl. *G. W. F. Hegel*, Enzyklopädie der philosophischen Wissenschaften I, Suhrkamp, 1986, S. 359 f.

24 *J. Neuner*, Die Rechtsfindung contra legem, 2. Aufl., C.H.Beck, 2005, S. 110; *Kriele*, Theorie (Fn. 19), S. 173.

25 Vgl. *B. Rüthers/C. Fischer/A. Birk*, Rechtstheorie und Juristische Methodenlehre, 12. Aufl., C.H.Beck, 2022, Rn. 813 ff.; *Neuner*, Allgemeiner Teil (Fn. 8), § 4, Rn. 44; *J. Lindner*, Rechtswissenschaft als Metaphysik, Mohr Siebeck, 2017, S. 85 f.; *R. Seinecke*, Methode und Zivilrecht bei Claus-Wilhelm Canaris, in: *J. Rückert/R. Seinecke* (Hg.), Methodik des Zivilrechts, 3. Aufl., Nomos, 2017, Rn. 1019, 1078.

26 Vgl. *G. Wagner*, Zivilrechtswissenschaft heute, in: *H. Dreier* (Hg.), Rechtswissenschaft als Beruf, Mohr Siebeck, 2018, S. 174.

Naturgesetz[27] – zielt von vornherein darauf ab, innerhalb eines bestimmten Problembereichs oder einer Fallgruppe eine begrenzte rechtliche Perspektive zu schaffen.[28] Es bietet niemals unmittelbar ein allgemeines Rechts- oder Gerechtigkeitskonzept wie ein Naturgesetz, sondern stellt lediglich begrenzte Maßstäbe zur punktuellen Lösung spezifischer Fallgruppen innerhalb der gesamten normativen Ordnung bereit. Es ist, als würde die Zeitlichkeit als eine unsichtbare Kraft durch die Räumlichkeit als eine begrenzte Ordnung ersetzt.

In diesem Zusammenhang stellt sich die Frage nach der Tragfähigkeit des teleologischen Denkens. Der hier diskutierte Charakter dieser Denkweise, wobei je nach Anwendungsbereich unterschiedliche Auffassungen bestehen können,[29] lässt sich als eine Perspektive verstehen, die primär die Überlegenheit des Denkens über den Zweck (*telos*) gegenüber dem Denken über die Ursache (*causa*) betont. Während Ersteres mit Fragen wie „Wohin" oder „Wozu" verknüpft ist und sich auf Erwartungen für die Zukunft oder die Rechtfertigung eines fremden, heteronomen Sollens bezieht, ist Letzteres mit der Frage nach dem „Woher" verbunden und reflektiert einen inneren oder selbstgesetzten Zweck.[30] Das bedeutet, dass die Teleologie weder über das Objekt selbst noch über die Bedingungen seiner realen Kausalität sprechen kann. Vielmehr betrachtet sie ein Objekt so, als sei es durch Zwecke hervorgebracht worden, und setzt implizit die Existenz eines diesem Objekt vorausgehenden Konzepts voraus. Infolgedessen zeigt die Teleologie nicht die tatsächlichen Kausalbedingungen eines Objekts oder Prozesses auf, sondern legt vielmehr die Bedingungen fest, unter denen etwas beurteilt wird.[31] Mit anderen Worten: Sie fungiert als regulative Idee und neigt dazu, eine Richtung vorzugeben, die willkürlich sowohl mit dem Anfang als auch mit dem Ende eines Objekts oder Verfahrens in Verbindung gebracht werden kann.[32] Letztlich führt diese teleologische Perspektive dazu, dass ein gegebenes Einzelgesetz in übertriebener Weise als etwas Organisches betrachtet wird, das über eine inhärente Fähigkeit

27 Vgl. *H. Kelsen*, Zur Lehre vom Gesetz im formellen und materiellen Sinn, mit besonderer Berücksichtigung der österreichischen Verfassung, in: *M. Jestaedt* (Hg.), Hans Kelsen Werke, Bd. 3, Mohr Siebeck, 2010, S. 236 f.

28 Vgl. *W. Hamacher*, Sprachgerechtigkeit, S.Fischer, 2018, S. 42.

29 *I. Kant*, Kritik der Urteilskraft, Felix Meiner, 2009, S. 335 f. (= B364 ff.).

30 *B. Hübner*, Der metaphysische Identitäts-Bruch: Einbruch des kausal-logischen in das teleo-logische Denken, Bd. 1, Passagen Verlag, 2010, S. 23; vgl. *N. Luhmann*, Gesellschaftsstruktur und Semantik, Bd. 3, Suhrkamp, 1989, S. 10 ff., 16.

31 *Lefebvre*, Image (Fn. 19), S. 27.

32 *Luhmann*, Gesellschaftsstruktur (Fn. 30), S. 19 ff., 23.

zur einheitlichen Selbstorganisation verfügt. In diesem Zusammenhang werden auch die inhaltlichen Grenzen des Gesetzes unscharf, wodurch es sich von dem Recht oder der Gerechtigkeit unterscheidet.

Der objektive Gesetzeszweck bleibt ebenso unklar wie seine begriffliche Bestimmung. Dies birgt die Gefahr, dass faktische Kräfte oder einige dogmatische Prinzipien übermäßig Einfluss ausüben, selbst wenn sie nicht in unmittelbarem Zusammenhang mit dem einzelnen punktuellen Gesetzesinhalt stehen. Diese Problematik ergibt sich aus der Prämisse der objektiv-teleologischen Gesetzesauslegung, wonach das Gesetz primär darauf abzielt, eine für den jeweiligen Fall angemessene Lösung zu finden. Der Gesetzesinhalt wird dabei an diesem Zweck oder Ziel ausgerichtet, was jedoch das Risiko einer übermäßigen Selbstrechtfertigung des Gesetzes in sich trägt. Ein solches Verständnis kann zu einer verzerrten Gesetzesauslegung führen, indem es den konkreten Gesetzesinhalt verkennt und stattdessen ein fiktives System konstruiert, das den Anschein erweckt, eine in sich geschlossene und harmonische Lösung zu bieten. Diese Auslegungsmethode, die auf einer derartigen ontologischen Bedeutungsebene beruht, hat zur Folge, dass sich die Interpretation vorrangig auf eine metaphysische Dimension des Gesetzes konzentriert und dabei dessen substanziellen sowie tatsächlich gegebenen Gehalt vernachlässigt. Infolgedessen wird kein methodischer Zugang zur Gesetzesauslegung eröffnet, sondern lediglich die ontologische Betrachtung des Gesetzes betont. Es bleibt fraglich, inwiefern diese Art des Verständnisses die Erfassung des gesetzlichen Sollens konkret beeinflussen kann.[33] So wie sich die Farbe nicht vom Objekt, das sie reflektiert, trennen lässt, lassen sich auch die Anhaftung an das Gesetzbuch und das Nachdenken über die inhärente Logik der Gesetzestexte – so selbstverständlich wie paradoxerweise – als notwendige Bedingungen verstehen, um rechtsethische Argumente im Gesetzesinhalt zu erfassen; nicht um das von jenseits Kommende zu betrachten, sondern um den Gegenstand der Interpretation, mit dem der Interpret Auge in Auge gegenübersteht,[34] als bereits gegebene[35] Simultaneität zu verstehen – eine Simultaneität, innerhalb derer der Interpretationsprozess des Interpreten aus antirealistischer Perspektive

33 *Lee*, Rechtsethische Auslegung (Fn. 4), S. 50 f.

34 Vgl. *E. Betti*, Zur Grundlegung einer allgemeinen Auslegungslehre, J.C.B.Mohr, 1988, S. 14 f.

35 Vgl. *O. Marquard*, Zukunft braucht Herkunft, Reclam, 2015, S. 74 ff.

weder mit dem Gegenstand identifiziert noch mit ihm verschmolzen werden darf.[36]

Wie die Gefahr einer übermäßigen Selbstrechtfertigung des Gesetzesinhalts zeigt, erkennt die objektiv-teleologische Auslegung bei der Berücksichtigung rechtsethischer Wertungen des Gesetzes nicht deren gesetzliche Bedeutung, sondern lediglich die Wertung als solche. Dies liegt daran, dass erst unter dieser Voraussetzung die Vorstellung einer harmonischen Lösung individuell entgegengesetzter rechtlicher Interessen leicht erreicht werden kann, was als charakteristisches Merkmal des teleologischen Denkens angesehen wird. Das bedeutet, dass der Zweckbegriff zwar nicht die gesamte Realität des Objekts konstituiert, jedoch als reflexive Grundlage dient, die es ermöglicht, die Einheit und Verknüpfung verschiedener Elemente als Ganzes zu bewerten. Dadurch wird letztlich anerkannt, dass das Ganze den einzelnen Teilen eine zweckmäßige Bedeutung verleiht.[37]

Auf diese Weise häuft das teleologische Denken unaufhörlich Zwecke aufeinander, negiert den ihm innewohnenden Widerspruch und strebt nach einem kohärenten System zur Selbsterhaltung. Dabei werden die konkreten, mit dem jeweiligen Fall verbundenen Inhalte nicht in ihrer tatsächlichen Bedeutung ernst genommen, sondern gewissermaßen neutralisiert.[38] Ein solches Verständnis verwässert die im Gesetz bereits enthaltenen rechtsethischen Minimalwertungen, die häufig als bloße Ausnahmen abgewertet werden, und transformiert sie zu übergeordneten Wertungen oder objektivierten Gesetzeszwecken. Diese rechtsethischen Minimalwertungen werden dann nicht mehr als Bestandteil des Gesetzesinhalts verstanden, sondern lediglich als außerhalb des Gesetzes existierende Prinzipien oder als wertende Aspekte, die sich ausschließlich auf die Rechtsfortbildung beziehen.

D. Rechtsethische Auslegung

Wie oben dargelegt, lässt die Gesetzesauslegung im Lichte des objektiven Gesetzeszwecks Raum für Missverständnisse bezüglich des Gesetzesinhalts. In diesem Kontext stellt sich die Frage, welche methodologische Perspekti-

---

36 Vgl. *H. Krämer*, Kritik der Hermeneutik, C.H.Beck, 2007, S. 14 ff., 201 ff.; *G. Figal*, Gegenständlichkeit, Mohr Siebeck, 2006, S. 95 ff., 126 ff.; *S. Lindroos-Hovinheimo*, Justice and the Ethics of Legal Interpretation, Routledge, 2012, S. 62.

37 Siehe dazu *Lefebvre*, Image (Fn. 19), S. 33.

38 Vgl. *J. Derrida* (übersetzt von *H. Brühmann*), Schurken, Suhrkamp, 2006, S. 173.

ve angenommen werden sollte, um einerseits eine vollständige Ethisierung des Gesetzes zu vermeiden und andererseits den wertbezogenen Sinn einzelner Gesetzesvorschriften präzise zu erfassen und anzuwenden.

Die punktuelle Einbeziehung rechtsethischer Argumente in die Gesetzesauslegung (rechtsethische Auslegung) sollte nicht als Versuch verstanden werden, ein einheitliches Bewertungssystem für die relevanten rechtsethischen Wertungen zu etablieren. Vielmehr gilt sie als eine Anpassung des Verständnisses des positiven Rechts an spezifische Interessenslagen innerhalb des Spannungsverhältnisses zwischen rechtsdogmatischem Verständnis und rechtsethischer Legitimation. Rechtsethische Wertungen, die sich auf die inhaltliche Rechtfertigung oder Kritik des positiven Rechts beziehen,[39] ermöglichen verschiedene inhaltliche Auslegungsansätze, die normative sowie empirische Erkenntnisse über das Bestehen und die Wirkungsweise des Rechts berücksichtigen. Aufgrund dieser Variabilität können beim Verständnis des Gesetzesinhalts punktuelle Widersprüche oder Konflikte zwischen rechtsethischen Wertungen entstehen. In diesem Zusammenhang ist es von entscheidender Bedeutung, dass solche Widersprüche und Diskontinuitäten ernst genommen und reflektiert werden, anstatt – wie es bei der Orientierung am objektiven Gesetzeszweck oft geschieht – sie übermäßig harmonisierend zu vereinheitlichen.[40]

Bei der Betrachtung der rechtsethischen Argumente wird schnell deutlich, dass Begriffe wie Treu und Glauben oder Gerechtigkeit äußerst abstrakt sind und eine Vielzahl unterschiedlicher Interessen und Wertungen umfassen können. Solche konzeptionell weit gefassten rechtsethischen Argumente können in konfligierenden Interessenslagen gleichermaßen von beiden Seiten herangezogen werden. Ein anschauliches Beispiel hierfür sind politische Auseinandersetzungen, bei denen gegensätzliche Interessengruppen auf der Straße demonstrieren und jeweils identische Plakate mit der Aufschrift „Wahrheit" oder „Gerechtigkeit" hochhalten.[41] Diese Mehrdeutigkeit zeigt, dass rechtsethische Argumente je nach Perspektive

---

39 Zur Rechtsethik vgl. *D. v. d. Pfordten*, Rechtsethik, 2. Aufl., C.H.Beck, 2011, S. 1, 7; *L. Kähler*, Begriff und Rechtfertigung abdingbaren Rechts, Mohr Siebeck, 2012, S. 230; *S. Kirste*, Rechtsphilosophie, 2. Aufl., Nomos, 2020, S. 23 ff.; *H. Dreier*, Rechtsethik und staatliche Legitimität, Universitas 4/1993, 377, 377; vgl. auch *F. Bydlinski*, Der Begriff des Rechts, Verlag Österreich, 2015, S. 227 ff.

40 *Lee*, Rechtsethische Auslegung (Fn. 4), S. 45; vgl. *I. Augsberg*, Methodisch verfahren, JZ 2024, 157, 163 f.

41 *M. Walzer*, Thick and Thin – Moral Argument at Home and Abroad, University of Notre Dame Press, 1994, S. 1.

unterschiedlich interpretiert werden können. Gerade angesichts dieser Problematik erweist sich ein minimalistischer Ansatz der rechtsethischen Argumente als sinnvoll.

Der rechtsethische Minimalismus zielt darauf ab, rechtsethische Wertungen so weit wie möglich auf differenzierte Rechtfertigungen zu beschränken. Die Berücksichtigung eines minimalen rechtsethischen Arguments an dieser Stelle steht nicht in direktem Zusammenhang mit dem Verständnis der Natur oder des Wesens des Rechts. Vielmehr dient sie lediglich als methodologischer Orientierungspunkt, um einen Zugang zu den gesetzlichen Inhalten zu ermöglichen. Im Kontext des rechtsethischen Minimalismus könnte die in der bisherigen rechtsphilosophischen Diskussion aufgeworfene Frage aufkommen, ob ein moralisches Minimum[42] als essenzieller und universeller Bestandteil des Rechts angesehen werden kann. In der vorliegenden Arbeit wird der Begriff des rechtsethischen Minimalismus jedoch nicht in diesem Sinne eines moralischen Minimums verstanden oder verwendet. Das bedeutet, dass es hierbei nicht notwendigerweise um ein essenzielles und universell gültiges Element des Rechts geht. Vielmehr steht im Vordergrund, dass rechtsethische Werte beim Verständnis gesetzlicher Inhalte partiell und punktuell einbezogen und berücksichtigt werden. So ist beispielsweise bei der Einbeziehung der Gerechtigkeit in die Gesetzesauslegung zu beachten, dass sie einerseits nicht die allgemeine und einheitliche Dimension des Rechts entfaltet und andererseits auch keine bloße Fortsetzung des Rechts darstellt.[43]

Aus dieser Perspektive existiert keine von vornherein festgelegte Hierarchie zwischen den rechtsethischen Minimalwertungen; sie bestehen in pluralistischer Weise.[44] Zudem können die zwischen ihnen auftretenden Widersprüche und Inkohärenzen in Betracht gezogen und berücksichtigt werden. Angesichts dieser Eigenschaft des rechtsethischen Minimums impliziert dies keine einseitige oder bereits vorab festgelegte Vollkommenheit rechtsethischer Werte. Es geht hier also nicht um eine bestimmte logische Kontinuität oder eine Grundlage, die zur Maximierung dieser rechtsethi-

42 Dazu vgl. *H. Kelsen*, Reine Rechtslehre, 2. Aufl., Franz Deuticke, 1960, S. 68; *H. L. A. Hart*, The Concept of Law, 3rd ed., Oxford University Press, 2012, S. 193 ff.; *L. Green*, The Morality in Law, in: *L. d'Almeida/J. Edwards/A. Dolcetti* (eds.), Reading HLA Hart's The Concept of Law, Hart Publishing, 2013, S. 184 ff.; vgl. *R. Forst*, Zwei Bilder der Gerechtigkeit, in: *R. Forst* u. a. (Hg.), Sozialphilosophie und Kritik, Suhrkamp, 2009, S. 218 ff.

43 Vgl. *B. Waldenfels*, Schattenrisse der Moral, Suhrkamp, 2006, S. 130.

44 Vgl. auch *F. Bydlinski*, System und Prinzipien des Privatrechts, Springer, 1996, S. 25 ff.

schen Werte führt, sondern lediglich um ihre Teilaspekte oder Fragmente, deren Realisierbarkeit jeweils von den konkreten Interessenlagen abhängt. Diese Fragmente spalten oder mindern jedoch nicht die Existenz eines zugrunde liegenden normativen Anspruchs der rechtsethischen Werte. Daher ist eine objektive und vollständige Rechtfertigung rechtsethischer Werte an dieser Stelle nicht zwingend erforderlich.[45] Stattdessen ist entscheidend, wie überzeugend minimale rechtsethische Argumente innerhalb der Pluralität dargelegt werden. Die Bewertung nach Kriterien wie Billigkeit, Gerechtigkeit und Verhältnismäßigkeit ist dabei grundsätzlich situationsbedingt und muss individuell sowie partiell vorgenommen werden. Der rechtsethische Minimalismus akzeptiert also keine rein regelhafte, neutrale oder uniforme Maßgabe für die Überzeugungskraft rechtsethischer Rechtfertigungen.[46]

Innerhalb des Bedeutungsspektrums einer rechtsethischen Wertung kann das rechtsethische Minimum als jener Teil verstanden werden, dessen Relevanz in einem bestimmten Kontext für alle offensichtlich sein muss.[47] Durch eine möglichst präzise und konkrete Formulierung rechtsethischer Wertungen steigt die Wahrscheinlichkeit, dass sie in spezifischen Interessenslagen angemessen berücksichtigt werden können. Entscheidender als die Frage, ob innerhalb der Gemeinschaft weitgehende Einigkeit über die rechtsethischen Wertungen besteht, ist die Intensität und Klarheit des rechtsethischen Minimums.[48] Selbstverständlich gibt es keinen formalen Algorithmus zur Bestimmung des rechtsethischen Minimums. Es hängt vielmehr vom jeweiligen Kontext und der Möglichkeit der Rechtfertigung spezifischer Interessenslagen ab. Im Streben nach einer harmonischen Einheit, die auf eine umfassende Wertung ausgerichtet ist, werden die Intensität und Klarheit tendenziell abgeschwächt. Je offener jedoch Widersprüche oder Konflikte mit anderen Minimalwertungen offengelegt werden, desto stärker treten die Intensität und Klarheit hervor. Dabei löst sich die Intensität von einer Denkweise, die nach einer in sich geschlossenen Erkenntnis strebt, und formuliert keine allgemeinen Prinzipien. Vielmehr manifestiert

---

45 Vgl. *L. Kähler*, Pluralismus und Monismus in der normativen Rekonstruktion des Privatrechts, in: *M. Grünberger/N. Jansen* (Hg.), Privatrechtstheorie heute, Mohr Siebeck, 2017, S. 125.

46 *Lee*, Rechtsethische Auslegung (Fn. 4), S. 62.

47 BeckOGK/*Kähler*, BGB § 242, Rn. 259.

48 *Lee*, Rechtsethische Auslegung (Fn. 4), S. 61; vgl. *Walzer*, Thick and Thin (Fn. 41), S. 6; *C. Sunstein*, Legal Reasoning and Political Conflict, 2nd ed., Oxford University Press, 2018, S. 35 ff., 45 ff.

sie sich als äußerste Differenz und verbrennt das, worauf etwas an sich selbst einfach zeigt.[49]

Eine solche Minimalisierung rechtsethischer Argumente im Rahmen der Gesetzesauslegung ermöglicht es, den impliziten Gesetzesinhalt aus verschiedenen Perspektiven zu erfassen. Sie richtet den Blick nicht nur auf die Selbstrechtfertigung des Gesetzes, sondern berücksichtigt auch die vielfältigen Differenzierungen und Modifikationen, die mit der Reduktion rechtsethischer Argumente einhergehen. Diese methodologische Perspektive befindet sich auf einer anderen Ebene als die Frage der Letztbegründung[50] rechtsethischer Werte. Statt sich mit solchen metaethischen Problemen zu befassen, betrachtet sie vielmehr die Möglichkeit alternativer Gesetzesauslegungen, die auf rechtsethischen Minimalwertungen basieren. Eine derartige Auslegungsmethode erweist sich als wirksam, indem sie die Realisierungsmöglichkeiten der im Gesetz enthaltenen rechtsethischen Wertungen einzeln überprüft. In diesem Sinne werden rechtsethische Argumente nicht pauschal in den objektiven Gesetzeszweck einbezogen, sondern weiterhin in ihren potenziellen Widersprüchen und Diskontinuitäten reflektiert. Gerade diese kritische Perspektive nimmt die rechtsethische Auslegung ernst.

In der Regel manifestieren sich rechtsethische Minimalwertungen in Form negativer Aussagen,[51] die aufzeigen, was mit ihnen nicht vereinbar ist, ohne jedoch unmittelbar eine spezifische Lösung vorzuschlagen. Angesichts dessen muss die rechtsethische Auslegung in reflektiver Weise erfolgen.[52] Zunächst wird eine rechtsethische Minimalwertung oder ein Rechtssatz im Zusammenhang mit einer bestimmten Gesetzesvorschrift formuliert und anschließend daraufhin geprüft, ob er zur betreffenden Interessenslage passt. Diese Rechtssätze werden experimentell vorgeschlagen und ihre Übereinstimmung überprüft – ähnlich wie bei der Hypothesenbildung in der empirischen Forschung. Es ist wesentlich, wie bei einem Experiment

---

49 Vgl. *M. Blanchot* (übersetzt von *G. Poppenberg/H. Weidemann*), Die Schrift des Desasters, Wilhelm Fink, 2005, S. 74.

50 Dazu vgl. *J. Lindner*, Rechtswissenschaft als Gerechtigkeitswissenschaft, RW 2011, 1, 9; *H. Albert*, Traktat über kritische Vernunft, 3. Aufl., Mohr Siebeck, 1975, S. 13 ff., 257 ff.; *K. Seelmann/D. Demko*, Rechtsphilosophie, 6. Aufl., C.H.Beck, 2014, § 9, Rn. 47 ff.; vgl. auch *M. Seel*, Theorien, 2. Aufl., S.Fischer, 2009, S. 128; *J. Nida-Rümelin*, Ethische Essays, Suhrkamp, 2002, S. 23.

51 Vgl. BeckOGK/*Kähler*, BGB § 242, Rn. 263.

52 Dazu vgl. *F. Kaulbach*, Experiment, Perspektive und Urteilskraft bei der Rechtserkenntnis, ARSP 1989, 447, 448, 455; *R. Zippelius*, Die experimentierende Methode im Recht, ARSP-Beiheft 44, 411, 412 ff.; vgl. auch *R. M. Hare* (übersetzt von *G. Meggle*), Freiheit und Vernunft, Suhrkamp, 1983, S. 106 ff.

mit Lackmuspapier, fortwährend rechtsethische Werte im Kontext der Rechtsdogmatik gegenüberzustellen.[53] Diese experimentelle Herangehensweise bei der Gesetzesauslegung strebt danach, aus den vielfältigen Möglichkeiten der rechtsethischen Rechtfertigung oder Kritik diejenigen zu ermitteln, die am überzeugendsten sind. Dies beruht letztendlich in gewissem Maße auf dem abduktiven[54] Denkansatz. Eine auf dieser Grundlage basierende rechtsethische Auslegung zielt letztlich zum Besserverstehen darauf ab, das bereits in gewissem Maße verstandenen Gesetz weiter zu vertiefen und sämtliche impliziten Bedeutungen maximal auszuschöpfen[55]. Dabei werden potenzielle Konflikte oder Widersprüche zwischen rechtsethischen Minimalwertungen innerhalb des Gesetzes ernst genommen und in den Auslegungsprozess einbezogen. Schließlich tragen diese Unstimmigkeiten oder Widersprüche dazu bei, die rechtsethischen Minimalwertungen als Teil des Gesetzesinhalts zu erkennen.

E. Methodologische Anwendung

Gemäß der experimentellen, auf Vergleich und Kontrast der rechtsethischen Minimalwertungen basierenden Auslegungsmethode sollte ihr Prozess an einem bestimmten Punkt innerhalb des Kontinuums der Auslegungsmöglichkeiten aktiv abgeschlossen werden, indem rechtsethische Argumente als Gesetzesinhalt erfasst werden. Entscheidend sind dabei nicht eine spezifische und eindeutige Bedeutung, die präzise zu einer Gesetzesvorschrift passt, sondern vielmehr die vielfältigen Relationen zwischen den Auslegungsmöglichkeiten. Zwar lässt sich empirisch feststellen, dass die Gesetzesauslegung für die Praxis erst dann als abgeschlossen gilt, wenn der Gesetzesinhalt auf die relevanten Sachverhalte angewendet wird.[56] Jedoch wird die als Gesetzesinhalt verstandene rechtsethische Minimalwertung aufgrund ihrer normativen Natur nicht nahtlos in die Sachverhalte eingefügt, sondern sie umfasst diese in einem weiteren Sinne. Die rechtsethische Auslegung konzentriert sich daher auf die Wechselbeziehungen,

---

53 „»Paßt das?« —Mach ein Experiment!" (*L. Wittgenstein* (übersetzt von *J. Schulte*), Vortrag über Ethik und andere kleine Schriften, Suhrkamp, 1989, S. 135).

54 *C. Peirce*, Collected Papers of Charles Sanders Peirce, Vol. V and VI, Harvard University Press, 1974, S. 105 ff.; vgl. *J. Habermas*, Auch eine Geschichte der Philosophie, Bd. 2, Suhrkamp, 2020, S. 703 ff.; *J. Lege*, Pragmatismus und Jurisprudenz, Mohr Siebeck, 1999, S. 398 ff., 438 ff.

55 Vgl. *Habermas*, Auch eine Geschichte der Philosophie (Fn. 54), S. 721.

56 Vgl. *S. Müller-Mall*, Verfassende Urteile, Suhrkamp, 2023, S. 161 f.

in denen rechtsethische Minimalwertungen sowohl beeinflussen als auch beeinflusst werden. Dementsprechend wird der Abschluss oder der Umfang der rechtsethischen Auslegung erst dann deutlich, wenn eine juristische Beurteilung der Sachverhalte unter Berücksichtigung der gegenseitigen Relationen rechtsethischer Wertungen sowie der Rechtsfortbildung erfolgt.

In der Regel erfolgt die Rechtsfortbildung, indem konkrete Lösungen außerhalb des Gesetzes geschaffen werden, wenn im Gesetz keine angemessene Auslegungsmöglichkeit besteht. Sie darf jedoch grundsätzlich nur dann vorgenommen werden, wenn sie durch anerkannte Rechtsgrundsätze oder rechtsethische Wertungen gerechtfertigt ist. Demgegenüber befasst sich die rechtsethische Auslegung mit der Frage, ob und inwieweit rechtsethische Wertungen als potenzieller und impliziter Gesetzesinhalt situationsbedingt verstanden werden können. Während die rechtsethische Auslegung und die Rechtsfortbildung aus formaler Sicht als voneinander getrennt erscheinen, ist diese Unterscheidung in der Praxis nicht immer eindeutig. Hieraus ergibt sich ein Spannungsverhältnis, das aus der Natur rechtsethischer Wertungen und insbesondere aus dem Prinzip der Gesetzesbindung resultiert; nämlich die Spannung zwischen der rechtsethischen Auslegung und der rechtsethischen Legitimation der Rechtsfortbildung. Daher kann die Rechtsfortbildung nicht unmittelbar erfolgen, ohne dass zuvor eine Auslegungsmöglichkeit auf Grundlage rechtsethischer Minimalwertungen innerhalb des Gesetzes berücksichtigt wurde. Darüber hinaus ist zu beachten, dass rechtsethische Minimalwertungen nicht ausschließlich auf den Gesetzesinhalt beschränkt sind. Vielmehr stehen die rechtsethische Auslegung des impliziten Gesetzesinhalts und die rechtsethische Legitimation der Rechtsfortbildung letztlich in einem Verhältnis der Gewichtung zueinander. Diese beiden methodologischen Prozesse durchdringen sich bis zu einem gewissen Grad gegenseitig, sodass eine Zunahme der einen Seite eine Abnahme der anderen bewirken kann und sie in einem Kontinuum wechselseitiger Beeinflussung stehen.[57] In diesem Sinne stellt die rechtsethische Auslegung selbst den Ausgangspunkt der Rechtsfortbildung bereit, während die Ergebnisse dieser Auslegung als inhaltliche Rechtfertigungselemente zur Legitimation der durch die Rechtsfortbildung geschaffenen Rechtskonstruktionen beitragen.

57 Vgl. *D. v. d. Pfordten*, Deskription, Evaluation, Präskription, Duncker & Humblot, 1993, S. 433 f.

Hierdurch sollte man sich von einer methodologischen Sichtweise verabschieden, die rechtsethische Wertungen im Rahmen der Gesetzesauslegung als objektive Gesetzeszwecke in ihrer übergeordneten Form – etwa als Rechtssicherheit, Verhältnismäßigkeit oder rationaler Konfliktlösung – betrachtet und zugleich kleinere, gegensätzliche oder widersprüchliche rechtsethische Argumente lediglich in Einklang bringt. Denn rechtsethische Wertungen in ihrer abstrakten Form stehen nicht in direktem Zusammenhang mit den gesetzlichen Inhalten für bestimmte Fallgruppen, da sie vielmehr dem Bereich des Rechts oder der Ethik zuzuordnen sind. Folglich liegt es im Bereich des Rechts, innerhalb umfassender rechtsethischer Wertungen eine Harmonie der Teile anzustreben – eine Aufgabe, die der Rechtsfortbildung zugewiesen ist. Im Spannungsverhältnis zwischen rechtsdogmatischen Gesetzesvorgaben und rechtsethischer Legitimation kann die durch die rechtsethische Auslegung erkannte rechtsethische Minimalwertung den Ausgangspunkt der Rechtsfortbildung legitimieren und deren Rechtfertigungslast im Vergleich zu anderen Fällen verringern. Zudem erfordert das Prinzip der Gesetzesbindung, dass die Rechtsfortbildung möglichst gesetzesnah[58] erfolgen muss. Dieser normativen Anforderung kann auch die rechtsethische Auslegung gerecht werden, die auf dem Konzept des rechtsethischen Minimalismus basiert.

Gestützt auf die rechtsethische Auslegung wird es wahrscheinlicher, dass die konkrete Rechtsfortbildung verstärkt in Richtung der Zulassung von Analogien als möglichst gesetzesnahe Form der Rechtsfortbildung erfolgt. Die unmittelbare Rechtfertigung des aus der Analogie resultierenden Ergebnisses gehört zwar zu den rechtsethischen Wertungen, die außerhalb des Gesetzes liegen. Wird jedoch ein Teil dieser rechtsethischen Wertungen auch als Gesetzesinhalt anerkannt, so verstärkt dies – im Zusammenhang mit dem Grundsatz der Gesetzesbindung – die Nähe der Rechtsfortbildung zum Gesetz und führt zu einer Analogie, die eine relativ geringere Rechtfertigungsanforderung als im Fall einer reinen Rechtsfortbildung hat. Insbesondere trägt die rechtsethische Auslegung dazu bei, rechtsethische Minimalwertungen gesetzlicher Inhalte in entsprechende Analogieschlüsse einzubeziehen. Dies gilt vor allem für solche Wertungen, die mit Ausnahmevorschriften im Gesetz verbunden sind.[59] In der bisherigen objektiv-te-

58 *C. Fischer*, Topoi verdeckter Rechtsfortbildungen im Zivilrecht, Mohr Siebeck, 2007, S. 493 f.

59 Es wird oft vertreten, dass Ausnahmevorschriften eng auszulegen sind und dass eine Analogie ihrem Wesen nach unzulässig ist (*singularia non sunt extendenda*). Aus

leologischen Auslegung wurden diese rechtsethischen Minimalwertungen hingegen häufig deshalb als bloße Ausnahmen in den Bereich der Rechtsfortbildung verdrängt, weil der objektive Gesetzeszweck eindimensional und abstrakt verstanden wurde. Dabei besteht eine hohe Wahrscheinlichkeit, dass nicht unmittelbar relevante faktische Kräfte oder etablierte dogmatische Prinzipien unter dem Vorwand des objektiven Gesetzeszwecks einen übermäßigen Einfluss ausüben. Dies liegt daran, dass die objektiv-teleologische Auslegung grundlegend davon ausgeht, dass eine der jeweiligen Situation angemessene Lösung zu finden ist und diese als Maßstab dient, um den Inhalt des Gesetzes zu bestimmen. Jedoch konzentriert sich diese Art der Gesetzesauslegung, wie zuvor erörtert, ausschließlich auf die ontologische Selbstrechtfertigung des Gesetzes und versäumt es, die darin enthaltenen individuellen und gegensätzlichen Bedeutungszusammenhänge zu betrachten. Schließlich ermöglicht die rechtsethische Auslegung eine methodische Distanzierung von der Denkweise, die die strikte Regel-Ausnahme-Struktur des Gesetzes auf der Grundlage eines abstrakten objektiven Gesetzeszwecks verfestigt. Stattdessen erlaubt sie es, Widersprüche oder Komplementarität der rechtsethischen Minimalwertungen sowie die darauf basierenden Auslegungsmöglichkeiten als Bestandteil des Gesetzesinhalts zu erfassen. Dadurch lässt sich der implizite Gesetzesinhalt näher an die jeweilige Interessenlage anpassen, ohne an ein formal-logisches Argumentationsverfahren gebunden zu sein, das bisher durch die Stabilität der Rechtsdogmatik gesetzliche Ausnahmen weitgehend verhinderte. Darin zeigt sich der methodische Vorteil der rechtsethischen Auslegung. Zudem erfüllt die rechtsethische Auslegung die Funktion, methodologisch sicherzustellen, dass gesetzliche Ausnahmen stets im Lichte rechtsethischer Minimalwertungen reflektiert werden.

Es gab einen Maler, der ausschließlich auf kleinen Leinwänden malte – etwa in der Größe von zwei aneinandergelegten Erwachsenenhänden. Es hieß, dies sei notwendig, um die Komposition im Griff zu behalten. Eine

---

methodologischer Perspektive ist es jedoch problematisch, einer derart generalisierten Behauptung uneingeschränkt zu folgen. Eine solche Argumentation beruht im Wesentlichen auf einem formal-logischen Ansatz und setzt lediglich die Vollständigkeit der Rechtsordnung voraus. Dazu vgl. MüKoBGB/*Säcker*, Einleitung, Rn. 123 ff.; *C. Herresthal/J. Weiß*, Fälle zur Methodenlehre, 2. Aufl., C.H.Beck, 2023, Rn. 197; *F. Müller/R. Christensen*, Juristische Methodik, Bd. I, 11. Aufl., Duncker & Humblot, 2013, Rn. 373; *M. Würdinger*, Die Analogiefähigkeit von Normen, AcP 2006, 946, 965 ff.

Methodik muss zumindest eine vergleichbare Ehrlichkeit aufweisen – sei es in der Kunst oder im Recht.

Grundriss der Rechtsgewinnungstheorie *Arthur Kaufmanns*

– Ein Quartett von Abduktion, Induktion, Analogie und Deduktion –

Su Gil An

I.

Arthur Kaufmann (1923–2001) ist ein großer Rechtswissenschaftler, der nach einem „dritten Weg" sucht: Zwischen Sein und Sollen, zwischen Naturrecht und Rechtspositivismus sowie zwischen Objektivität und Subjektivität versucht er einen dritten Weg einzuschlagen, der nicht auf „Entweder-oder", sondern auf „Sowohl-als-auch" basiert.[1]

Seine Bemühung, zwischen zwei Extremen die goldene Mitte zu finden, ist auch bei seiner juristischen Methodenlehre deutlich spürbar. Er lehnte die herkömmliche Sichtweise ab, die zwischen Rechtsphilosophie zum einen und Methodenlehre zum anderen scharf unterscheidet. Traditionell hat man die Frage „Was ist Recht?" (Was?) einerseits und die Frage „Wie erkennt man Recht?" (Wie?) andererseits voneinander getrennt und dann die erste Frage dem Bereich der Rechtsphilosophie zugeordnet und die zweite dem der Methodenlehre. Danach beschränkt sich die Aufgabe der juristischen Methodenlehre nur darauf, bereits vorhandenes positives Recht formal-logisch auszulegen und auf den Fall anzuwenden. Dagegen wendet *Kaufmann* ein, dass „Was"-Frage und „Wie"-Frage nicht so getrennt untersucht werden sollen. So strebt er danach, eine neue dynamische Methodenlehre aufzubauen, welche Rechtsidee (Sollen) und Rechtsrealität (Sein) miteinander abstimmen und dadurch ein richtiges, lebendiges Recht gewinnen kann.[2]

---

1 *A. Kaufmann*, Rechtsphilosophie, 2. Aufl., München 1997, S. 40 ff.; *S.-I. Liu*, Arthur Kaufmanns „Dritter Weg" zwischen Naturrecht und Rechtspositivismus. Eine Skizze, in: U. Neumann/W. Hassemer/U. Schroth (Hrsg.), Verantwortetes Recht. Die Rechtsphilosophie Arthur Kaufmanns. Tagung 10. bis 11. Mai 2003 in München, Stuttgart 2005, S. 39 ff.

2 *A. Kaufmann*, Rechtsphilosophie (Fn. 1), S. 9 f.; *Y.-W. Kim*, Die personale Rechtslehre von Arthur Kaufmann, Hanyang Law Review 26 (4), 2009, 49 (49 ff.).

Kaufmanns neuartige Methodenlehre zur Rechtsgewinnung[3] besteht aus vier Elementen, die mit jeweils unterschiedlichen Rollen aufs Engste miteinander kooperieren – nämlich: Deduktion, Induktion, Abduktion und Analogie.[4] In dieser Hinsicht bezeichnet *Robert Alexy* die Rechtsgewinnungstheorie *Kaufmanns* als „*Kaufmannsche* Quaternität“: In *Kaufmanns* Quaternität ist die „Deduktion [...] die Magd, die Analogie der König, die Induktion die fleißige Ministerin und die Abduktion ein fahrender Ritter, dessen Lebendigkeit und Wagemut verhindern, dass die Mannschaft einschläft.“[5]

Alexys Beschreibung ist meiner Meinung nach ganz korrekt. Zudem bin ich der Überzeugung, dass „*Kaufmanns* Quarternität“ dazu entscheidend beitragen kann, die juristische Methode aus einer neuen Sicht zu betrachten und damit tiefer zu verstehen. In Korea ist jedoch *Kaufmanns* Methodenlehre noch nicht ernsthaft untersucht worden. Daher möchte ich hier ihre Bausteine und Funktionsweise kurz umreißen und meine koreanischen Kolleginnen und Kollegen bitten, ihre Aufmerksamkeit auf *Kaufmanns* Rechtsgewinnungstheorie zu schenken.

II.

Zunächst wird erklärt, wie Deduktion, Induktion, Analogie und Abduktion ablaufen und wie sicher sie sind. In den folgenden Schemata bedeuten:[6]

---

3 *Kaufmann* verwendet den Begriff „Rechtsgewinnung“ als Oberbegriff, der die Begriffe „Rechtsfindung“ und „Rechtsanwendung“ im Sinne des herkömmlichen Sprachgebrauchs umfasst. *A. Kaufmann*, Das Verfahren der Rechtsgewinnung – Eine rationale Analyse: Deduktion, Induktion, Abduktion, Analogie, Erkenntnis, Dezision, Macht, München 1999, S. 12 f.

4 *A. Kaufmann*, Rechtsphilosophie (Fn. 1), S. 69 f.; *ders.*, Rechtsgewinnung (Fn. 3), S. 51 ff.

5 *R. Alexy*, Arthur Kaufmanns Theorie der Rechtsgewinnung, in: U. Neumann/W. Hassemer/U. Schroth (Hrsg.), Verantwortetes Recht (Fn. 1), S. 47.

6 *A. Kaufmann*, Die Rolle der Abduktion im Rechtsgewinnungsverfahren, in: G. Britz/H. Jung/H. Koriath/E. Müller (Hrsg.), Grundfragen staatlichen Strafens. Festschrift für Heinz Müller-Dietz zum 70. Geburtstag, München 2001, S. 349 (353).

R: Regel (Norm)
F: Fall
E: Ergebnis
——————→ sicherer Teil des Schlusses
··················→ unsicherer Teil des Schlusses
←··············→ Zirkel bzw. Spirale

1. Deduktion

Die Deduktion ist der Schluss vom Allgemeinen auf das weniger Allgemeine, das Besondere. Sie hat die folgende Struktur:[7]

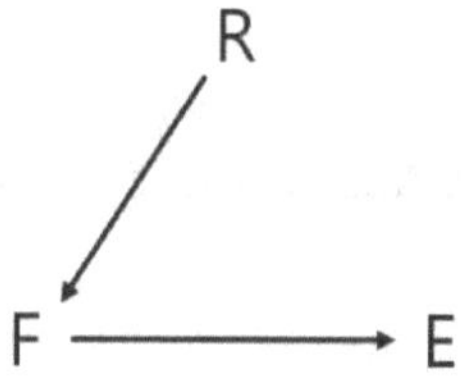

Mit dem berühmten Bohnenbeispiel hat *Charles Sanders Peirce* die Form der Deduktion folgendermaßen formuliert:

Das Bohnenbeispiel von *Peirce*:[8]

R: Alle Bohnen aus diesem Sack sind weiß (All the beans from this bag are white)
F: Diese Bohnen sind aus diesem Sack (These beans are from this bag)
E: Diese Bohnen sind weiß (These beans are white)

Um die Eigenschaft des deduktiven Schlusses zu veranschaulichen, hat *Kaufmann* dem Bohnenbeispiel das folgende Beispiel hinzugefügt:[9]

7 *A. Kaufmann*, Rechtsgewinnung (Fn. 3), S. 51 ff.; *ders.*, Abduktion (Fn. 6), S. 349 (353).
8 *C. S. Peirce*, Deduction, Induction, and Hypothesis, The Popular Science Monthly XIII, 1878, 470 (472).
9 *A. Kaufmann*, Rechtsphilosophie (Fn. 1), S. 75; *ders.*, Rechtsgewinnung (Fn. 3), S. 51.

Das Beispiel von *Kaufmann*:

R: Alle vom Gesetzgeber formal korrekt erlassenen Normen sind Recht
F: Die NS-Rassegesetze sind vom Gesetzgeber formal korrekt erlassen
E: Die NS-Rassegesetze sind Recht

Die Deduktion beginnt bei der Regel und zielt auf das Ergebnis. Bei der Deduktion ist der ganze Schluss sicher; bei den anderen Schlüssen ist nur derjenige Schritt sicher, der der Deduktion entspricht. Der deduktive Schluss ist daher zwingend; jedoch ist er nur analytisch, sodass er nichts Neues erbringt, also unser Wissen nicht erweitert. Die Regel selbst findet man mittels Induktion; es muss bedacht werden, dass die Regel auch autoritativ (durch Macht) festgesetzt sein kann (so beim zweiten Beispiel von *Kaufmann*).[10]

2. Induktion

Die Induktion ist der Schluss vom Besonderen auf das Allgemeine. Sie hat die Form:[11]

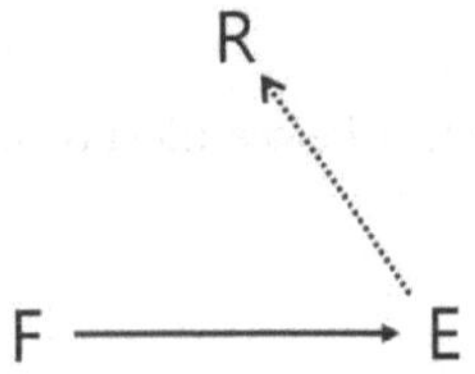

Das Bohnenbeispiel von *Peirce*:[12]

F: Diese Bohnen sind aus diesem Sack
E: Diese Bohnen sind weiß
R: Alle Bohnen aus diesem Sack sind weiß

10 *A. Kaufmann*, Rechtsphilosophie (Fn. 1), S. 75; *ders.*, Rechtsgewinnung (Fn. 3), S. 51, 54 f.

11 *A. Kaufmann*, Rechtsgewinnung (Fn. 3), S. 52 ff.; *ders.*, Abduktion (Fn. 6), S. 349 (354).

12 *C. S. Peirce*, Hypothesis (Fn. 8), 470 (472).

Das Beispiel von *Kaufmann*:[13]

> F: Die NS-Rassegesetze, das BGB, das StGB ... sind vom Gesetzgeber formal korrekt erlassen
> E: Die NS-Rassegesetze, das BGB, das StGB ... sind Recht
> R: Alle vom Gesetzgeber formal korrekt erlassenen Normen sind Recht

Die Induktion ist ein synthetischer Schluss; sie erbringt neue Kenntnisse und erweitert damit unser Wissen. Je größer die Zahl der Fälle ist, die in die Induktion einbezogen werden, desto sicherer wird die Induktion. Die Induktion ist jedoch nicht zwingend; zwingend wäre sie nur dann, wenn alle Exemplare beobachtet werden, was jedoch in der Tat unmöglich ist. Wie die obige Grafik zeigt, ist der Schritt vom Fall nach Ergebnis sicher, der Schritt vom Ergebnis nach Fall aber nicht. Folglich kann der induktive Schluss zu einem falschen Ergebnis führen – im Bohnenbeispiel ist es möglich, dass es im Sack auch nicht weiße Bohnen gibt.[14]

3. Abduktion

Die Abduktion ist der Schluss vom Besonderen über das Allgemeine auf das Besondere. Sie lässt sich so darstellen:[15]

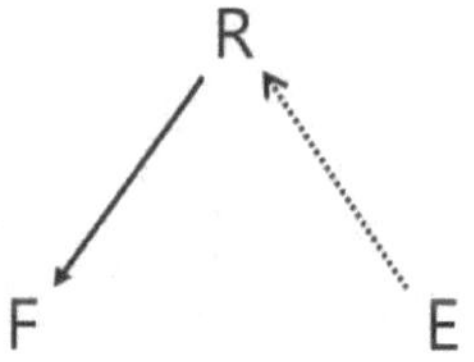

Das Bohnenbeispiel von *Peirce*:[16]

> E: Diese Bohnen sind weiß
> R: Alle Bohnen aus diesem Sack sind weiß
> F: Diese Bohnen sind aus diesem Sack (könnte aus diesem Sack sein)

---

13 *A. Kaufmann*, Rechtsphilosophie (Fn. 1), S. 76; *ders.*, Rechtsgewinnung (Fn. 3), S. 51.

14 *A. Kaufmann*, Rechtsgewinnung (Fn. 3), S. 52, 56 f.; *ders.*, Abduktion (Fn. 6), S. 349 (354).

15 *A. Kaufmann*, Rechtsgewinnung (Fn. 3), S. 53, 57 ff.; *ders.*, Abduktion (Fn. 6), S. 349 (357).

16 *C. S. Peirce*, Hypothesis (Fn. 8), 470 (472).

Das Beispiel von *Kaufmann*:[17]

E: Die NS-Rassegesetze sind Recht
R: Alle vom Gesetzgeber formal korrekt erlassenen Normen sind Recht
F: Die NS-Rassegesetze sind vom Gesetzgeber formal korrekt erlassen (könnten vom Gesetzgeber formal korrekt erlassen sein)

Die Abduktion ist ein Schluss vom Ergebnis über die Regel zum Fall. Wie die Figur illustriert, ist der Schritt vom Ergebnis nach Regel unsicher. Die Abduktion ist also ein riskanter Schluss, dessen erster Schritt schon unsicher ist; sie ist ein gewagter Schluss, der nur problematische Urteile erbringt, sodass sich jederzeit seine Unrichtigkeit herausstellen kann, da die Bohnen doch nicht aus diesem Sack stammen, die NS-Rassegesetze doch nicht korrekt erlassen sind. Wichtig ist dennoch, dass die Abduktion der Induktion vorausgeht und eine Hypothese produziert, die uns hilft, das endgültige Ergebnis zu erarbeiten. Die Abduktion leistet eine erste Orientierungshilfe.[18]

4. Analogie

Die Analogie geht vom Besonderen aus und führt dann über das Allgemeine zum Besonderen. Sie verfährt nicht linear, sondern zirkulär (spiralenförmig); ihre Struktur sieht so aus:[19]

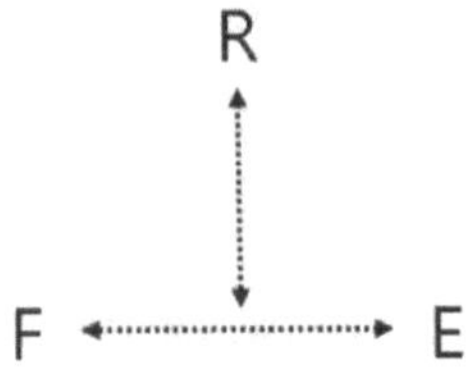

17 *A. Kaufmann*, Rechtsgewinnung (Fn. 3), S. 52.
18 *A. Kaufmann*, Rechtsphilosophie (Fn. 1), S. 76; *ders.*, Rechtsgewinnung (Fn. 3), S. 52, 57 f.
19 *A. Kaufmann*, Rechtsgewinnung (Fn. 3), S. 54, 59 ff.; *ders.*, Abduktion (Fn. 6), S. 349 (354).

Das Bohnenbeispiel von *Kaufmann*:[20]

> F: Diese Bohnen a, b, c sind aus diesem Sack; die Bohnen c, d, e sind ebenfalls aus diesem Sack, und sie sind weiß
> R: Alle Bohnen aus diesem Sack sind weiß
> E: Die Bohnen a, b, c sind weiß

Das Beispiel von *Kaufmann*:[21]

> F: Die NS-Rassegesetze sind vom Gesetzgeber formal korrekt erlassen; das BGB, das StGB, das HGB ... sind ebenfalls vom Gesetzgeber formal korrekt erlassen, und sie sind Recht
> R: Alle vom Gesetzgeber formal korrekt erlassenen Normen sind Recht
> E: Die NS-Rassegesetze sind Recht

Anders als Deduktion, Induktion und Abduktion lässt sich die Analogie nicht in linearer Weise darstellen. Sie ist kein logischer Schluss, der lediglich in einer Richtung verläuft, sondern ein Vergleich bzw. eine Gleichsetzung, die bei Fall, Regel und Ergebnis zugleich sowie wechselseitig stattfindet und stets gemeinsam mit Deduktion, Induktion und Abduktion auftritt. Zu beachten ist, dass die Analogie kein „Niveauschluss", also kein Fallvergleich ohne Regel, sondern ein Vergleich zwischen Fall und Ergebnis unter der Regel (*Tertium Comparationis*) ist. Je nach der Wahl des *Tertium Comparationis* können entgegengesetzte Ergebnisse erfolgen. Das heißt: Wo Analogie möglich ist, ist Umkehrschluss (*Argumentum e Contrario*) auch immer möglich. Denn alle Dinge sind einander sowohl gleich (ähnlich) als auch ungleich (unähnlich). Deswegen können Fall und Ergebnis zu Unrecht gleichgesetzt werden; dunkle Bohnen mit weißen, die NS-Rassegesetze mit Recht. Insofern ist Analogie noch unsicherer als Induktion und Abduktion. Wie man der Grafik entnehmen kann, ist bei der Analogie alles unsicher; kein Schritt entspricht der Deduktion. Aber ohne Analogie, bei der es darauf ankommt, von der Übereinstimmung in einigen Merkmalen zur Übereinstimmung auch in unbekannten anderen Merkmalen zu schließen, kann man nicht ins Unbekannte vorstoßen.[22]

---

20 Da *Peirce* Analogie nicht behandelt hat, hat *Kaufmann* selbst dieses Bohnenbeispiel formuliert. *A. Kaufmann*, Rechtsphilosophie (Fn. 1), S. 76.

21 *A. Kaufmann*, Rechtsphilosophie (Fn. 1), S. 76.

22 *A. Kaufmann*, Rechtsgewinnung (Fn. 3), S. 52, 59 f.

III.

In der zeitgenössischen Methodenlehre, wie *Kaufmann* betont, ist die Auffassung kaum mehr haltbar, dass die Subsumtion des Falles unter eine Norm das einzige oder das wichtigste Mittel zur Rechtsgewinnung ist. Im Prozess der Rechtsgewinnung findet allerdings immer die Subsumtion (Deduktion) statt. Bevor aber die Subsumtion stattfindet, müssen zunächst einmal die Prämissen des deduktiven Schlusses gewonnen sein.[23] Das Verfahren, in dem solche Prämissen gewonnen werden, erläutert *Kaufmann* mit dem „Salzsäurefall" des BGH (BGHSt 1, 1) wie folgt:

> Salzsäurefall des BGH:
>
> Der Täter hat einer Kassiererin, die auf einer Sparkasse einen größeren Geldbetrag einzahlen sollte, verdünnte Salzsäure ins Gesicht geschüttet und ihr dann die Geldtasche entrissen, die sie unter dem offenen Mantel trug. Dabei hat der BGH die Frage gestellt, ob Salzsäure hier als „Waffe" im Sinne des schweren Raubes nach § 250 StGB a.F. angesehen werden kann – und er hat sie bejaht.[24]

Die Feststellung, ob im obigen Fall Salzsäure eine Waffe ist, kann nicht allein durch die Subsumtion erfolgen. Denn nach dem Wortlaut des § 250 StGB a.F. sowie nach dem möglichen Wortsinn von „Waffe" ist Salzsäure keine Waffe. Auf die Frage, ob hier Salzsäure eine Waffe im Sinne des § 250 StGB a.F. ist, kann man nur dann stoßen, wenn man das Geschehen als einen möglichen Fall des schweren Raubes „vorversteht". Vorversteht man das Geschehen anders, beispielsweise als versuchte Tötung, dann kommt es nicht in Betracht, ob Salzsäure eine Waffe ist.[25] Dies zeigt offensichtlich, dass die Interpretation des Gesetzes und die Feststellung des Sachverhalts untrennbar und zirkulär sind. „Die Gestaltung einer Gesetzesnorm zu einem Tatbestand (Interpretation) geschieht am Fall, die Gestaltung des Falles zu einem Sachverhalt (Konstruktion) geschieht an der Gesetzesnorm."[26] Um die Frage zu beantworten, ob Salzsäure unter Waffe im Sinne des schweren Raubes subsumiert werden kann, muss man zuerst

---

23 *A. Kaufmann*, Rechtsgewinnung (Fn. 3), S. 1 ff.; *ders.*, Abduktion (Fn. 6), S. 349.

24 *A. Kaufmann*, Rechtsgewinnung (Fn. 3), S. 9, 11.

25 *A. Kaufmann*, Rechtsphilosophie (Fn. 1), S. 89; *ders.*, Rechtsgewinnung (Fn. 3), S. 74, 86.

26 *A. Kaufmann*, Rechtsgewinnung (Fn. 3), S. 75.

den Obersatz (Tatbestand) und den Untersatz (Sachverhalt) des deduktiven Schlusses gewinnen.[27]

1.

Der Obersatz enthält die Herstellung der sogenannten konkreteren Norm, nämlich des Tatbestands, der die schon im Hinblick auf den Fall konkretisierte Norm (Fallnorm) darstellt. Logisch ist die Herstellung des Obersatzes eine **Induktion**; mittels der Induktion sucht man die Regel („Alle Fälle des schweren Raubes sind Raub mittels Waffen"). Weil es indessen praktisch unmöglich ist, alle Exemplare (alle möglichen Fälle von schwerem Raub) zu beobachten, ist die vollständige Induktion auch unmöglich. Die Induktion kann insoweit zu einem falschen Ergebnis führen; nicht alle Fälle, in denen beim Raub gefährliche Mittel angewendet werden, sind *de lege lata* Fälle des schweren Raubes.[28]

2.

Die Herstellung des Untersatzes erfolgt durch Fallvergleich. Der zweifelhafte Salzsäurefall, der gelöst werden soll, wird hier mit Fällen verglichen, bei denen es zweifellos um Waffen geht (Gewehr, Pistole, Revolver, Handgranate usw.). Dabei wird geprüft, in welchen Merkmalen Salzsäure mit eindeutigen Waffen übereinstimmt und in welchen nicht. Der Fallvergleich geschieht immer in der Weise, dass das weniger Bekannte mit dem Bekannteren verglichen wird – und dann: Aufgrund der übereinstimmenden Merkmale wird das weniger bekannte Merkmal mit dem bekannteren gleichgesetzt; aufgrund der nicht übereinstimmenden Merkmale wird das weniger bekannte Merkmal mit dem bekannteren nicht gleichgesetzt.[29]

Der weniger bekannte Fall – Raub mittels Salzsäure (Fall 2) – wird mit den bekannteren Fällen – Raub mittels Gewehre, Pistolen usw. (Fall 1) – verglichen, und zwar unter dem Vergleichspunkt (*Tertium Comparationis*). Der Vergleich des weniger Bekannten mit dem Bekannteren ist **Analogie**. Sie ist, wie gesehen, unsicher und riskant, denn alles Irdische ist einander

27 *A. Kaufmann*, Rechtsgewinnung (Fn. 3), S. 74 f.; *ders.*, Abduktion (Fn. 6), S. 349 (349).

28 *A. Kaufmann*, Rechtsgewinnung (Fn. 3), S. 56; *ders.*, Abduktion (Fn. 6), S. 349 (354 f.).

29 *A. Kaufmann*, Abduktion (Fn. 6), S. 349 (350).

sowohl gleich als auch ungleich, sodass bei Fallvergleich statt Analogie immer auch der Umkehrschluss möglich ist. Die Gültigkeit der Analogie hängt wesentlich von der Wahl des Vergleichspunkts ab, also von den Merkmalen, die verglichen werden; diese Wahl beruht vorwiegend nicht auf einer rationalen Erkenntnis, sondern überwiegend auf Dezision und somit auf Ausübung von Macht, was allermeist unreflektiert geschieht. Bei der Analogie, wie gesagt, können entgegengesetzte Ergebnisse resultieren: Vergleicht man unter dem Gesichtspunkt „Waffen sind gefährlich" den Fall 2 mit dem Fall 1, dann kann man so feststellen, dass Fall 2 mit Fall 1 übereinstimmt; vergleicht man demgegenüber unter dem Gesichtspunkt „Waffen sind mechanisch" den Fall 2 mit dem Fall 1, kann man daraus schließen, dass Fall 2 (chemisch) mit Fall 1 (mechanisch) nicht übereinstimmt.[30]

3.

Die Herstellung des Obersatzes erfolgt durch die Induktion; die Herstellung des Untersatzes durch Analogie. Genauer gesagt: Die induktive Ermittlung des Tatbestands kann nur in Bezug auf den Fall geschehen; der Fallvergleich nur in Bezug auf eine bestimmte Norm. Wenn man den Salzsäurefall als eine versuchte Tötung ansieht, dann würden Ober- und Untersatz der Subsumtion erheblich anders aussehen als bei Annahme eines möglichen schweren Raubes. „Die Aufbereitung des Falles an der Norm zu einem Sachverhalt und der Norm am Fall zu einem Tatbestand (konkretere Norm) geschieht wechselbezüglich aneinander im Modus des Zugleich".[31] Wenn man durch dieses ständige „Hin- und Herwandern des Blickes zwischen Obersatz und Lebenssachverhalt"[32] entschieden hat, ob

30 In der Tat hat der BGH den Fall 2 mit dem Fall 1 gleichgesetzt; er ist davon ausgegangen, dass Fall 2 mit Fall 1 übereinstimmt in einigen Punkten (Raub, gefährlich, die Absicht, Widerstand zu verhindern). Im Gegensatz dazu hat die herrschende Lehre Salzsäure auch bei solchem Gebrauch nicht als Waffe erachtet, da sie es für verbotene Analogie gehalten hat, hier Salzsäure mit Waffe gleichzusetzen. Der Gesetzgeber hat das BGH-Urteil für fehlerhaft angesehen, aber die Verwendung der Salzsäure beim Raub für strafwürdig im Sinne des § 250 StGB a.F. Folglich hat er den § 250 StGB entsprechend geändert. *A. Kaufmann*, Rechtsgewinnung (Fn. 3), S. 71; *ders.*, Abduktion (Fn. 6), S. 349 (354 f.).

31 *A. Kaufmann*, Abduktion (Fn. 6), S. 349 (351).

32 *K. Engisch*, Logische Studien zur Gesetzesanwendung, 3. Aufl., Heidelberg 1963, S. 15.

Salzsäure mit Waffe im Sinne des § 250 StGB a.F. gleichgesetzt wird oder nicht, dann ist die **Deduktion** ein einfacher und zwingender Schluss.[33]

4.

Bisher haben wir gesehen, wie beim Verfahren der Rechtsgewinnung Ober- und Untersatz des Subsumtionsschlusses durch Induktion und Analogie gebildet werden und wie es mit der Deduktion endet. Dennoch bleibt es noch ein Problem. Wie beginnt dieses Verfahren? Es ist klar, dass man mit einem Fall beginnen muss – aber: Mit was für einem Fall soll man anfangen? Wie kann man auf die Idee kommen, dass der Salzsäurefall ein Fall von schwerem Raub sein könnte?[34]

Dass Vorurteile Bedingungen des Verstehens sind, hat *Hans-Georg Gadamer* verdeutlicht. Alles Verstehen beginnt mit einem „hermeneutischen Vorurteil".[35] Dies gilt auch für das Rechtsverstehen. Ohne Vorurteil bzw. Vorverständnis können wir nicht wissen, in welcher Richtung wir den Fall ermitteln und die Beweise erheben sollen. An eine Sache, die wir verstehen wollen, gehen wir nicht mit Unkenntnis heran, was sie bedeuten könnte, sondern immer mit Vorverständnis, was wir bei ihr zu finden trachten. Das Vorverständnis dient als Ansatzpunkt für die Rechtsgewinnung. Seine logische Struktur ist zwar noch nicht ausreichend erklärt worden. Klar ist aber, dass sie weder Induktion noch Deduktion entspricht.[36]

Im späten 19. Jahrhundert hat *Peirce* herausgefunden, dass es neben Deduktion und Induktion noch einen dritten logischen Schluss gibt, der der Induktion vorausgeht – nämlich: **Abduktion**.[37] Während die Deduktion das Herleiten von der Regel ist und die Induktion das Hinleiten zur Regel, ist die Abduktion das Ableiten über die Regel. Die Abduktion geht vom Ergebnis aus und bildet damit eine Regel, die den Fall erklären kann. Sie produziert also eine Hypothese: Im Salzsäurefall könnte es um einen schweren Raub gehen, wenn man Salzsäure bei diesem Gebrauch als Waffe im Sinne des § 250 StGB a.F. anzusehen ist. Da aber die Abduktion ein unsicherer und riskanter Schluss ist, ist auch die von ihr gebildete Hypothe-

---

33 *A. Kaufmann*, Abduktion (Fn. 6), S. 349 (352).

34 *A. Kaufmann*, Abduktion (Fn. 6), S. 349 (355).

35 *H.-G. Gadamer*, Wahrheit und Methode. Grundzüge einer philosophischen Hermeneutik, Tübingen 1986, S. 270 ff.

36 *A. Kaufmann*, Abduktion (Fn. 6), S. 349 (356 f.).

37 *C. S. Peirce*, Hypothesis (Fn. 8), 470.

se unsicher und nur vorläufig. Daher muss man im Verfahren der Rechtsgewinnung ständig überdenken, ob man die Hypothese noch korrigieren muss.[38] Dennoch braucht man sie unbedingt, um einen Ausgangspunkt zur Rechtsgewinnung zu finden.[39]

IV.

Kaufmann hat plausibel dargestellt, dass das Verfahren der Rechtsgewinnung aus den vier Bausteinen besteht: zuerst **Abduktion**, dann zugleich **Induktion** und **Analogie**, und zuletzt **Deduktion.**[40]

Verfahren der Rechtsgewinnung bei Kaufmann:

Abduktion → Induktion + Analogie → Deduktion

1. Abduktion: Herstellung von Hypothesen
2. Induktion: Herstellung von Obersatz des Schlusses
   Analogie: Herstellung von Untersatz des Schlusses
3. Deduktion: Schlussfolgerung

Das Verfahren der Rechtsgewinnung beginnt immer mit dem Vorverständnis, nämlich mit der Abduktion, die ein unsicherer und riskanter Schluss ist. Dabei sollen wir uns stets überlegen, ob wir die durch die Abduktion gebildete Hypothese noch korrigieren sollen. Induktion und Analogie, die den Ober- und den Untersatz der Subsumtion bilden, beinhalten Unsicherheit, wo sich die „Einfallstore für Dezision, Macht und Willkür“[41] befinden. Wie *Kaufmann* hervorhebt, sollen wir uns stets bewusst sein, in welchem Schritt wir uns genau befinden und wie sicher ein solcher Schritt ist, wenn wir die Rationalität der juristischen Methodenlehre sichern wollen.[42]

Alles in allem: Unsichere, irrationale Schritte im Rechtsgewinnungsverfahren, die nicht völlig eliminiert werden können, müssen wir möglichst genau lokalisieren und möglichst vernünftig reflektieren. „Die Wissen-

38 Vgl. Fn. 30.
39 *A. Kaufmann*, Abduktion (Fn. 6), S. 349 (356 ff.).
40 *A. Kaufmann*, Abduktion (Fn. 6), S. 349 (358).
41 *A. Kaufmann*, Rechtsgewinnung (Fn. 3), S. V; *ders.*, Abduktion (Fn. 6), S. 349 (353).
42 *A. Kaufmann*, Abduktion (Fn. 6), S. 349 (358).

schaftlichkeit der Rechtswissenschaft kann nur in einer rationalen Analyse des nicht allenthalben rationalen Rechtsgewinnungsverfahrens liegen."[43]

43 *A. Kaufmann*, Rechtsgewinnung (Fn. 3), S. 42.

The Meaning and Role of Non-finite Aspect of Law

Wu Ye Kang

A. Introduction

The non-finite aspect of law is swept under the carpet but is always on the lookout for an opportunity to turn up. It cannot be identified by way of ordinary methods of application of law, because it is amorphous. Nonetheless, no solid and rational conceptual structure of law can prevents its' appearance and impact. Paradoxically, its' appearance and its' being cannot be clearly or precisely identified and predicted. Let me talk about an historical fact. right after the French Revolution, to control their court aristocrats the representatives of citizens have set up the determinate and absolute sentencing scheme in which a judge did not have any discretion. As soon as that penal law was applied, it was realized that the sense of justice of that era could not allow them to stick to the strict standard. In other words, the modern form of the rule of law established by the Revolution was seriously challenged by the pressure of individualized justice that can never be eradicated to deal with real cases, which are endlessly reinterpreted and reconstructed by mainly judges, lawyers and also any kind of lay persons.

Herewith, the important question is how we can deal with or control a non-finite aspect of laws in our legal system. If it cannot be cut off from the legal system, it must be questioned how possible it is to take it into consideration in regard with legal standards. The traditional method of law looks lethargic in dealing with it, because it nullifies any conceptual and categorical formality that is necessary to achieve the rule of law. Also, it does not let a formal logic work well. It dumps out a consistency of legal standards and simultaneously bring a contradiction that challenges an exciting rule of law.

Then, it seems reasonable to start from the question of when such a non-finite aspect of law comes to appear. First, we should analyze the process of legal reasoning that lies in the core understanding of a legal standard but ironically is never possibly mechanically expressed. Second, the higher rank of legal standard that is always necessary to bring about a new standard or fix up an existing standard should be paid attention to and analyzed in detail to access its' true form and nature. Third, the issue of universality and individuality of justification seems to reveal another aspect of it, in that it leads to the abyss of amorphous substance of law. Fourth, the individualized justice or the principle of proportionality in the United States' death penalty law, which has shown its' strong characteristic to break up all the forms of categorical restraints, is the most distinctive proof of the non-finite aspect of law.

B. Some Examples of Non-finite Aspects of Law, A Threat to the Rule of Law?

I. Limits of Statutory Interpretation

A noble dream of the modern rule of law based on democracy must have found its' ground on the statutory provisions that were written down by legislative process. This type of approach that controls the persons who apply laws, such as judges, prosecutors, lawyers, any governmental officials, has extended to formation of well-organized structures of laws. The most distinctive example is the tree-step structure of Verbrechenssystem formulated by German academics of criminal law. German academics must have dreamed of the idealistic conceptual entity that can effectively realize the rule of law. Moreover, the idea of delivering the meanings inside hard and fast rules without any distortion must have turn its' attention to the formal logic, which, however, is not so popular and moreover very unpersuasive.

Unfortunately, any legal concept that is statutorily provided or derived through its' interpretation does not contain its' meaning like a water in a bowl or does not deliver it without any loss through legislation. In fact, it seems often unsuccessful to argue for the principle of legality against Korean Supreme Court's expansion of a statutory meaning. Already, driving a car comes within the conception of 'bearing and carrying a dangerous object'.[1] Also, having a victim lapse into unconsciousness through injection of drug or alcohol is classified as a sort of serious violence for robbery or rape.[2]

As a matter of semantic perspective, there is no serious distinction between prohibited analogy and permitted interpretation. When interpreting

1 *See e.g.* Korean Supreme Court 5.30.1997, 97도597.

2 As for a rape case, *see e.g.* Korean Supreme Court 6.29.2017. 2017do3196. About a robbery case, *see e.g.,* Korean Supreme Court 12.11.1984. 84do2324.

a statutory word, a judge relies on a analogical method by comparing a fact and another one. We, human beings, does not print out the meaning within a statutory word into a factual situation. Rather, the process of clarification of a conception of a legal word is parallel with the process of understanding a meaning of a factual situation. Those two processes come simultaneously.[3] Therefore, a deductive reasoning is another expression and aspect of an analogical reasoning. The standard of controlling an analogical reasoning is not predetermined but nonfinitely generated.[4] This is why so many simple and strict arguments of legality do not effectively persuade jurists in lots of cases.

This inextinguishable aspect of legal interpretation seems to remind us of something behind the formal standards, which are clearly identified or described. The force of endless analogy may not be completely eradicated in a legal system. It draws a deep shadow for the background of typical conceptual and formal standards.

II. Gaps of Law

Filling out a gap of statutory provisions cannot go completely within the positive legal system. In other words, it always poses a threat to a strict sense of the rule of law. A judge who is obliged to fill out a gap of law should identify a legal standard which occurs anywhere inside or outside of a legal system. Of course, many jurists and legal scholars comment that a judge should always consult the meanings within the legal system to fill out a gap of law. That is, it is argued that to support the principles of legality and democracy, a legal practitioner should not decide any case outside of laws.[5]

It does not seem so simple to stand up for the rule of law when identifying and filling out a gap of law. The one of the main reasons is that no legal standard to supplement a gap of law does preexist as clear formality in a legal system. A judge facing a gap of law should find out a conceptual standard by rely on very general principles beyond a formal

---

3 *See e.g.* Sangdon Lee, The limit of Interpretation of Criminal Law, 29(2) Justice 7 (1996); *see also* Cheonsoo Lee, The limit of Interpretation of Criminal Law, 379 Human Right and Justice 144 (2008).

4 Wuye Kang, Analysis of Analogical Reasoning in Anglo-American Law, 23(1) Korean Journal of Legal Philosophy 287, 315–316 (2020).

5 Jinwan Park, Law Formation as the Problem of Relation between Constitutional Interpretation and Statutory Interpretation, 71 Law Journal 1, 46–49, 52 (2020).

rule. It is simply because a gap of law means no clear rule there inside of the legal system. For example, Korean Supreme Court get outside of Korean Code of Criminal Procedure[6] to identify the defendant's right to argue for the appellate process although he has directly filed for Korean Supreme Court and was frustrated by the prosecutor's appeal, of which result is clearly provided in Korean Code of Criminal Procedure. In other words, to justify such a consequence, Korean Supreme Court should go to the level of Korean constitution that does not have a directly written legal consequence unlike the prosecutor's right to appeal in Korean Code of Criminal Procedure and so is considered as a matter of weight. Also, a social norm outside of the legal system has been often introduced by such a general standard of law. Korean Supreme Court has considered a changed social norm to understand the contemporary meaning of human dignity and sexual autonomy in the context of homosexual relationships. Korean Supreme Court has narrowed the scope of punishment for the case of homosexual relations based on the contemporary conception of the fundamental rights that have been seriously affected by the changed version of a social norm about it.[7] The general principles and standards, such as fundamental rights, general clauses in statutes, general principle derived from many specified formal rules, and also a general principle of morality, which make analogical reasoning possibly vary and cannot be exhaustively enumerated.[8]

Fundamentally, an analogical reasoning principally based on the general standard shall be named as a main method in filling out a gap of law. As a matter of fact, a mechanical or strict standard to control such an analogical process has not been suggested by anybody, any authority or any good material. In other words, it is a legal reasoning that could not be completely formalized and thus unpredictable before considering a concrete case. To achieve an acceptable conclusion in a particular case, a process of searching a reasonable standard that is not yet provided in a statute shall be started.[9]

---

6 Korean Supreme Court 7.17.2023, 2021do11126.

7 Korean Supreme Court 4.21.2022, 2019do3047.

8 Wuye Kang, The Meaning and Nature of Constitution-Conforming Interpretation of Penal Provision, 34(4) Korean Journal of Criminal Law 395 (2022).

9 Wuye Kang, A Critique of Principles and Practices of a Judge's Formation of Legal Standards, 26(3) Korean Journal of Legal Philosophy 99 (2023).

III. General Standard of Law

Every single legal standard contains a certain level of generality and universality. To treat similar cases alike, generality and university based on formal conceptual standards of law are inevitable. Nonetheless, a formal standard cannot appear as a universal sense in all aspects. Therefore, a higher level of generality and abstractness is necessary when a judge meets a limit of a particular rule of law based on factual consideration of a case.

For instance, Korean Supreme Court has relied on the concept of alternative possibility of an lawful act, which is the most general and universal standard in the stage of considering criminal blameworthiness. It is well-known but still interesting that the criteria of criminal blameworthiness of alternative possibility is not written in Korean Code of Criminal Law. Korean Supreme Court declares not guilty the soldiers who lied in ambush against the armed communist guerrilla but took a 2-hours nap by turns during their execution of duty because they had just slept only 3~5 hours for 4 day long. That is, their violation of duty as a military soldier is partial and trivial but is not blameworthy based on a humane perspective.[10] This shows that a more universal approach sometimes should be derived to alternate or change a strict rule of statute.

As already partially mentioned, Korean Supreme Court often relies on Korean Constitution to correct the wrong practice of criminal procedure. For example, for the case that a court-appointed lawyer mistakenly misses a deadline of appeal, Korean Supreme Court supports a defendant's right to effective assistance of counsel, which is not clearly posited in Korean Constitution as well as even in Korean Code of Criminal Procedure. To realize an actual meaning of a defendant's right to counsel, Korean Supreme Court established the additional process that the appellate court should cancel the appointment of the counsel who fails to appeal and reappoint a new counsel to make a valid appeal with a newly extended deadline of appeal.[11] It is a clear example that a fundamental right in Korean Constitution can be flexibly understood to avoid an unjustifiable and unacceptable consequence of a case.

The most universal standard comes from the concept of the whole system of law (Gesamt-Rechtsordnung). The standard of the whole system of law tends to be used to correct or change too strict rules of each legal area.

10 Korean Supreme Court 3.11.1980, 80do141.

11 Korean Supreme Court 2.16.2012, 2009do1044.

Therefore, rather than conceptual standards, an individual consideration of concrete case is used as the most important approach when the standard of the whole system of law is cited. That is, the two different principles of universality and individuality should be satisfied at the same time. Thus, the sub-concepts, which the principle of trust and good faith and the socially accepted rules belong to, under the standard of the whole system of law try to overcome the narrow meanings of common statutory standards toward the more universal but less stable consideration of law.[12]

It is interesting that the general standards of law not only stay in individualized and simultaneously universal reasonableness but also come closer to support the fundamental rights. Recently, Korean Supreme Court supported workers' collective right to consent to a revised rule of labor, rather than simply approved the validity of the rule based on the standard of objective reasonableness. In that case, Korean Supreme Court took the principle of trust and good faith differently than before.[13] Also, Korean Supreme Court stroke down many social norms that is the main source of Korean Family Law especially about the family membership, the right to family religious service, the right of graveyard, on the basis of the constitutional right to equality.[14] Moreover, it has been decided that the fundamental rights to personal autonomy, privacy and human dignity that has changed the social norm about homosexuality narrow down the scope of criminal punishment against homosexual activities between military members. All these cases have been decided based on the principle of the whole system of laws, which is never to be definable.

IV. Legal Justification

Korean Criminal Code has a distinctive and unique clause of 'socially accepted rules (社會常規)'. According to Korean Supreme Court, the concept of 'socially accepted rules' means the act that can be acceptable based on social morals and common sense that lies behind the spirit of the whole system of laws. Based on this definition, the standard of 'socially accepted rules' not only get to the conception of the whole system of laws but also go outside it to draw any other social norms.

12 Wuye Kang, *supra* note 8), at 119.

13 Korean Supreme Court 5.11.2023, 2017da35588.

14 Korean Supreme Court 7.21.2005. 2002da1178; Korean Supreme Court 1.19.2017, 2013-da17292; Korean Supreme Court 11.56., 2013, 2018da248616.

Most of all, the Article 20th of Korean Criminal Code that contains 'socially accepted rules' as a requirement of justification represents the universal conception of law. It means that once an act is considered justifiable, though it satisfies elements of a crime, it should be also treated as lawful in a matter of any other legal area. For example, although a practice of hand acupuncture that is classified as a medical treatment and thus should be treated by a licensed doctor of korean medicine, Korean Supreme Court justified a practice of hand acupuncture by an unlicensed and lay person, because it does not cause any serious harm to a patient. What should be cautious is that such a practice of hand acupuncture is not simply justified based on the fact of low-level danger but also the consideration of so many factors, such as motive, purpose, method, times, knowledge, experience and background, age and physical state of patient, possibility of side effect, and moreover social ethics and social norm.[15] This flexible standard is supported by 'socially accepted rules' posited in the Article 20th of Korean Criminal Code. Because of the universal nature of 'socially accepted rules', the practice of hand acupuncture cannot be taken unlawful by any other laws, including administrative law or civil law, although such an unlicensed practice actually causes any kind of damages to other medical doctors or patients.

As we have already seen, the standard of 'socially accepted rules' for the case of hand acupuncture is so flexible to adapt itself to any concrete and specific consideration of a case in question. The reason why such an individualized approach of 'socially accepted rules' can survive and dominate in the doctrine of justification is because the universal perspective that transcends the conceptual limit of the requirements in the criminal law is necessary. In other words, the real universal consequence of law cannot be completely achieved by any well-defined and well-organized formal requirements of law. In Korean Supreme Court decisions, this universal aspect of 'socially accepted rules' has shown enormous influential powers. Based on the name of 'socially accepted rules', the weak cases of self-defense and necessity can be justified without referring to the Article 21st or the Article 22nd of Korean Criminal Code.[16] In addition, sometimes, 'socially accepted rules' is cited to support justifications in tort law or administrative discipline. What should be cautious is that this prosperity of 'socially

15 Korean Supreme Court 4.25.2000, 98do2389.

16 *See e.g.* Korean Supreme Court 1.16.2014. 2013do6761; *see also* Korean Supreme Court 12.14.2009. 2007do6243; *see also* Korean Supreme Court 7.22.1986, 86do751.

accepted rules' has been seriously challenged because it is negating the principle of rule of law.

V. Sentencing Law

The individualized justice that vitiates the conceptual standards of law appeared most distinctively in the United States Supreme Court's cases of the death penalty law. In the Supreme Court's case of McGautha v. California, Justice Harlan declared that "to identify before the fact those characteristics of criminal homicides and their perpetrators which call for the death penalty, and to express these characteristics in language which can be fairly understood and applied by the sentencing authority, appear to be tasks which are beyond present human ability."[17] This non-finite nature of individualized justice did destruct and sweep away any formality of sentencing law in American death penalty. For the capital punishment to be proportional to crime and criminal, not only the conceptual and formal *ex ante* definition of crime generally proportional to punishment but also the very individualized *ex post* consideration of blameworthiness specifically proportional to circumstances of crime and criminal. It means a strong pressure of lawlessness is inescapable in the death penalty law. In other words, McGuatha has cast a wonderful skepticism on the establishment of the rules and the standard used in the capital sentencing area. McGautha is a kind of expression about the agnostic power that cannot be easily disposed of but should be taken most seriously if we want to go forward to the more rational decisions that the law always requires. In short, you cannot completely define who will be subject to death penalty before facing and considering a particular case.[18]

This individualized aspect of justice does not only have its presence in capital punishment cases. Rather, it warns that any type of extremely mechanical system of sentencing will not be successful. In fact, the United States Supreme Court declared unconstitutional some mechanical Sentencing Guidelines and also attack the binding force of the Federal Sentencing Guidelines. This shows how hard it is to define a particular blameworthi-

---

17 McGautha v. California, 402 U.S. 183 (1971).

18 Wuye Kang, Analysis of sentencing guidelines and sentencing trial based on the principle of proportionality between crime and punishment, 24(4) Korean Journal of Comparative Criminal Law 453, 458–459 (2023).

ness of crime and criminal to achieve the ideal of rule of law based on conceptual and formalistic means of language. As a matter of fact, the failure of the Federal Sentencing Guidelines that has a structure of so strict and complex formality opened up the discussion about the inevitable existence of lawlessness.[19]

It looks enigmatic that this power of agnosticism is not simply limited to the area of sentencing guidelines but also lurk under the idealistic carpet of rule of law, being ready to pop out from any ocean deep of laws. What seems difficult is that it has been never known how effectively this aspect of law can be dealt with through a typical method of law. Probably, the void and non-finite aspect of law may be a real battlefield to liberate and transcend any suppressing conditions, including conceptual aspect of rule of law and thus to achieve the dignity of every single individual human being and the harmonious and peaceful relations between them.

C. The Reasons or the Mechanism of Non-finite Legal Standards

I. Substance over Form

It is so interesting that legal meanings are not completely stuck inside the formality of laws. Ironically, the rule of law could capture reasonable conclusions for various legal issues not simply based on a written black-letter laws. The formal standards of laws that are conceptually divided and relatively isolated within its extension could not perfectly express the real merits of legal issues.

Most of formal standards does not completely correspond to a purpose behind of it. There always appears under-inclusiveness or over-inclusiveness of a formal standard over a purpose or an aim of it, which is understood as substance under its' formality. By the way, the fundamental substance of death penalty law does not seem to easily allow for strict formality. As already mentioned before, Justice Harlan in McGautha v. California has justifiably given up the establishment of a good formal standard to determine what is the best substantive requirement for the capital punishment. Moreover, Justice Stevens's project of setting up the legal standards for the death penalty cases, which are the peak of pyramid of heinous murder

19 *Id.*, at 460–463.

cases,[20] does not seem successful in the following cases of the United States Supreme Court. The categorical *ex ante* definition of which criminals and crimes should be subject to capital punishment is contradictory to the real merit of the sentencing law of death penalty. Let us extend this field of vision, such that a total context of a legal case that should be considered to achieve a real justice is not always well understood by conceptual means of laws.

No matter how strict and well-organized the legal formality is, a new legal meaning always lurks under the carpet of it. In other words, a well-organized formality of law does not directly lead to a particular legal consequence.[21] If there is no leeway or discretion to apply a law to a case, it must turn to be a mechanical legality, not a human or humane approach of law. For a justification of an act, the traditional method to define what is legal or illegal is not enough. The determining process of a justification of an act opened up the way to consider the universality of it. In other word, without the sufficient ground of universality, it seems unacceptable to vitiate a legislative definition of a crime.[22] That is, a whole system of law is necessary to determine whether an act is legitimate or not especially as a matter of exclusion of illegality.

II. Subjectivity over Objectivity

A legal concept of a whole system of law that is understood as an objective form does conceal a subjective perspective within itself. As a matter of law, a concept of a whole system of law transcends the totality of entire legal standards inside of it but functions as reforming and reinterpreting them. Therefore, a legal issue can be treated differently depending on which concept of whole systems of laws is chosen.

For example, since Korean civil law system was established, the social norms or customs regarding a membership of a family, a right to worship supervisor, a right to graveyard has been accepted as valid laws by Korean Supreme Court. Recently, however, the perspective of the whole system of law especially about fundamental rights, such as equality, plays a central

20 Walton v. Arizona, 497 U.S. 639 (1990); Arizona v. Ring, 200 Ariz. 267, 280, 25 P.3d 1139, 1152 (2001).

21 *See generally* Wuye Kang, *supra* note 4).

22 *See supra* at the part of "Universality and Individuality of Legal Justification".

role in recognizing those rights as a part of civil law system. Also, it was by the case of Korean Supreme Court that the part of meaning of criminal elements punishing homosexuality in military camp was eradicated based on the perspective of the social norms entangled with fundamental human dignity, recognizable inside as well as outside of the positive laws. In short, a whole system of law can contain positive laws as well as unwritten laws. Therefore, the laws cannot be exhaustively enumerated by any means that has been written by languages. The apex of unwritten laws is occupied by subjective perspectives, which should be, however, close to universality.[23]

Ironically, the most universal approach attracts the most individualized justice, attacking the formal approaches of laws, whose aim is to achieve the treatment of the similar things alike through generalization and abstractness, not the bare individualization. For instance, reliance on the general principles opened up the way to the concept of whole system of law. The more general is a standard, the more individualized consideration can be possible. That is, when a universal conclusion is asked for, a limit of linguistic concept tries to be leaped over. There are tons of cases and examples that can prove it. Most of all, as already mentioned, the determination of justification tends to universal but individualized, of which phenomenon are distinctively represented by the concept of 'socially accepted rules' of the Article 20th of Korean Criminal Code. Simply put it, the standard of 'socially accepted rules' itself is equal to the whole system of law which is formed by and also conveys a subjective perspective. The principle of 'trust and good faith' also required so flexible and individualized consideration of cases.[24] In other words, it brings a very contextual approach that fixes and modifies a formality of a legal standard or a contract. For example, although a customer made a contract with a lawyer about a particular level of attorney fee, on the consideration of the circumstances, such as the relation between the lawyer and the customer, the process of taking the case, the level of difficulty of the case, the value of the subject-matter in the litigation, the effort of the lawyer, the value of winning the case, etc, the attorney fee can be reconsidered to determine its excessiveness as an exception of the principle of freedom of contract and also for the principle of 'trust and good faith'. In the recent cases of Korean Supreme Court

23 *See generally* Wuye Kang, A Conception and Nature of the Concept of the Whole System of Law in Korean Supreme Court, 27(2) Korean Journal of Legal Philosophy 139 (2024).

24 Korean Supreme Court 10.14. 2022, 2018da210690.

that support the fundamental rights of workers, equality, autonomy, and the newly formed social norms so entangled with concrete social realities are necessary to change, reform or vitiate the already established rules and standards.[25] In addition, it is noteworthy that the strongest form of state's violence has woken up the most serious respect for the fundamental right of an individual defendant. In the sentencing law of death penalty in the United States, the most fundamental and individual consideration for the right of every single defendant is required the most intensively. As already mentioned before, Justice Harlan pointed out the impossibility of perfection of formality in sentencing guidelines of death penalty. It is because, any trivial factor ought not to be disregarded for the benefit of a defendant's dignity and a balanced consideration of the most serious type of a case. Also, a defendant threaten to kill never wants to skip over any minor mistake and error in legal standard. In the context of capital punishment, the principle of individualized justice smells bloody.[26]

Conceptual categories does not provide a perfect and objective structure of legal standards and thus must face the area of indeterminacy, which a concrete case continues to convey into formality of law. For this reason, a well-organized hierarchy of legal interests has never been perfectly successful. Korean Supreme Court sometimes does not place an absolute superiority of right to life over right to body or right to self-determination. For example, no medical doctor is considered to possess a right to force a third party's blood donation to save a patient life which is even in critical moment. Also, Korean Supreme Court rejected to criminally blame a doctor who did not show an absolute respect for a patient's life, who asked the doctor to do surgery without blood transfusions.[27] The right to the self-determination of the patient is not lower than the right to life that is often considered to have infinite weight.

When reviewing a legal standard or a government policy, the idea of incommensurability prevails over the standard of interests balance. In the sense of the entire legal history, the workable and effective criteria of balancing of conflicting interests has never been developed and thus told. In

25 *See* Kang, *supra* note 23).

26 Wuye Kang, Critical Analysis of the Principle of Proportionality -Based on American Cases Theories-, 20(1) Korean Journal of Criminal Policy Study 393 (2009); Wuye Kang, The Death Penalty Laws in America, 31(1) Law Review of Jurisprudence 295 (2007).

27 Korean Supreme Court 6.26.2014, 2009do14407.

fact, Korean Constitutional Court has seldom relied on the principle of interest balance but has resorted to the principle of minimum infringement. Nonetheless, Korean Supreme Court has still compared the seriousness of inflicted interests under the name of minimum infringement. For example, Korean Supreme Court pointed out that if an amount of infliction of fundamental right while applying a statutory word surpass an amount of infliction on the principle of stability of law that a new understanding of the statutory word can cause, then it may be in violation of the principle of minimum infringement and the principle of proportionality.[28]

What should not be lost is that for such a determination we still do not have any reliable scale. Generally, to strike a balance of conflicting interests, we often faces the situation of determining a fact and a value without any workable formal standards. Because the standard of interests balancing is the most important and ultimate principle of legal issues in the hierarchy of legal system and methodology, it must be clearly understood that jurists cannot escape the non-finite pressure in doing law and justice. The extra examples of the non-finite aspect of law are not scarce but plentiful, such as the issue of the concepts of justice, liberty, reasonableness, foreseeability, social policy and the problem of a gap of a law, and general concepts in law, etc. The aim of this paper is to find out the way of describing the amorphous and non-finite aspect and nature of law. To make out a legal conclusion in wisdom, we should learn about how to deal with it. Not often but sometimes, the empty space of legal meaning will help to achieve a more reasonable and justifiable conclusion of a legal issue. But, it is very clear that it is not easy to achieve, because the amorphous and non-finite aspect and nature of law must reject the ordinary methodology of law with formal concepts and categories. This paper hopes to lay a small corner stone to develop such a innovative way to effectively discuss about the aspect of law.

III. A Free Person Perspective

No matter how well-organized a legal dogmatic become, it is unavoidable to face the human factors, such as will and intention. Any legal system cannot perfectly eradicate the subjective aspect inside of itself. This indeterminate

28 Korean Supreme Court 5.19.2022, 2021do17311; Korean Supreme Court 11.1.2018, 2016do10912.

factor help a judge to strike a real balance and flexibly adapt an existing dry rule into a concrete case.

The real equilibrium is not given before considering legal and factual issues of cases. Kantian and also Rawlsian approach to interest balancing is based on the project of liberalism. That is, the initial principle that a free and equal person should take part in a process of determination should be taken as the most dominating and highest. No matter how well-formed a standard is, it cannot control a particular legal consequence without any consideration of a free person.[29] The modern legal system plants an indeterminate and thus non-finite aspect of law into itself, instead of mechanically strict connections of conceptual rules and standards. Human beings with free-will seem to necessarily and inescapably face their own shapes inside of the legal systems they have established.

D. Conclusion

When a judge simply tries to understand a best standard of a law, he must be ignorantly digging into an endless abyss inside of and around it and finding it void and empty at last. Therefore, if the most rigorously and thoroughly analyzed, every single formal standard of law may lose its' firm ground. The chain of conceptual connections does not allow any isolated and complete definition of rule and principle.

However, if he starts to get a good resolution of case and controversy by relying on a good standard. It means that a jurist should not alienate the nonfinite aspect from a legal system but ought to consider it as a part of itself. What is necessary and important is doing a law, not simply digging out an objective meaning of it. A non-finite aspect of law should be properly bore in mind to have a jurist and a system of law not ignore each other. In conclusion, a balancing approach should not be simply about between written laws and principles but also about between a written and an unwritten. It opens up a democratic process of debate about what should be chosen as the most fundamental of law for a concrete case in question. Probably and generally, any suppression of a minor and subordinate group or person is taken the most seriously in doing law at this particular moment in Korea. This process should not be exhaustive. This is a strange loop of normativity we never escape from.

---

29 Wuye Kang, Analysis of 'Reflective Equilibrium' of John Rawls, 23(2) Korean Journal of Legal Philosophy 69 (2020).

Bibliography

Kang, Wuye, The Death Penalty Laws in America, 31(1) Law Review of Jurisprudence 295 (2007).

__________, Critical Analysis of the Principle of Proportionality -Based on American Cases Theories-, 20(1) Korean Journal of Criminal Policy Study 393 (2009).

__________, Analysis of 'Reflective Equilibrium' of John Rawls, 23(2) Korean Journal of Legal Philosophy 69 (2020).

__________, An Analytical Study on Analogical Method in Anglo-American Law, 23(1) Korean Journal of Legal Philosophy 287 (2020).

__________, The Meaning and Nature of Constitution-Conforming Interpretation of Penal Provision, 34(4) Korean Journal of Criminal Law 395 (2022).

__________, A Critique of Principles and Practices of a Judge's Formation of Legal Standards, 26(3) Korean Journal of Legal Philosophy 99 (2023).

__________, Analysis of sentencing guidelines and sentencing trial based on the principle of proportionality between crime and punishment, 24(4) Korean Journal of Comparative Criminal Law 453 (2023).

__________, A Conception and Nature of the Concept of the Whole System of Law in Korean Supreme Court, 27(2) Korean Journal of Legal Philosophy 139 (2024).

Lee, Cheonsoo, The limit of Interpretation of Criminal Law, 379 Human Right and Justice 144 (2008).

Lee, Sangdon, The limit of Interpretation of Criminal Law, 29(2) Justice 7 (1996).

Park, Jinwan, Law Formation as the Problem of Relation between Constitutional Interpretation and Statutory Interpretation, 71 Law Journal 1 (2020).

Einführung in die juristische Methodenlehre in Korea

Young-Whan Kim

I. Begriff und Funktion der juristischen Methodenlehre

Es braucht kaum noch erwähnt zu werden, dass Korea zum kontinental europäischen Rechtskreis gehört, in dem das geschriebene Recht als die wichtigste Rechtsquelle angesehen wird. Daher liegt es nahe, dass die koreanische juristische Methodenlehre gerade von der sog. Anwendungslehre des positiven Rechts ausgeht.[1] Während im angelsächsischen Rechtskreis die Rechtsfindung anhand der Präjudizien eine dominierende Stellung

---

1 Literatur zur juristischen Methodenlehre in Korea; 1) Zur Übersetzung *Hyung Bae Kim*, Die juristische Methodnelehre(*Zippelius*, Einführung in die juristische Methodenlehre), 1976; *Il Tae Huh*, Die jurisische Methodenlehre(*Larenz/Canaris*, Methodenlehre der Rechtswissenschaft), 2000; *Sung Bang Hong*, Theorie zur Rechtsgewinnung(*Kriele*, Theorie zur Rechtsgewinnung), 2013; *Zai Wang Yoon*, Die juristische Methodenlehre(*Engisch*, Einführung in das juristische Denken), 2011; *Chun Kyu Choi*, Die juristische Methodenlehre (*Kramer*, Juristische Methodenlehre), 2022. 2) Zur Fachliteratur *Do Kyun Kim*(Hrsg.), Die koreanische Rechtsordnung und deren Auslegungslehre, 2013; *Kye Il Lee*(Hrsg.), Die juristische Methodenlehre, 2017; *Hak Tae Kim*, Die Auslegung des Gesetzes und deren Anwendung, 2017; *Young Whan Kim*, Grundproblem der Rechtsphilosophie, 3. Aufl., 2012, S. 253–342(Kap. 7, 8, 9, 10); *Jong Oh Kim/Bong Cheol Choi/Hyun Cheol Kim/Dong Ring Shin/Chun Soo Yang/ Kye Il Lee*, Rechtsphilosophie, 3. Aufl., 2022, S. 241–318(Kap. 11, Die juristische Methodenlehre in USA, Kap. 12, Die juristische Methodenlehre in Deutschland, Kap 13, Die juristische Methodenlehre in Korea); *Dae Whi Kim*, Rechtsphilosophie und Rechtstheorie, 2.Aufl. 2023, S. 239–330(Kap 9, Recht und Sprache, Methodenlehre); *Seo Hyuk Oh*, Die juristische Methodenlehre, 2024.
Zur wichtigsten Literatur in Deutschland; *Engisch*, Einführung in das juristische Denken, 12. Aufl., 2018; *Larenz*, Methodenlehre der Rechtswissenschaft, 4. Aufl., 1979; *Larenz/Canaris*, Methodenlehre der Rechtswissenschaft, 3. Aufl., 1995; *Bydlinski*, Juristische Methodenlehre und Rechtsbegriff, 2 Aufl. 1991; *Pawlowski*,: Methodenlehre für Juristen, 2. Aufl. 1991; *Esser*, Vorverständnis und Methodenwahl in der Rechtsfindung, 2. Aufl. 1972; *Raisch*: Vom Nutzen der überkommenen Auslegungskanonen für die praktische Rechtsanwendung, 1988; *Zippelius*, Juristische Methodenlehre, 12. Aufl., 2021; *Kaufmann*, Das Verfahren der Rechtsgewinnung, 1999; *Koch/Rüßmann*, Juristische Begründungslehre, 1982; *Kramer*, Juristische Methodenlehre, 4. Aufl., 2013.

einnimmt[2], steht hier dagegen die Auslegung des positiven Rechts und deren Anwendung auf den konkreten Fall im Mittelpunkt. Ungeachtet dieser unterschiedlichen Methodik der Rechtsgewinnung ist jedoch nicht zu verkennen, dass es in den beiden Rechtskreisen letztlich darauf ankommt, die Sache „Recht" herauszufinden.[3]

Wenn die juristische Methodenlehre die Reflexion auf das eigene Tun darstellt, nimmt sie einen gewissen Abstand in Anspruch, von dem aus dieser Prozess der Rechtsgewinnung betrachtet werden kann. Hier steht die Frage im Mittelpunkt, was vor sich geht, wenn ein Gesetz interpretiert oder wenn eine Gesetzeslücke ausgefüllt wird. Dabei kommt es auch darauf an, unter welchen Bedingungen eine Interpretation des geltenden Rechts oder dessen Lückenausfüllung als zutreffend beurteilt werden kann. Wenn sie hiernach dazu dienen soll, das richterliche Urteil auf seine methodische Begründetheit zu überprüfen, verwundert es nicht, dass die juristische Entscheidungspraxis grundsätzlich durch sie begleitet wird, indem bestimmte Anforderungen an das Vorgehen der Gerichte gestellt werden, die wiederum deren Argumentationsweise und Begründungsstil mitbestimmen. Also die juristische Methodenlehre stellt eine „normative Lehre" dar, nämlich eine Metadisziplin, die prädikativ sagt, wie der Interpret auf Grund gewisser rechtlicher Vorgaben verfahren sollte, wenn es gerade um die Rechtsgewinnung geht[4].

Gegen die juristische Methodenlehre erhebt sich das Bedenken, in dem die Rolle anderer Kriterien als positiv rechtliche Prämisse bei der Rechtsgewinnung betont wird[5]. Dazu gehört vor allem die Ansicht von *Esser*, dass der Richter mit einem gewissen Vorverständnis an den Fall herantritt, dessen Konstitution bereits durch eine Art Vorentscheidung bestimmt ist. Das Vorverständnis des Richters setzt dann nicht nur den Verstehensprozess

2 Nach *Fikentscher* ist das Kernstück der englischen Rechtsmethode das Prinzip „stare decisis, nach dem man Präzedenzfälle zu befolgen hat, soweit ihre jeweilige „ratio decidendi" reicht, die die juristische Aussagekraft eines entschiedenen Falles enthält. Dagegen bedeutet „obiter dictum" lediglich eine unwesentliche Beigabe für die juristische Entscheidung. Von „distinguishing" als Aufzeigung rechtlicher Unterschiede zwischen zwei Fällen ist zu trennen das „overruling" als ausgesprochene Zurückweisung eines Präzedenzfalls. Dazu *Engisch*, Einführung (Fn. 1), S. 255 f.

3 *Larenz/Canaris*, Methodenlehre (Fn. 1), S. 65. In diesem Sinne behauptet *Engisch* auch, dass die juristische Methodenlehre in die Rechtsphilosophie einmündet. Näher dazu *Engisch*, Einführung (Fn. 1), S. 252 ff.

4 Dazu vor allem, *Kramer*, Methodenlehre (Fn. 1), S. 39, 47.

5 Zur gesamten Kritik an die juristische Methodnelehre *Bydlinski*, Juristische Methodenlehre (Fn. 1), S. 140 ff.

in Gang, sondern steuert nach der Methodenwahl den Prozess auf das in der Richtigkeitsüberzeugung des Richters vorweggenommene Ergebnis hin. Darum dient die schuldgerechte Gesetzesinterpretation lediglich zu einer nachträglichen Stimmigkeitskontrolle, nämlich einer Scheinlegitimierung des in Wirklichkeit nach den außerpositiven Kriterien gewünschten Ergebnis.[6] Da die klassische juristische derart die Handlungsbedingen der juristischen Praxis verfehlt, erweist sie sich als nutzlos.[7]

Beifall findet die detaillierte Analyse von *Esser* darüber, wie der Richter tatsächlich verfährt. Dabei zeigt sich, dass es keine klaren Regeln der Rechtsmethodik oder der Auslegungsstandards gibt, sondern eine große Bandbreite an plausiblen Interpretationen, in der die persönliche Einschätzung des Richters die endgültige Entscheidung trifft. Aber daraus folgt nicht, dass der Richter in der Weise vorgehen darf. Denn diese methodologische Ansicht verstößt gerade gegen den Grundsatz „der Bindung des Richters an Gesetz", das überall in der Verfassung vorgeschrieben ist[8]. Nach diesem Gebot soll der Richter seine Entscheidung primär an den Maßstäben der Rechtsordnung orientieren[9]. Daneben stellt sich auch heraus, dass die von *Esser* vorgeschlagene Rationalitätskontrolle bei tatsächlicher Rechtsfindung – wie Konsens über Gerechtigkeit, Vernünftigkeit, Plausibilität – weitgehend hinter dem Niveau der traditionellen juristischen Methodenlehre zurückbleibt, weil deren Kriterium zu vage erscheint[10]. Hier stellt sich die skeptische Ansicht von *Esser* als unbefriedigend heraus.

In diesem Zusammenhang ist auch der Vorschlag von Neumann zu erwähnen, die juristische Methodenlehre durch die Argumentationslehre abzulösen. Ihm ist insofern zuzustimmen, als die juristische Methodenlehre vom Modell der einzig richtigen Entscheidung ausgeht und die Rechtsfindung als Akt der Erkenntnis begreift, während es bei der juristischen Argumentationstheorie um die Begründung der gerechten Entscheidung geht.

---

6 Vor allem *Esser*, Vorverständnis (Fn. 1), S. 132 f., 175 f.

7 *Esser*, Vorverständnis (Fn. 1), S.7.

8 Artikel 103 der koreanischen Verfassung, die lautet: „Richter urteilen unabhängig nach ihrem Gewissen und im Einklang mit der Verfassung und den Gesetzen." Vgl dazu auch Art 20 Abs. 3 in der deutschen Verfassung, die vorgibt, „...die vollziehende Gewalt und die Rechtsprechung sind an Gesetz und Recht gebunden."

9 Aus diesem Grund ist es dringlich vonnöten, die beiden folgenden Fragen, nämlich „questio facti" und „questio iuris" strikt voneinander zu unterscheiden Dazu *Engisch*, Einführung (Fn. 1), S. 79.

10 *Esser*, Vorverständnis (Fn. 1), S.8, 162 ff. Ausführlich dazu *Bydlinski*, Juristische Methodenlehre (Fn. 1), S. 155 f.

In der Tat gerät die juristische Methodenlehre wegen dieses Denkansatzes viel mehr als die juristische Argumentationslehre in die Schwierigkeiten, die Handlungsbedingen der Praxis einzulösen[11]. Dennoch bin ich der Ansicht, dass diese beiden Lehren nach demselben Ziel strebt, die richtige Entscheidung zu finden, so dass eine friedliche Koexistenz möglich wäre. Der Unterschied zwischen beiden liegt also lediglich in dem Weg dazu, nämlich zum einen das methodische Mittel dazu festzulegen, zum anderen die argumentative Begründung der Entscheidung klarzustellen. Sollte die juristische Methodenlehre also lediglich das konzeptionelle Rahmen zur Rechts-gewinnung darstellen, erweist sie sich als unentbehrlich, weil sie vor allem den Prozess der Rechtsgewinnung transparent macht. Aufgrund des positiven Rechts steht hier das logisch-erkenntnistheoretische Problem im Mittelpunkt, unter welchen formalen Voraussetzungen das Ergebnis der Rechtsgewinnung wahr oder nicht. Um diese Wichtigkeit der juristischen Methodenlehre deutlich zu machen, soll im Folgenden ihr grundlegendes Denkmuster in Korea mit Beispielen aus der Rechtsprechung erörtert werden.

II. Das Hauptschema der juristischen Methodenlehre

Wenn man die juristische Methodenlehre noch näher betrachtet, dann fällt auf, dass sich die Rechtsgewinnung auf zwei Wegen vollzieht, nämlich sowohl durch die Rechtsfindung als auch durch die Rechtsfortbildung, die sich herkömmlich anhand des Kriteriums des möglichen Wortsinns voneinander unterscheide[12]. Danach bewegt sich die Rechtsfindung im Rahmen des möglichen Wortsinnes, um den entscheidenden Maßstab durch die Auslegung des Gesetzes herauszufinden (secundum oder intra legem). In diesem Sinne ist die Rechtsfindung mit der Auslegung im üblichen Sinne gleich. Dagegen kann die Rechtsgewinnung über die Wortlautgrenze hinausgehen oder vom Wortsinn abweichen, weil das Gesetz in diesem Fall keine nach ihrem möglichen Wortsinn anwendbare Regel enthält,

11 Dazu *Neumann*, Juristische Methodenlehre und Theorie der juristischen Argumentation, Rechtstheorie 32, 2/3, 2001, S. 239 ff.

12 *Heck*, Gesetzesauslegung und Interessenjurisprudenz, 1914, S. 33; *Engisch*, Einführung (Fn. 1), S. 259; *Canaris*, Die Feststellung von Lücken im Gesetz, 2. Aufl., 1983, S. 23; *Kramer*, Methodenlehre (Fn. 1), S. 55 f.; *Larenz/Canaris*, Methodenlehre (Fn. 1), 143f. Nach diesen soll eine Deutung, die nicht mehr im Bereich des möglichen Wortsinnes liegt, nicht mehr Ausdeutung, sondern Umdeutung sein.

also eine Gesetzeslücke vorliegt. Eine solche Rechtsgewinnung lässt sich beispielsweise durch Analogie oder teleologische Reduktion vollziehen, was als Rechtsfortbildung genannt wird (praeter legem). Also der mögliche Wortsinn markiert die Grenze, woran sich die Rechtsfindung und die Rechtsfortbildung unterscheiden lassen. Auch wenn die Grenzziehung zwischen den beiden Bereichen offensichtlich unscharf ist, weil der Wortlaut neben einem Bedeutungskern einen nach den Rändern verschwimmenden Begriffshof besitzt[13], basiert die juristische Methodenlehre in Korea dennoch auf dieser Unterscheidung[14].

Gegen das Kriterium des möglichen Wortsinnes erheben sich gravierende Einwände[15]. Zwar erscheint es fast unmöglich, eine klare Grenze dieses Maßstabes festzulegen, weil sie sprachlich kaum genau auszumachen ist, zumal sich ähnliche methodische Vorgänge sowohl in der Rechtsfindung als auch in der Rechtsfortbildung abspielen und auch die Auslegung bereits ein wertendes Element enthält[16]. Dennoch hat die auf dem Kriterium der Wortgrenze aufbauende Unterscheidung gute Gründe für sich. Zum einen überzeugt nicht vollends das Gegenargument, dass sich nur der fließende Übergang zwischen der Rechtsfindung und der Rechtsfortbildung finden

13 Zum Begriff von Begriffskern und Begriffshof *Heck*, Gesetzesauslegung und Interessenjurisprudenz, 1914, S. 173.

14 . Siehe zur skeptischen Ansicht *Hyung-Bae Kim*, Die Auslegung des Gesetzes und die Ausfüllung der Lücke – anhand des Zivilrechts, in, ders., Zivilrechtliche Untersuchung(民事法研究), 1986, S. 41ff.; *Hyun-Sup Shim*, Juristische Methodenlehre in rechtsphilosophischer Hinsicht, Seoul National University, Rechtswissenschaft Bd. 24 Heft 1, 1983, S. 10ff.. Zur abweichenden Meinung, *Jong Oh Kim/Bong Cheol Choi/ Hyun Cheol Kim/Dong Ring Shin/Chun Soo Yang/ Kye Il Lee*, Rechtsphilosophie (Fn. 1), S. 266, 272 f. Trotz des Skeptizismus gegen die Grenzfunktion des möglichen Wortsinnes hält *Seo Hyuk Oh* die Differenzierung zwischen Rechtsfindung und Rechtsfortbildung für unerlässlich. Dazu *ders.*, Die juristische Methodenlehre (Fn. 1), S. 406.

15 Besonders zur Diskussion über das Analogieverbot im Strafrecht in Deutschland *Sax* und *Arthur Kaufmann* zweifeln ein Analogieverbot im herkömmlichen Sinne an, Während *Sax* behauptet, dass ein Analgieverbot nicht bestehe, geht *Kaufmann* noch weiter, indem er sagt, dass es ein solches Analogieverbot im Strafrecht überhaupt noch nie gegeben habe. Stattdessen finde die Analogie ihre Grenze nur im Unrechtstypus, der dem gesetzlichen Tatbestand zugrunde liegt. An der Ansicht von *Kaufmann* wurde sich weitgehend angeschlossen; *Hassemer, Stratenwerth* und *Hruschka*. Dazu *Engisch*, Einführung (Fn. 1), S. 259 Anm. 49.; *Young-Whan Kim*, Die strafrechtliche Auslegung und die Grenze zur Analogie, in: *Dong-Eun Shin* (Hrsg.), Die Grenze der gesetzlichen Auslegung, 2000, S. 29 f.

16 *Canaris*, Die Feststellung von Lücken (Fn. 12), S. 23; *Kramer*, Methodenlehre (Fn. 1), S. 56 f.; *Bdlinski*, Methodenlehre (Fn. 1), S. 470 f.

lässt, weil die Grenze zwischen den beiden Bereichen in überwiegenden Fällen leicht herauszufinden ist. Zum anderen besteht die praktische Funktion dieser Unterscheidung gerade darin, die jeweilige Rechtsgewinnung rechtsstaatlich zu rechtfertigen. Im Fall der Rechtsfindung braucht man kaum besondere methodologische Gedankengänge, wohingegen in der Rechtsfortbildung erneut auf ihre Rechtfertigung geprüft werden soll. Sonst würden die Gerichte eine ihnen nicht zustehende Gewalt usurpieren[17].

Hier sei noch erwähnt, dass in der Theorie und Praxis in Korea eine weitgehende Vermengung von der Rechtsfindung mit der Rechtsfortbildung obwaltet. Ein gutes Beispiel dafür ist, dass in der richterlichen Entscheidung ausnahmslos der Begriff „analogisierende Auslegung“ verwendet wird[18]. Darüber hinaus scheint der Oberste Gerichtshof Koreas auch nicht in der Lage zu sein, „die restriktive Auslegung“ von „teleologischer Reduktion“ zu unterschieden.[19] Daneben lässt sich auch beobachten, dass hier die juristische Methodenlehre zwar anhand der einzelnen Beispiele entwickelt, aber gar nicht zu einem systematischen Konzept theoretisch herausgebildet wird. Anstatt dessen werden unterschiedliche Rechtsgewinnungen allein anhand des Wortlauts oder des Ergebnisses des Urteils klassifiziert. An diesem problematischen Zustand ändert sich auch in der Praxis nichts[20].

---

17 Zu beachten ist hier das Argument von *Kye Il Lee*, dass diese Unterscheidung letztlich auf das verfassungsrechtliche Gebot der Bindung des Richters an das Gesetz zurückgeht. Auch wenn sich der mögliche Wortsinn im Prozess der Rechtsgewinnung konstituiert, so ist er schließlich feststellbar. Dazu ausführlich *ders.*, Eine Studie über die Systematik der Rechtsfortbildung des Richters, Recht und Gesellschaft, Bd. 56, 2017, S. 303 ff.

18 Seit 1965 verwendet der Oberste Gerichtshof Koreas koreanische höchste Gericht den Begriff der analogisierenden Auslegung. Vgl. dazu Oberste Gerichtshof 1954.5.5. 4287Minsnag271.

19 Auch in Deutschland wird darauf hingewiesen, dass diese öfters miteinander vermengt werden, wobei hervorzuheben ist, dass es bei teleologischer Reduktion um die Einschränkung des zu weit gehenden Anwendungsbereichs der betreffenden Norm nach der ihr eigenen Teleologie geht, was mit der sprachlichen Formulierung wenig zu tun hat. Dazu *Larenz/Canaris*, Methodenlehre (Fn. 1), S. 211.

20 Ausführlich dazu *Young Whan Kim*, Theorie und Praxis der juristischen Methodenlehre in Korea, in: Bu (Hrsg.), Juristische Methodenlehre in China und Ostasien, 2016, S. 280 ff.; Zur Problematik der juristischen Methodenlehre in Korea – Rechtsfindung und Rechtsfortbildung, ausdehnende Auslegung und Analogie, eingeschränkte Auslegung und teleologische Reduktion, rechtsphilosophische Studie, Bd. 18, Heft 2, 2015, S. 145 ff.

III. Die Auslegung von Gesetzen

1. Das Auslegungsziel, Gesetzgeber oder Gesetz?

Nach dem Wortgebrauch wird unter Auslegung Auseinanderlegung und Darlegung des im Text beschlossenen Sinnes verstanden. Der Gegenstand der juristischen Auslegung ist also der Gesetzestext als Träger des in ihm niedergelegten Sinnes, um dessen Verständnis es in der Auslegung geht. Durch die Auslegung wird dieser Sinn mit anderen Worten deutlicher ausgesagt und mittelbar gemacht. Blickt man auf die Geschichte der juristischen Methodenlehre in Deutschland zurück, werden bereits Ende des 19. Jahrhunderts zwei Theorien über das Ziel der Auslegung vertreten, nämlich die subjektive und die objektive Theorie[21]. Während die subjektive Theorie auf die Ermittlung des Willens des historischen Gesetzgebers abzielt, kommt es bei der objektiven Theorie darauf an, den dem Gesetz immanenten Sinn zu erschließen. Dabei betont die subjektive Theorie die rechtsstaatliche Anforderung „die Bindung des Richters an das Gesetz" und behauptet, dass die Aufgabe der Justiz gerade darin liegt, den Willen des Gesetzgebers wiederzufinden und dementsprechend den Sinn des Gesetzestextes zu interpretieren. Dagegen hält die objektive Theorie die gerechte Entscheidung im konkreten Fall für ausschlaggebend, indem sie die Rechtsgewinnung als die Herstellung des der Gegenwart angemessenen Gesetzessinnes begreift[22].

Jeder der beiden Theorien liegt eine Teilwahrheit zugrunde. Einerseits ist gegen die subjektive Theorie darauf hingewiesen worden, dass sich der Wille des Gesetzgebers schwer feststellen lässt. Daneben wird auch hervorgehoben, dass sie nicht dazu geeignet ist, das gegenwärtige Problem richtig zu bewältigen, weil das Gesetz relativ alt ist. Andererseits ist an der objektiven Theorie kritisiert worden, dass sie das Gesetz zu weit auslegt, so dass die Bindung des Richters an das Gesetz vernachlässigt wird[23]. Deswegen wird heute versucht, die beiden Ansätze in einer vermittelnden

---

21 *Larenz* zufolge ist die objektive Auslegungstheorie in der zweiten Hälfte des 19. Jahrhunderts von *Kohler*, *Binding* und *Wach* vertreten worden. Dazu *ders.*, Methodenlehre (Fn. 1), S. 35f.

22 Dazu *Engisch*, Einführung (Fn. 1), S. 133 ff.; *Larenz/Canaris*, Methodenlehre (Fn.1), 137 ff.

23 Dazu *Young-Whan Kim*. Das Grundproblem der Rechtsphilosophie, 3. Aufl., 2012, S. 300ff.

Ansicht zum Ausgleich zu bringen, wobei der Akzent mal eher auf dem subjektiven[24], mal eher auf dem objektiven Element liegt[25].

Wenn ich recht sehe, lässt sich in Korea eine intensive Diskussion um das Auslegungsziel schwer finden. Dabei fällt auf, dass früher die Rechtsprechung häufig den Begriff „die Absicht der Gesetzgebung (立法取旨)" verwendet. Aber es scheint nicht ganz klar zu sein, was damit gemeint ist, denn er impliziert sowohl die tatsächliche Absicht des Gesetzgebers (die subjektive Theorie) als auch das Ziel des Gesetzes (die objektive Theorie). Festzuhalten bleibt, dass die juristische Methodenlehre in Korea auf dieser Weise der Auseinandersetzung um das Auslegungsziel ausweicht. Aber dieses Bild ändert sich allmählich, weil sich in Gegenwart eine zunehmende Neigung zur objektiven Theorie in der Rechtsprechung beobachten lässt, wo die Ansicht von *Radbruch* sogar zitiert worden ist[26], dass das Gesetz viel klüger als der Gesetzgeber ist.[27] Allerdings wird diese objektive Meinung dahingehend scharf kritisiert, dass sie die Prinzipien der Gesetzesauslegung überschreitet, die vor allem auf dem Wortlaut sowie dem System des Gesetzes beruht, was gemeinsam danach strebt, den Ausgleich zwischen der Rechtssicherheit und der Fallgerechtigkeit zu ermöglichen[28]. Im Ganzen genommen ist nun ein breiteres Spektrum nicht zu verkennen. Zur objektiven Theorie neigt nun das jüngste Urteil zu sexuellem Missbrauch in der militärischen Einrichtung[29] und die Mindermeinung zum Urteil über Arbeitsunfälle[30]. Dagegen tendieret das Urteil zur Feiertagsvergütung zur subjektiven Theorie[31].

24 Beispielsweise *Engisch*, Einführung (Fn. 1), S. 172f.

25 Zum Beispiel *Larenz/Canaris*, Methodenlehre (Fn. 1), S. 139f.

26 *Radbruch* hat behauptet: „Der Ausleger kann das Gesetz besser verstehen, als es seine Schöpfer verstanden haben, das Gesetz kann klüger sein als sein Verfasser – es *muss* sogar klüger sein als seine Verfasser." Dazu *ders.*, Rechtsphilosophie, 8. Aufl., 1973, S. 207.

27 Das Urteil zur Militärverweigerung, Oberster Gerichtshof, 1.11.2018,2016do10912. Hier geht es darum, die ‚berechtigten Gründe' in §188 Abs. 1 des Wehrdienstgesetzes zu interpretieren. Da die Verpflichtung des Wehrdienstes durch dessen Kriminalisierung gerade die Gewissensfreiheit als Grundrecht des Betroffenen beeinträchtigt, wird darunter auch die Wehrdienstverweigerung von Zeugen Jehovas verstanden und also nicht bestraft.

28 Siehe die Mindermeinung von *So Young Kim, Hee Dae Jo, Sang Ok Park, Ki Taek Lee* in diesem Urteil.

29 Oberster Gerichtshof, 21.4.2022, 2019do3047.

30 Oberster Gerichtshof, 9.9.2021, 2017du45933.

31 Oberster Gerichtshof, 21.6.2018, 2011da11239.

2. Kriterien der Auslegung; sog. Auslegungscanones

Sollte die Auslegung nicht dem Gutdünken des Auslegers überlassen bleiben, sondern in einer nachprüfbaren Weise vor sich gehen, bedarf es bestimmter Auslegungskriterien, nach denen sich der Auslegende richten soll. Solche Kriterien sind aber in der juristischen Methodenlehre bereits entwickelt worden, nämlich das grammatikalische, das systematische, das historische und das teleologische Element.[32]

Jede Auslegung eines Textes beginnt mit dem Wortsinn. Dies versteht sich von selbst, weil der Wortlaut des Gesetzes das primäre und wichtigste Indiz für den Normsinn darstellt. Daher gibt es in jedem Land unzählige Beispiele für die grammatikalische Interpretation und Korea ist keine Ausnahme davon. Fraglich ist aber, was unter dem Wortlaut zu verstehen ist, der gerade ausgelegt werden soll. Dabei stellt sich die Frage, was die Umgangssprache oder die Fachsprache, tatsächlicher oder möglicher Sinn und der Sprachgebrauch im Zeitpunkt des Gesetzeserlasses oder der heutige Sprachgebrauch bedeutet? Ein Beispiel für die grammatikalische Interpretation ist die Frage, ob der Transsexuelle auch als ein Tatobjekt der Vergewaltigung angesehen werden kann, weil das Strafrecht nur die Frau als Tatbestandsmerkmal vorsieht[33].

Als das zweite Element kommt die Systematik des Gesetzes in Betracht. Dahinter steht der Gedanke, dass die einzelnen Normen nicht unverbunden nebeneinanderstehen, vielmehr als System konsistenter Wertentscheidungen zu begreifen sind, deren Einzeltatbestände nicht isoliert, sondern im Zusammenhang mit den dazugehörigen anderen Normen interpretiert

32 Nachdem *Savigny* dafür das grammatikalische, das logische, das systematische und das historische Element aufgestellt hat, wird heute das teleologische Element hinzugefügt, indem das logische und das systematische zu einem systematischen Element zusammengefasst werden. Dazu *ders.*, Das System des römischen Rechts, Bd. 1, 1840, S. 212f.

33 Ausgehend von der biologischen Betrachtungsweise, die auf die weiblichen Geschlechtsorgane abhebt, hat der Oberste Gerichtshof Koreas früher den sexuellen Missbrauch von Transsexuellen nicht als Vergewaltigung gewertet. (Oberster Gerichtshof 1996. 6. 11. 96do791). Danach hat es seine Ansicht geändert, nachdem zum biologischen Faktor auch der soziologische Aspekt hinzugenommen wurde, unter dem die psychologische Einstellung des Opfers, sich als eine Frau zu fühlen, und dessen sozial anerkanntes Selbstverständnis mitberücksichtigt werden. (Oberster Gerichtshof 2009.9.10. 2009da3580.) Dieses Problem ist nun vollends gelöst, weil das Strafrecht inzwischen das Tatbestandmerkmal „Frau“ durch das „des fremden Menschen“ ersetzt hat.

werden. Nur auf diese Weise lassen sich die Wertungswidersprüche vermeiden. Dieses Element wird wiederum in ein äußeres und ein inneres System eingeteilt, wobei das innere System ein konsistentes System von Wertungsentscheidung bedeutet, wohingegen sich das äußere System auf den formalen Aufbau des Gesetzes bezieht. Ein Beispiel für das innere System, das auf den Bedeutungszusammenhang abstellt, ist die Entscheidung des Obersten Gerichthofs über das Verhältnis zwischen §29 Abs 1 des koreanischen Grundrechts und §2 Abs. 1 und Abs. 2 des Staatshaftungsrechts in Bezug auf die Staatshaftung[34].

Drittens ist es naheliegend, die Regelungsabsicht des Gesetzgebers zu erforschen, wenn die oben genannten beiden Elemente nicht dazu taugen, den Sinn des Gesetzes deutlich zu machen. Da die Entstehungsgeschichte vielfach Auskunft über die Normvorstellung des Gesetzgebers gibt, wird dies als das historische Element bezeichnet. Mit ihm sind aber die Vorstellungen gemeint, die der Gesetzgeber tatsächlich gehabt hat, auch wenn deren vollständige Ermittlung kaum möglich erscheint. Da aber in Korea früher nicht genügend Gesetzesmaterialien vorhanden sind, scheint es Schwierigkeiten zu bereiten, Beispiele dafür zu finden. Als ein Beispiel dafür ist dennoch die Entscheidung des Obersten Gerichthof Koreas, „der sog. Betragsfall" zu nennen[35].

34 Dabei werden drei Ansichten vertreten: Nach der Mehrheitsmeinung, die die staatliche Haftung und das zivilrechtliche Schadensersatzprinzip vermittelt, soll die Amtshaftung den Beamten nur zuerkannt werden, wenn sie vorsätzlich oder grob fahrlässig gehandelt haben. Für das leicht fahrlässige Unrecht der Beamten soll der Staat die Verantwortung übernehmen. Dagegen behauptet die Sondermeinung, dass der Beamte nach dem zivilrechtlichen Schadensersatzprinzip in allen Fällen zur Verantwortung gezogen werden muss, ungeachtet der leichten oder groben Fahrlässigkeit. Die letzte Ansicht beruht schließlich auf dem staatlichen Haftungsprinzip, nach dem der Staat für das sämtliche Unrecht der Beamten verantwortlich sein soll, so dass §29 Abs 1 des koreanischen Grundrechts lediglich den Regress der staatlichen Haftung gegen den Beamten bedeutet. Dazu Oberster Gerichtshof 1996. 2. 15. 95da38677.

35 Oberster Gerichtshof 1978. 4. 25. 78do246. In Frage kommt hier §55 Ab, 1 Nr. 6 des koreanischen Strafrechts, die lautet: Wenn eine Geldstrafe gemildert werden soll, so wird sie um die Hälfte ihres Höchstbetrages herabgesetzt. Nun ist die Frage, ob mit diesem Merkmal nicht nur die Obergrenze, sondern auch die Untergrenze des Betrags gemeint sein kann. Die Mehrheitsmeinung bejaht dies, indem sie den sog. Redaktionsfehler des Gesetzverfassers beim Vorgang der Gesetzgebung offen zugegeben hat. Auch wenn die Entstehungsgeschichte und die Absicht des Gesetzes in diesem Fall relativ unklar ist, so kann dies doch als ein historisches Element der Auslegung angenommen werden.

Viertens bedeutet Telos Zweck oder Ziel. Somit ist die teleologische Interpretation die Auslegungsmethode, die nach der ratio legis fragt. Wenn die Auslegung des Gesetzes dazu dienen soll, gerade eine billige Entscheidung in Einzelfällen zu ermöglichen, verwundert es nicht, dass diese Methode am häufigsten verwendet wird, so dass ihr vorrangige Bedeutung zukommt. Hier sind zwei Gruppen objektiver Kriterien zu konstatieren, die den Ausschlag geben müssen.: Zum einen geht es um die Struktur des geregelten Sachbereichs, an der der Gesetzgeber selbst nichts ändern kann, und zum anderen um die hinter einer Regelung stehenden rechtsethischen Prinzipien, in denen der Sinnbezug auf die Rechtsidee begreifbar wird. Objektiv-teleologisch wird dieses Kriterium deshalb genannt, weil sich der Gesetzgeber dieser Bedeutung nicht immer bewusst gewesen ist. Ein Beispiel, das den Verdacht erweckt, ob er sich bei dieser Entscheidung nicht um eine verbotene Analogie handelt, ist der Fall über das Wort „bei sich führen[36].

Hier sei auch erwähnt, dass das oberste Gericht öfters den Begriff der gesamt-systematischen Interpretation verwendet hat[37]. Dabei zeigt sich, dass diese mal eine Mehrheitsmeinung, mal eine Minderheitsansicht darstellt. Auf jeden Fall tut es not, diesen Begriff auszudifferenzieren, weil es zu vage wäre, was damit gemeint ist. Da diese Interpretation letztlich auf die Fallgerichtigkeit abzielt, lässt sie sich als eine Abart der „systematisch-teleologische Auslegung“ bezeichnen.

Letztlich kommt auch die verfassungskonforme Auslegung in Betracht, die in den jüngsten Entscheidungen stetig an Bedeutung gewonnen hat. Früher wurde sie als eine besondere Form der systematischen Auslegung verstanden, die auf dem Prinzip der Einheit der Ordnung beruht. Sie ist berufen, bei mehrdeutigem Wortlaut unter den möglichen Deutungen

---

36 Oberster Gerichtshof 1997. 5. 30. 97do597. Hier kommt folgender Fall in Frage: Der Angeklagte ist an das die Abschleppdienstgebühr verlangende Verkehrspersonal mit seinem Personenkraftwagen angefahren und hat ihn 1m lang geschleppt, so dass er auf dem Boden gefallen und daher verletzt ist. Nachdem das Fahrzeug als ein gefährliche Werkzeug gemäß §3 Abs. 1 des Gesetzes gegen das Gewalttätigkeitsverbrechen interpretiert wird, hat der Oberste Gerichtshof entschieden, dass mit dem Wort „bei sich führen“ nicht nur „bei sich haben“, sondern auch „verwenden oder benutzen“ gemeint ist und daher der Angeklagte bestraft werden soll. Diese Entscheidung ist stark kritisiert worden, weil die Interpretation des Wortes „bei sich führen“ als „zum Verbrechen benutzt“ weit über die Wortlautgrenze überschreitet hat. Dazu *Yong-Hyun Gang*, die Gewalttaten mit dem Fahrzeug und „Bei Sich Führen“ gefährlicher Werkzeuge, Strafrechtliche Fallstudie Bd. 7, 1999, S. 238ff.

37 Oberster Gerichtshof 1994.12.20, 94mo32., 2004. 11.28., 2004do1228.

diejenige auszuwählen, die die mit der Verfassung in Einklang steht[38]. Das Gebot verfassungskonformer Auslegung verlangt also, von mehreren möglichen Normdeutungen, die teils zu einem verfassungswidrigen, teils zu einem verfassungsmäßigen Ergebnis führen, diejenige vorzuziehen, die den Sinn der Verfassung besser wiedergibt. Anders als die Vergangenheit, wo die verfassungskonforme Auslegung meistens dazu dient, auf die Verfassungsmäßigkeit des bestimmten Gesetzes zu überprüfen[39], lässt sich in Korea neulich beobachten, dass die verfassungskonforme Interpretation nicht nur eine Auslegung des Gesetzes, sondern auch eine Rechtsfortbildung umfasst, die in Berufung auf den später noch darzustellen Rechtsgrundsatz erfolgt[40]. Hinzu kommt auch eine Diskussion über die Unterscheidung der verfassungsorientierten von der verfassungskonformen Auslegung. Allerdings unterliegt sie den hierfür geltenden methodischen Grenzen wie Wortlaut wie dem Zweck des Gesetzes[41]. Als Beispiel für die verfassungskonforme Auslegung in Korea sind die oben dargestellten Fälle anzuführen; nämlich das Urteil zur Militärverweigerung(Oberster Gerichtshof, 1.11.2018,2016do10912) und das jüngste Urteil zu sexuellem Missbrauch in der militärischen Einrichtung (Oberster Gerichtshof, 21.4.2022, 2019do3047).

3. Rangordnung der Auslegungselemente

An der juristischen Methodenlehre in Deutschland ist stark bemängelt worden, dass eine gesicherte Rangordnung unter den eben genannten Auslegungselementen bis jetzt noch nicht vorhanden ist. In der gerichtlichen Praxis ist zwar öfters zu beobachten, dass von Fall zu Fall diejenige Auslegungsmethode verwendet wird, die zum befriedigenden Ergebnis führt. Auch wenn es noch nicht zur herrschen Lehre gehört, verfährt die überwiegende Ansicht wie folgt vor: Der Wortsinn bildet den Ausgangspunkt der Auslegung, dann kommt das systematische Auslegungselement zum

38 *Engisch*, Einführung (Fn. 1), S. 124.

39 Verfassungsgerichtshof, 1990.4.2. 89hzunga 113, 2002.11.28. 98hzunba 101, 2002.11.28, 98hyunba 101/ 98hyunba8.

40 Hier liegt es nahe, weshalb *Bydlinski* diese Auslegung als eine Abart der systematisch-teleologischen Interpretation bezeichnet. Dazu *ders.*, Juristische Methodenlehre (Fn. 1), S. 455.

41 Ausführlich dazu *Kye Il Lee*, Eine methodologische Untersuchung über die Typen des verfassungskonformen Urteils, Recht und Gesellschaft, Bd. 60, 2019.

Zuge. Im Fall der mehreren Auslegungen ist diejenige Auslegung vorzuziehen, die dem Willen des Gesetzgebers am ehesten gerecht wird. Reichen die bisher genannten Kriterien dennoch nicht aus, so wird letztlich auf die objektiv-teleologischen Kriterien zurückgegriffen.[42]Letztlich sei erwähnt, dass die Auseinandersetzung über das Auslegungsziel in Deutschland nun zur Frage nach der Rangfolge der verschieden Auslegungselemente gewechselt zu sein scheint[43].

Wenn es um die Rechtsfindung in Korea geht, bleibt zu beobachten, dass eine theoretische Auseinandersetzung mit dem Auslegungselement lediglich in geringem Umfang vorhanden ist[44]. Neulich fällt auf, dass die einzelnen Auslegungselemente im Urteil erwähnt werden. Und in Bezug auf Rangfolge der Auslegungselemente bleibt es zu beobachten, dass die Rechtsprechungen vielmals auf die Grundsatzentscheidung rekurriert, in der das Auslegungsziel und die Auslegungselemente zusammengesetzt sind. Sie lautet: „Das Ziel der Gesetzesauslegung liegt darin, innerhalb der Grenzen, die die Rechtssicherheit gefährden, eine Fallgerechtigkeit zu finden. In diesem Prozess gilt es, die im Gesetz verwendeten Wörter so getreu wie möglich der gewöhnlichen Bedeutung auszulegen und darüber hinaus durch die systematische und logische Interpretations-methoden, die den gesetzgeberischen Zweck und Zweck des Gesetzes.... berücksichtigen, eine vernünftige Auslegung sicherzustellen."[45]

Dabei stellt sich heraus, dass es in den Entscheidungen des Obersten Gerichts in Korea zwei gegensätzliche Positionen gibt. Eine Position, die vom Gesetzestext ausgeht und die Rechtssicherheit, nämlich die gleiche Rechtsanwendung betont, wohingegen eine andere Position vom einzelnen Fall ausgeht und auf konkrete Billigkeit der Entscheidung, nämlich die Fallgerechtigkeit in den Vordergrund stellt. In Bezug auf die argumentative Struktur zeigt sich, dass für eine Position „der Gesetzestext-die gleiche

---

42 *Engisch*, Einführung (Fn. 1), S. 147ff. 172ff.; *Larenz/Canaris*, Methodenlehre (Fn. 1), S. 332ff.

43 Dazu vor allem *Koch/Rüßmann*, Begründungslehre (Fn. 1), S. 178f.

44 *Jin_Su Yune*, Erstes Kapital, Allgemeiner Teil, in: Yong-Dam Kim(Hrsg.), Kommentar zum Zivilrecht Bd.1, 2010, S. 85ff; *Young-Whan Kim*, Grundprobleme (Fn. 1), S. 253ff.; *Hak-Tae Kim*, Die Grenze der Gesetzesauslegung: Eine kritische Untersuchng der juristischen Methode anhand der gerichtlichen Entscheidung, Hanguk Unversity of Foreign Studies., Rechtswissenschaft Bd. 22, 2006, S. 177ff.; *Dong-Jin Park*, Eine Studie über die klasssische juristische Methodenlehre, Justizverwaltung, 1997 S. 7ff.; *Seo-Hyuk Oh*, Die Auslegung des Gesetzes (Fn.15), S. 20ff.

45 Oberster Gerichtshof, 23.4.2009, 20o6da81035.

Rechtsanwendung für den jeweiligen Fall-Rechtsstabilität“ bezeichnend ist, dagegen für eine andere Position „der konkrete Fall-die Rechtsgestaltung für den betreffenden Fall-Fallgerechtigkeit“. Um diese gegensätzliche Position zu begründen, sind verschiedene Auslegungselement in Bezug genommen. Welches die Mehrheitsansicht vertritt, hängt nun lediglich von der Stimmenzahl der Richter ab. Sollte aber alle Auslegungselemente hier ohne die feste Rangfolge berücksichtigt werden, verwundert es nicht, dass der Eindruck entsteht, als ob die Auslegungskriterien beliebig nach dem erwünschten Ergebnis ausgewählt werden. Das hat sich sehr deutlich am strafrechtlichen Analogieverbot gezeigt[46].

IV. Methoden richterlicher Rechtsfortbildung

1. Rechtsfortbildung als Fortsetzung der Rechtsfindung

Auch wenn die Auslegung des Gesetzes gerade die zentrale Aufgabe einer der Praxis zugewandte Rechtswissenschaft ausmacht, hat sich diese nicht darin erschöpft. Denn es hat sich immer gezeigt, dass auch ein sorgsam bedachtes Gesetz nicht für jeden Fall eine Lösung zur Verfügung hat. Also jedes Gesetz ist unvermeidbar lückenhaft, wofür der Richter eine bestimmte Methode der Rechtsgewinnung braucht. Daher versteht es sich von selbst, dass die Ausfüllung dieser Lücke ein wichtiges Anliegen der Jurisprudenz darstellt. Beim näheren Zusehen zeigt sich aber, dass die Auslegung grundsätzlich nicht strikt von der Rechtsfortbildung unterschieden ist. In der Tat bedeutet jede Konkretisierung eines Begriffs durch die Auslegung insofern eine Rechtsfortbildung, als sie eine unter mehreren Bedeutungen als zutreffend kennzeichnet und damit eine bestehende Ungewissheit beseitigt. Angenommen, dass sich jede Interpretation auch durch eine schöpferische Leistung des verstehenden Subjekts vollzieht, ist dieser kreative Teil schon in der Auslegung vorhanden. Wenn daher zwischen der Auslegung und der Rechtsfortbildung nur ein gradueller Unterschied besteht, dann setzt sich jene bruchlos in dieser als der Lückenausfüllung fort[47]. Auch in Korea ist die Befugnis des Richters zur Rechtsfortbildung weitgehend anerkannt. Freilich bedarf richterliche Rechtsfortbildung der methodisch geleiteten

---

46 Zu diesem Methodensynkretismus *Young Whan Kim*, Theorie und Praxis der Juristische Methodenlehre in Korea (Fn. 20), S, 281, Anm. 7.

47 *Larenz/Canaris*, Methodenlehre (Fn.1), S. 188f.

Begründung, weil die Gerichte ohne diese in den Bereich der Gesetzgebung eingreifen würden, wie es oben bereits dargestellt wurde.

2. Begriff und Art der Gesetzeslücke

Wie erwähnt, kennzeichnet der Begriff der Gesetzeslücke die Grenze der Rechtsfortbildung. Und er zeichnet sich in doppelter Hinsicht aus. Zum einen weist er auf eine „Unvollständigkeit" hin. Daher kann man von einer Gesetzeslücke nur dann sprechen, wenn dieses für einen bestimmten Bereich eine einigermaßen vollständige Regelung anstrebt. Zum zweiten lässt sich die Frage, ob eine Lücke vorliegt, in Bezug auf die „Planwidrigkeit" des Gesetzes beurteilen. Dabei ist der ihm zugrunde liegende Regelungsplan aus dem Gesetz selbst im Wege der Auslegung zu erschließen. Hier spielt die Teleologie des Gesetzes allerdings eine entscheidende Rolle, wobei hervorzuheben bleibt, dass sie nicht zu eng verstanden werden darf. Eine Gesetzeslücke bedeutet also "eine planwidrige Unvollständigkeit des Gesetzes"[48].

Bei vielen Unterscheidungen ist besonders die von der offenen und der verdeckten Lücke von besonderer Bedeutung. Offene Lücken liegen dann vor, wenn das Gesetz entgegen seinem Zweck für eine bestimmte Fallgruppe keine Regel enthält, die auf sie anwendbar wäre. Dagegen kommen verdeckte Lücken in Frage, wenn das Gesetz zwar auch Fälle geregelt hat, die aber seinem Sinn und Zweck nach eigentlich nicht erfasst werden sollten. Der Wortsinn des Gesetzes schießt hier über das Ziel hinaus. Hier besteht die Lücke gerade im Fehlen einer Einschränkung des zu weit formulierten Sinnbereichs des Gesetzes[49].

3. Analogie als die Ausfüllung der offenen Lücke

Wenn es um eine offene Lücke geht, so geschieht ihre Ausfüllung überwiegend im Wege der Analogie. Unter einer Analogie wird eine solche

48 Dazu *Canaris*, Die Feststellung von Lücken (Fn. 13), S. 39; *Larenz/Canaris*, Methodenlehre (Fn. 1), S. 191ff, 194.; *Engisch*, Einführung (Fn. 1), S. 236ff.; *Bydlinski*, Methodenlehre , (Fn. 1), S. 472f; *Kramer*, Methodenlehre, S. (Fn. 1), 137ff.

49 *Kramer* findet den herkömmlichen Sprachgebrauch merkwürdig, weil es hier keine Regelung fehlt. Wenn die Lücke hier gerade darin besteht, eine gesetzliche Einschränkung vermissen zu lassen, dann sollte er anstatt der verdecke Lücke „Ausnahmenlücke" bezeichnet werden. *Kramer*, Methodenlehre (Fn. 1), S. 143f.

Rechtsgewinnung verstanden, in der die für einen Tatbestand A oder mehrere ähnliche Tatbestände anwendbare Regel auf einen vom Gesetz nicht geregelten, aber ihm ähnlichen Tatbestand B übertragen wird. Diese Übertragung beruht darauf, dass beide Tatbestände in der maßgebenden Hinsicht gleich zu bewerten sind, also auf der Forderung der Gerechtigkeit, Gleichartiges gleich zu behandeln. Gegen die Analogie wird behauptet, dass es dabei nicht um einen Schluss vom Besonderen auf Besonderes, sondern vom Besonderen auf das Allgemeine, d.h. Induktion geht[50]. Zuzustimmen ist dem Einwand, dass sie ein problematisches Verfahren darstellt. Doch stellt sich heraus, dass sie ein hybrider, nämlich aus Deduktion und Induktion zusammengesetzter Schluss ist. Mit anderen Worten: Hier lässt sich nicht unmittelbar von einem Besonderen auf ein Besonderes, sondern durch die Vermittlung des den beiden Tatbeständen Gemeinsamen schließen, was für ihre Bewertung ausschlaggebend ist[51].

Ein besonders qualifizierter Fall des Analogieschlusses ist das sogenannte „argumentum a maiore ad minus“ (argumentum a fortiori). Es besagt, dass eine Rechtsfolge, die für einen weniger gewichtigen Sachverhalt angeordnet ist, umso mehr für einen wertungsmäßig gewichtigeren Fall gelten muss, der aber nicht geregelt ist. Kurz; Wenn es verboten ist, dass zwei mit einem Fahrrad fahren, gilt dies „erst recht“ für den Fall, dass drei mit einem Fahrrad fahren. Ein bekanntes Beispiel dafür ist die Entscheidung des Obersten Gerichtshofs über den Fall „der fahrlässigen Brandstiftung“[52].

---

50 *Canaris*, Die Feststellung der Lücken (Fn. 13), S. 97ff.; *Engisch*, Einführung (Fn. 1), S.248ff.; *Bydlinski*, Methodenlehre (Fn.1), S. 478f.

51 *Kaufmann*, Das Verfahren (Fn.1), S.60f.; *Engisch*, Einführung (Fn. 1), S.249f.: *Larenz/Canaris*, Methodenlehre (Fn. 1), S. 205f.

52 Oberster Gerichtshof 1994. 12. 20. 94mo32. Hier geht es um folgenden Fall: Bei windigem Wetter hat der Angeklagte das trockene Heu gesammelt, um damit seine Zigarette anzuzünden. Wegen des dadurch entstandenen Brandes ein großer Teil des Apfelobstgartens zum Opfer. Die einschlägige Vorschrift für diesen Fall ist §170 Abs.2 des koreanischen Strafrechts, die lautet: “Der vorangehende Absatz ist auf denjenigen anzuwenden, der fahrlässig einen ihm selbst gehörigen in §166 und §167 genannten Gegenstand verbrennt und dadurch eine Gemeingefahr verursacht“. In Frage kommt es nun, wie das Tatbestandsmerkmal “einen ihm selbst gehörigen in §166(allgemeine Gebäude) und §167(allgemeine Sache) genannten Gegenstand” zu interpretieren ist. Entgegen dem allgemeinen Sprachgebrauch, diesen Satz als eine Konjunktion zu verstehen, hat die Mehrheitsansicht des Gerichts diese Vorschrift als distinktiv ausgelegt, so dass dieser Tatbestand nicht nur seinen eigenen in §166 genannten Gegenstand, sondern auch die in §167 genannten Sachen unabhängig von deren Zugehörigkeit erfasst und daher der Angeklagte bestraft werden soll. Es liegt nahe, dass diese Schlussfolgerung auf dem Gedanken von argumentum a fortiori

Dabei fällt aber auf, dass das argumentum a fortiori in Korea hier nicht als der Analogie verwand, sondern vielmehr eher als eine Art der systematischen Auslegung begriffen wird[53].

Das Pendant zum Analogieschluss und zum argumentum a fortiori ist der Umkehrschluss (argumentum e contrario). Danach gilt die Rechtsfolge R für andere Tatbestände nicht, weil sie nur an den Tatbestand A geknüpft ist. Hier spielt die Ähnlichkeit der beiden Tatbestände keine Rolle, so dass der Umkehrschluss die Ablehnung der Analogie bedeutet. Allerdings ist die Frage, ob eine gesetzliche Regel einen Umkehrschluss erlaubt oder die Grundlage für die Analogie bildet, nicht eine Frage der formalen Logik, sondern der in ihr zum Ausdruck kommenden Wertung. Ein Beispiel für das Verhältnis zwischen beiden ist die Entscheidung des Obersten Gerichtshofs über den Begriff des „Mieters"[54].

4. teleologische Reduktion zur Ausfüllung der verdecken Lücke

Bekanntlich gehören Analogie und teleologische Reduktion zur Rechtsfortbildung. Sie stellen quasi zwei wichtige Säule von ihr dar. Wie gesagt, bezeichnet eine verdeckte Lücke einen solchen Fall, in dem eine gesetzliche

---

beruht. Das heißt: Wenn die fahrlässige Bestrafung des eigenen Gegenstandes bestraft wird, gilt dies umso mehr für die der fremden Sachen.

53 So nennt das höchste Gerichts Gericht ausdrücklich eine „gesamt-systematische Auslegung". Dazu Oberster Gerichtshof 1994. 12. 20. 94mo32.

54 Hier liegt folgender Fall vor: Weil ein über siebzig Jahre alten Mann mit der Pflege seiner schwerkranken Frau beschäftigt war, hat er seiner Tochter das Sparbuch gegeben mit der Bitte, an seiner Stelle den Vertrag über eine Mietwohnung abzuschließen. Nach dem Mietwohnungsgesetz in der alten Fassung kann der Mieter in einer Frist(5 Jahre) nach dem Abschluss dieses Mietvertrages einen Antrag auf die Übertragung des Eigentums an der Wohnung stellen, wenn er den Mietvertrag in seinem Namen abgeschlossen und in dieser Wohnung gewohnt hat. Aufgrund des sog. „materiellen Mieters", der mit seinem Geld den Mietvertrag abgeschlossen und jahrelang in der Wohnung gelebt hat, hat das Tae-Jeon Oberlandesgericht(die zweite Instanz) diesem alten Man das Wohnungseigentum bewilligt, auch wenn er rechtlich dazu nicht berechtigt ist, weil der Vertrag in Namen seiner Tochter geschrieben wurde. Dazu Oberlandesgericht Taejeon 2006na1846. Diesen Fall hat der Oberste Gerichtshof anders entschieden und zwar mit der Begründung, dass der Mieter in §15 Abs. 1 des Mietwohnungsgesetzes lediglich denjenigen bedeutet, mit dem der Mietvertrag tatsächlich abgeschlossen wurde. Darum verstößt ein solcher Umgang mit dem Gesetz gegen den Grundsatz der Auslegung, deren Ziel darin liegt, zur billigen Entscheidung insoweit zu dienen, als diese nicht die Rechtssicherheit beeinträchtigt. Wenn der Sinn des Gesetzes eindeutig feststeht, dann ist eine davon abweichende Interpretation grundsätzlich ausgeschlossen. Dazu Oberster Gerichtshof 2009, 4.23. 2006da81035.

Regel gemäß der immanenten Teleologie des Gesetzes einer Einschränkung bedarf. Die Ausfüllung einer solchen Lücke geschieht also durch die Hinzufügung der sinngemäß geforderten Einschränkung. Weil hiermit die im Gesetz enthaltene, nach ihrem insoweit eindeutigen Wortsinn zuweit gefasste Regel auf den ihr nach dem Sinnzusammenhang des Gesetzes zukommenden Anwendungsbereich zurückgeführt wird, spricht man von einer teleologischen Reduktion. Kurz: Bei ihr geht es darum, einen zu weit gefassten Wortsinn auf den Anwendungsbereich zu reduzieren, der der ratio legis entspricht. Ein Beispiel dafür ist die Entscheidung über die Selbstanzeige nach der Entdeckung der Tat.[55] Mir scheint diese Art der Rechtsfortbildung eine der schwierigsten Methoden zu sein, denn sie hat den Anschein contra legem, als ob sie unmittelbar gegen das Gesetz verstößt[56].

Wie der Umkehrschluss die Analogie ablehnt, ist auch bei der teleologischen Reduktion eine solche Grenze dort sichtbar, wo „eine sog. formale Ordnungsschrift" in Frage kommt, die strikt auszulegen ist. Dahinter steckt der Gedanke des Schutzes des Vertrauens der Rechtsgenossen in die Beständigkeit und Voraussehbarkeit der Rechtsausübung, also „Ordnung

55 Oberste Gerichtshof 1997. 3. 20. 96do1167. Hier geht es um folgenden Fall; A hat vom Wahlkampfmanager B ungefähr 7.8 Million Won erhalten, damit er als Wahlkampfhelfer die Wahlkampagne für C macht. Er sollte mit diesem Geld den Wählern einen vermögensrechtlichen Vorteil anbieten, um die Wahl für C zu gewinnen. Wegen dieser Tat wurde er wegen der Bestechung der Wahl angeklagt und dann polizeilich verfolgt. Da er floh, wurde diese Anklage eingestellt. Erst danach ging er zur Polizei, um das Geständnis abzulegen. In Frage kommt es nun, ob die Rechtsfolge des Gesetzes zur Amtswahl und deren Verhinderung, nämlich "Absehens von der Strafe" lediglich für "die Selbstanzeige vor der Entdeckung der Tat" gilt. Nachdem A in der Vorinstanz bestraft wird, macht nun die Mehrheitsansicht im obersten Gericht ihn zum Freispruch, denn sie sieht die Einschränkung der Rechtsfolge auf die Selbstanzeige vor der Entdeckung der Tat als eine unzulässige teleologische Reduktion an. Da das Gesetz selbst keine zeitliche Grenze vorschreibt, ist diese Restriktion mithilfe des möglichen Wortsinnns allein nicht zu bewerkstelligen. Nur sei erwähnt, dass hier ein Begriff „die limitierte Analogie" anstatt der teleologischen Reduktion verwendet wird.

56 *Engisch* zufolge wird das Gesetz hier durch contra legem korrigiert. Und es gibt zwei Fälle, die voneinander strikt zu unterscheiden ist. Danach soll die Gesetzesberichtigung, die sich um den wahren Willen des Gesetzgebers vom möglichen Wortsinn des Gesetzes zu befreien, erlaubt sein. Problematisch ist es dagegen, wenn sich diese Gesetzeskorrektur stattdessen auf die außerpositive Rechtsidee bezieht. Dazu *Engisch*, Einführung (Fn. 1), S. 248ff. Um die Bedeutung von contra legem hervorzuheben, schlägt *Kye Il Lee* den Begriff „gesetzeskorrigierende Rechtsfortbildung"' vor, was meines Erachtens zu kompliziert und daher unnötig erscheint. Dazu *Kye Il Lee*, Systematik der Rechtsfortbildung (Fn. 18), S. 325ff.; *Jong Oh Kim/Bong Cheol Choi/Hyun Cheol Kim/Dong Ring Shin/Chun Soo Yang/ Kye Il Lee*, Rechtsphilosophie (Fn. 1), S. 281ff.

um der Ordnung willen". Danach hat sich der Richter diesen Formalvorschriften schweigend zu beugen, mögen sie ihm im Einzelfall auch sinnlos erscheinen. Also sie beansprucht mit Rücksicht auf das Rechtssicherheitsinteresse ein Reduktionsverbot[57]. Ein Beispiel dafür ist die Entscheidung des Obersten Gerichtshofs über die Gültigkeit des nationalen Wechsels ohne die Angabe des Ausstellungsortes[58]

5. Rechtsfortbildung mit Rücksichten auf allgemeine Grundsätze des Rechts oder die Bedürfnisse im Rechtsverkehr

Sollten diese beiden wie Analogie und teleologischer Reduktion nicht ausreichen, die gesuchte Entscheidung zu finden, dann wird zur Ausfüllung der Rechtslücke empfohlen, etwa auf allgemeine Grundsätze des Rechts zu rekurrieren. Dazu gehören „allgemeine Rechtsgrundsätze" wie „Geist der

---

57 Hier sei auch der relativ neue Fall erwähnt, in dem die Formvorschrift nun beachtet wird. In Frage kommt hier, ob das ohne Siegel aufgefasste Testament erbrechtlich als ungültig angesehen werden soll. Da der Oberste Gerichtshof die Gültigkeit dieses mangelhaften Testaments abgelehnt hat, ist dieser Fall auch vom koreanischen Verfassungsgericht entschieden worden und zwar mit dem Ergebnis, dass das das Siegel als eine notwendige Form vorschreibende Gesetz verfassungsgemäß sein soll. Dazu der Oberste Gerichtshof 2006. 9. 8.2006da25103. Die Entscheidung des koreanischen Verfassungsgerichts 2008.3. 27. 2006hyunba82, Plenumsentscheidung.

58 Oberster Gerichtshof 198.4.23. 95da36466. Hier geht es um folgenden Fall: Das koreanische Wechselgesetz schreibt in §1 des Wechselrechts die einzelnen Voraussetzungen der Gültigkeit des Wechsels, bzw. Nr. 7 die Angabe des Ausstellungsortes vor und definiert in §2 den mit diesem Formmangel behafteten Wechsel als ungültig. Ausgehend davon, dass dieses Merkmal im Hinblick auf die Gerichtsbarkeit nicht für den nationalen, sondern nur für den internationalen Wechsel von Bedeutung ist, hat die Mehrheitsansicht dieses Gerichts den nationalen Wechsel ohne den Ausstellungsort als gültig entschieden. In methodischer Hinsicht ist diese Entscheidung zweispurig, was das Gericht anscheinend nicht angemerkt hätte. Sie bedient sich zum einen teleologischer Reduktion, zum andern der Berufung auf das Bedürfnis im ständigen Rechtsverkehr. Bezüglich teleologischer Reduktion wird diese Entscheidung in der Weise rekonstruiert, dass die ratio leis von §1 darin liegt, die internationale Gerichtsbarkeit des Streits klarzustellen, weshalb dieser Zweck für den nationalen Wechsel belanglos ist. In dem Maß soll daher der Anwendungsbereich dieser Regelung reduziert werden (sog. teleologische Reduktion). Fraglich ist allerdings, ob diese Berichtigung mittels der teleologischen Reduktion rechtfertigt werden kann, weil sie gegen das Reduktionsverbot verstößt. Darüber hinaus wäre auch diese Entscheidung deswegen problematisch, weil sie zwei verschiedenen Argumentationsformen – zum einen die rechtsimmanente Rechtsfortbildung und zum anderen die rechtstranszendente Rechtsfortbildung -, die sich nicht miteinander harmonisieren, gleichseitig verwendet.

Rechtsordnung", „die Natur der Sache" und „legitime Mittel für legitime Zwecke". Worauf diese Rechtsgrundsätze basieren und wie das Präferenzverhältnis zwischen ihnen aussieht, lässt sich jedoch nicht vorab einheitlich beantworten. Klar ist jedoch, dass allgemeingültige Rechtsgrundsätze wie das „Verantwortungsprinzip" in engem Zusammenhang mit der Frage der Rechtsphilosophie stehen. Dahingegen erfordert die Abwägung von Nutzen und Pflichten im Zusammenhang mit dem Grundsatz „legitime Mittel für legitime Zwecke", eine teleologische Diskussion, die individuelle historische Umstände berücksichtigt. Ab und zu werden hier auch die ständigen Bedürfnisse des Geschäftsverkehrs in Bezug genommen[59]. Während es in Deutschland relativ viele Beispiele für diese Lückenausfüllung gibt[60], sind in Korea Beispiel dafür leider schwer zu finden. Ein Beispiel dafür ist, die Entscheidung des Obersten Gerichtshofs über die Änderung des Geschlechts eines Transsexuellen im Personenstandbuch[61].

In Bezug auf die Rechtsfortbildung in Korea zeigt sich, dass die Rechtsprechung überhaupt nichts von der Lücke erwähnt und diese meistens mittels der Auslegung zu ergänzen versucht. Konkret: Auch wenn offensichtlich eine Lücke vorliegt, wollen die meisten Richter diese Tatsache nicht wahrnehmen, sondern zu Unrecht durch eine berichtigende Auslegung zu ergänzen versuchen, die sich auf den ganzen Bedeutungszusam-

---

59 Dazu den eben erwähnten Fall über die Gültigkeit des nationalen Wechsels ohne die Angabe des Ausstellungsortes. Als ein Beispiel ist in Deutschland die Sicherungsübereinigung angeführt. Dazu *Larenz/Canaris*, Methodenlehre (Fn. 1), S. 233ff. Hervorzuheben sei hier, dass sich *Engisch* anders als *Larenz/Canaris* dieser sog. gesetzesübertragenden Rechtsfortbildung gegenüber sehr zurückhaltend verhält. *Engisch*, Einführung (Fn. 1), S. 303ff.

60 Beispiele dafür sind der Verbotsirrtum, die Euthanasie und die Schwangerschaftsunterbrechung aufgrund des Güterabwägungsprinzips. Dazu *Engisch*, Einführung (Fn. 1), S. 260ff.

61 Oberster Gerichtshof 2006.6.22. 2004sue42 Plenumsentscheidung. Hier liegt folgende Fall: ein Transsexueller stell einen Antrag darauf, dessen Geschlecht von einem Mann zu einer Frau umzuwandeln. In der Tat hat der Gesetzgeber einen solchen Fall nicht vorgesehen, so dass es gesetzlich unmöglich ist, das bei der Geburt eingetragene Geschlecht nachträglich im Personenstandbuch zu korrigieren. Dennoch hat die Mehrheitsansicht des Obersten Gerichtshofs das frühere Geschlecht nach dem Verfahren von §120 des Personenstandesbuchgesetzes(戶籍法) im Personenstandbuch korrigiert. Es geht hier also um die Lückenausfülling, in der die Menschenwürde der transsexuellen und das Streben nach dem Glück die volle Geltung erlangen sollen. Hier stellt sich dieser Fall als eine verfassungskonforme Rechtsfortbildung heraus, weil dies Lücke in Berufung auf die in der Verfassung vorgeschriebene Menschenwürde ausgefüllt wird. Dagegen wird freilich von der Gegenmeinung vertreten, dass das Korrigieren des Geschlechts gesetzliche Reform erfordert.

menhang des Gesetzes bezieht[62]. Daneben ist auch nicht klar, auf welchem Wege – nämlich mittels der Analogie oder teleologischer Reduktion? – sich die Rechtsfortbildung vollzieht. Vermutlich liegt der Grund für das Misstrauen gegenüber dem Lückenbegriff darin, dass die Entscheidung unnötigerweise kompliziert wird, wenn die Lücke offengelegt wird. Freilich ist die Schwierigkeit in der Praxis wohl verständlich. Aber damit ist noch nicht gesagt, dass sie weiter in einer solchen Weise verfahren darf.

Nun wird das bisher dargestellte im folgenden Bild zusammengestellt.

Das gesamte Denkschema der juristischen Methodenlehre

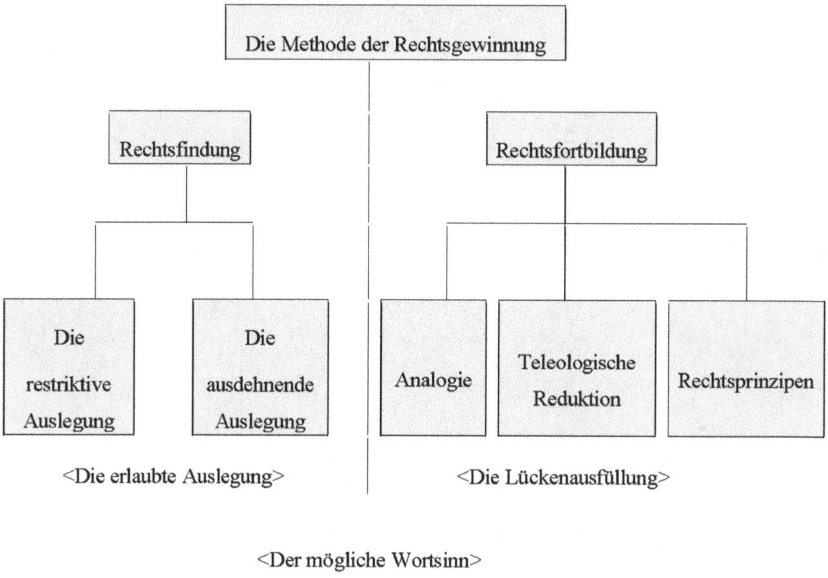

62 Zur selben Ansicht *Seo-Hyuk Oh*, Die Auslegung (Fn. 14), S. 436f.

Autorenverzeichnis

Prof. Dr. Young Whan Kim
Prof. em. an der Hanyang Universität in Seoul
<kimyw@hanyang.ac.kr>

Prof. Dr. Kye Il Lee
Prof. an der Yonsei Universität in Seoul
<kilee@yonsei.ac.kr>

Prof. Dr. Sung Bum Lee
Prof. an der Seoul National Universität in Seoul
<lsb0516@snu.ac.kr>

Prof. Dr. Su Gil An
Prof. an der Myongi Universität in Seoul
<sugilan@hotmail.com>

Prof. Dr. Hyun Jung Lee
Prof. an der Erlangen-Nürnberg Universität in Deutschland
<hyun.jung.lee@fau.de>

Prof. Dr. Joon Kyu Choi
Prof. an der Seoul National Universität in Seoul
<kyu77@snu.ac.kr>

Dr. Hyun Kyung Lee
Wissenschaftiche Mitarbeiterin an der Seoul National Universität in Seoul
<yvette912@snu.ac.kr>

Dr. Bum Jin Kim
Rechtsanwalt in der Kanzlei Primus
<bj1627@naver.com>

Prof. Dr. Doo Hyun Kong
Prof. an der Seoul National Universität in Seoul
<kd-02@hanmail.net>

Prof. Dr. Wu Ye Kang
Prof. an der Korea Maritime & Ocean Universität in Pusan
<wykang@kmou.ac.kr>